A Cookbook

for Serving the

Internet

UNIX Version

Philip E. Bourne

An Internet-Enhanced Book:
http://www.sdsc.edu/pb/Cookbook/UNIX

To join a Prentice Hall PTR internet mailing list, point to
http://www.prenhall.com/register

Prentice Hall PTR, Upper Saddle River, New Jersey 07458
http://www.prenhall.com

Library of Congress Cataloging in Publication Data

Bourne, Philip E.
  A cookbook for serving the Internet : UNIX version / Philip E.
Bourne.
    p.   cm.
  Includes bibliographical references and index.
  ISBN 0-13-519992-1
  1. Client/server computing.   2. Internet (Computer network)
3. UNIX (Computer file) I. Title.
QA76.9.C55B68 1997
005.7'137682--dc21   96-47269
                                  CIP

Editorial/production supervision: *Nicholas Radhuber*
Cover design: *Anthony Gemmellaro*
Manufacturing manager: *Alexis Heydt*
Acquisitions editor: *Mike Meehan*
Marketing manager: *Stephen Solomon*
Editorial Assistant: *Tara Ruggiero*

© 1997 by Prentice Hall PTR
Prentice-Hall, Inc.
A Simon & Schuster Company
Upper Saddle River, New Jersey 07458

The Publisher offers discounts on this book when ordered in bulk quantities.
For more information, contact:
          Corporate Sales Department
          Prentice Hall PTR
          1 Lake St.
          Upper Saddle River, NJ 07458
          Phone: 800-382-3419 Fax: 201-236-7141
          E-mail: dan_rush@prenhall.com

Printed in the United States of America
10 9 8 7 6 5 4 3 2 1

ISBN 0-13-519992-1

Prentice-Hall International (UK) Limited, *London*
Prentice-Hall of Australia Pty. Limited, *Sydney*
Prentice-Hall Canada, Inc., *Toronto*
Prentice-Hall Hispanoamericana S.A., *Mexico*
Prentice-Hall of India Private Limited, *New Delhi*
Prentice-Hall of Japan, Inc., *Tokyo*
Simon & Schuster Asia Pte. Ltd., *Singapore*
Editora Prentice-Hall do Brasil, Ltda., *Rio de Janeiro*

To Roma and Scott
for unselfishly also giving up their weekends.

Contents

List of Tables

List of Figures

Preface

If you have decided it is time to serve some information, either to the whole Internet community or to a single organization, small or large (i.e., via an *Intranet*), this **may** be the book for you. My first job is to turn the **may** into a yes or a no. If you have been in a bookstore and seen shelves upon shelves of Internet-related books, you will likely appreciate this direct approach. If you want a succinct (i.e., short and inexpensive) guide to establishing a network-based information server on a UNIX® system, read on. If you want a pseudo-novel where the details of serving information are buried amid a mass of anecdotes and personal tales of woe, then put this back before you get the cover dirty.

SCOPE

Let us begin by making sure you understand the scope of the material that is presented within these pages.

> *Emphasis on information servers, not clients.* Going out onto the Internet and (for example) downloading a file with ftp, sending mail, or reading someone's home page are client activities and are initiated using client software resident on the local computer. Setting up a secure ftp environment, redistributing an incoming mail message to members of a mailing list, or writing and making available a Web *home page* are server activities and require special software resident on the server. The majority of Internet-related books deal ONLY with the client aspect of Internet information access. This is NOT a book about using Web browsers like Mosaic, Netscape, and HotJava, nor is it a book that attempts to be a dictionary of servers to go and visit. This IS a book about designing and maintaining a server to support anonymous and enhanced ftp, Listservers, and Web-based access. Having said that, one chapter (Chapter Five) is devoted to obtaining and configuring client software, since it is required (1) to get the server software you need, and (2) to review the information on your own server as it is added.

> *Emphasis on the organization of the information.* What makes a good server is not necessarily fancy presentation, but the quality and organization of the information. This book cannot

help you with the quality of your information; however, it can make it easier to navigate and find the information.

Establishing an information server on a UNIX system. While many of the principles are the same, irrespective of whether the operating system is a UNIX variant, Microsoft Windows 3.1®, Microsoft Windows 95®, Microsoft Windows NT®, Apple Macintosh® operating system, etc., I have chosen to restrict the discussion to all versions of UNIX to remain more focused. Windows and possibly Macintosh-specific versions of this book will be available in the future.

PREREQUISITES

Degree of UNIX administrative experience required. You have to have root access to the system (either yourself or working with the UNIX system administrator) and understand the rudimentary aspects of file system layout, UNIX security, script programming, *daemons* and so on. It would also help to be familiar with writing code using the Perl interpretive language. In short, the intended audience is most likely folks who look after their own UNIX workstations or servers, but that task is only a prerequisite for getting your real job done. Now your real job involves, in addition, providing information to remote network clients. This could be as simple as providing your own demographic information for an electronic directory maintained by your organization, to providing teaching materials, to providing a complex front-end supporting iterative query of an underlying information resource.

Internet access assumed. There is not a detailed technical discussion in this book for getting connected to the Internet. That is, getting physically connected, getting an Internet address and being able to resolve addresses. I will show you how to determine whether you have met all the prerequisites for being connected, and if not, where to go for more information on types of connectivity, Internet providers, etc.

FORMAT

If you are still reading, either you are lucky enough to have too much time on your hands, or you have met the prerequisites and belong to the intended audience. The next question to ask yourself is whether the format of this book is going to be helpful to you? To answer this question, consider my motivation in writing the book.

Over the past couple of years, I have been responsible for establishing and supporting information and information servers on UNIX platforms. What frustrated me in the beginning was the lack of a good overview of what software I should be installing, where I could get it, and how I could organize my information to make its presentation most effective. I would be misleading you if I said sources, either online or printed, were not available today to help. In fact, the opposite is true. The problem is that there is *so much* information, it is hard to know where to start.

My goal is to make this cookbook that place to start. You decide with my help what to cook and then gather a set of ingredients—software obtained free from the Internet, optional commercial software, and, of course, the information itself. You put these ingredients together using the right utensils, and follow steps a through z. The result should be an Internet feast for a world of information consumers.

This cookbook goes one step further in that it contains a global recipe—a recipe of recipes—to get you to all the other recipes. You can also think of the global recipe as a roadmap. With a traditional map, you begin with something that covers a large area (the introduction in this book) and gradually homes in on where you need to go (individual chapters and sections).

Choosing the route raises questions. Do I go on the Interstate? Do I take the scenic route? The analogy with the Information Superhighway (no pun intended) leads to questions like: Should I provide support for video clips? Is gopher support still necessary? Which is the most secure of the World Wide Web (WWW) servers? Should I support a WWW forms interface? Should I support Java *applets* for access from Java-ready browsers?

Beyond answering the global questions, each chapter takes pieces of the global recipe, provides a list of software ingredients and where you can get them, and describes in a step-by-step fashion how to put them together to get the job done.

Getting the software installed is the beginning, not the end of the process. This book details how to organize your information for effective access by the various tools, create meaningful links between items of data, and effectively use graphics, frames, and clickable maps to facilitate navigation and convey the information. Information access on the Internet started as a passive process—reading of static text and images. It is now possible to engage in an active dialog, enter queries and get a response that can be subsequently refined as part of a more explicit query. Further, this whole process can involve sight, sound, and animation.

I devote a significant portion of this book discussing how you can support all these features. How sophisticated you want your server to be depends on how much you want to learn about such tools as Perl, HTML frames, and Java. People learn best from examples, so I include several scenarios, real and imaginary, to illustrate what can be achieved. For the real ones, code can be downloaded from the information server associated with this book and used as a template for your own exciting and innovative information servers.

If you are still undecided about whether this book meets your needs, look at the Global Recipe and its description and the Table of Contents (which is the more traditional form for presenting this recipe) and possibly the Introduction. You can do this either by further reading this book, or by visiting the information server.

YOUR OBLIGATION

Setting up an information server can be fun and rewarding if accessed by lots of folks or by the few people you really want to access it. Remember, however, that *how* the information is presented is a minor issue compared to the question of *what* information is presented. Just as I have an obligation to write the best possible book I can so that I am not taking your money under false pretenses, I also have an obligation to serve up the best information on my Internet server so as not to waste anyone's time. The community at large has, so far, fulfilled this obligation admirably.

SHARE THE EXCITEMENT

These are exciting times, in some ways reminiscent of a gold rush. We make up rules as we go, and what appears as a rich area of inquiry one day, with many people staking a claim, is forgotten the next. The end result of a gold rush, when the dust finally settled—or more correctly ran out—was an infrastructure of towns and cities that spurred economic development and social accomplishment. When the dust begins to settle on the Internet we will have a similar, albeit virtual infrastructure, that places a significant part of the total body of human knowledge at our fingertips. Who knows what we can achieve with such a resource? I am proud to help you become an active contributor to that resource.

Philip E. Bourne
San Diego, September 1996

Acknowledgments

Many people have contributed to this book, both directly and indirectly. Thanks to Jim Binder, Brigitte Carrabin, Mike Gannis, Mike Gribskov, Pamela Puckett, Ilya Shindyalov, and Stephanie Sides, who contributed directly by reading and commenting on all, or large parts, of the manuscript. Additional thanks to Ilya Shindyalov, my long time scientific colleague, who also contributed indirectly through many a lunchtime discussion on how best to use the Internet in our own research, and whose ideas and thoughts found their way into the pages. Thanks to Rich Toscano who got lumbered with translating ideas into code when he would have preferred to have been playing his guitar. Thanks to Philippe Youkharibache for many useful discussions had while we should have been improving our tennis game.

Indirectly, many of the superb staff at the San Diego Supercomputer Center (SDSC) have provided input. Michael Gribskov and Lynn Ten Eyck, as my colleagues in computational biology, deserve mention for their unique perspectives on using the Internet. While there are too many others to mention all of them, Nancy Wilkins-Diehr, Aaron von Hungen, Joshua Polterock and Ann Redelfs deserve mention. Josh, the SDSC Webmaster, still does not believe me when I tell him he will soon be the most important person in the organization. Perhaps he knows I have been wrong before.

Lastly, I must thank the many anonymous people who have contributed to this book and do not even know it. The information behind the many URLs cited in this book required a great deal of time and energy to develop. In many cases I am sure the effort in no way related to the developer's job requirements, but was done as a community service. Thanks to you all.

Conventions

Convention	Definition
http://www.sdsc.edu/pb/Cookbook/UNIX	*Uniform Resource Locator* (URL) for finding information on the Web.
ftp://ftp.sdsc.edu/pub	A URL beginning ftp may also be accessed using *anonymous ftp*.
http://www.sdsc.edu/- *cookbook*	URLs spanning more than one line are hyphenated following a slash (/). Hyphens located elsewhere in a URL are part of the URL.
Netscape *./xv* *../bin/mosaic*	Relative names of programs and files.
/etc/hosts	Absolute name of a program or file.
% **command**	UNIX shell command.
<TEXTAREA NAME="name" ROWS="size" COLS="size"> optional text </TEXTAREA>	HTML tag. For a single character or word as the value of an argument, double quotes are not obligatory, but good coding practice, nevertheless.

UNIX OPERATING SYSTEMS

UNIX is not a single operating system, but a class of operating systems with variants that run on 16-, 32-, and 64-bit hardware architectures. The major UNIX variants mentioned in this book are shown in the following table.

UNIX Variant	Supplier	Description
AIX	International Business Machines (IBM)	Supports R6000-based processors
Digital UNIX	Digital Equipment Corp. (DEC)	Supports DEC Alpha processors
FreeBSD	Various	Supports Intel 386, 486, and Pentium processors (see *http://www.freebsd.org/- welcome.html)*
HP/UX	Hewlett-Packard	Supports HP PARC RISC processors
Irix	Silicon Graphics Inc.	Supports Mips processors, R8000, and R10000 series processors
Linux	Various	Supports Intel 386, 486, and Pentium processors (see *http://sunsite.unc.edu/mdw/- linux.html*
NetBSD	Various	A variant of FreeBSD (see *http://www.public.iastate.edu/- ~gendalia/NetBSD.html)*
OSF/1	Open Software Foundation	Supports various processors. A number of UNIX variants, e.g., Digital UNIX, are derived from OSF/1
Solaris	Sun Microsystems Inc.	Supports SPARC processors
SunOS	Sun Microsystems Inc.	Supports SPARC processors; slowly being replaced by Solaris
Ultrix	Digital Equipment Corp. (DEC)	Supports Mips processors; obsolete, replaced by Digital UNIX
UnixWare	Novell Inc.	Supports various processors, notably Intel-based

What is an Internet-Enhanced Book?

While this book offers a concise description of building and maintaining an Internet information server, it cannot hope to stay current for long, given the speed at which the Internet is evolving. Having a CD-ROM stuck in the back helps because it provides more information than in the book, but it too becomes dated quickly. "Internet-enhanced" means, in effect, that I use the Internet as a book supplement, which can be updated continuously and available to you long after the book has been published. The following diagram indicates how this works.

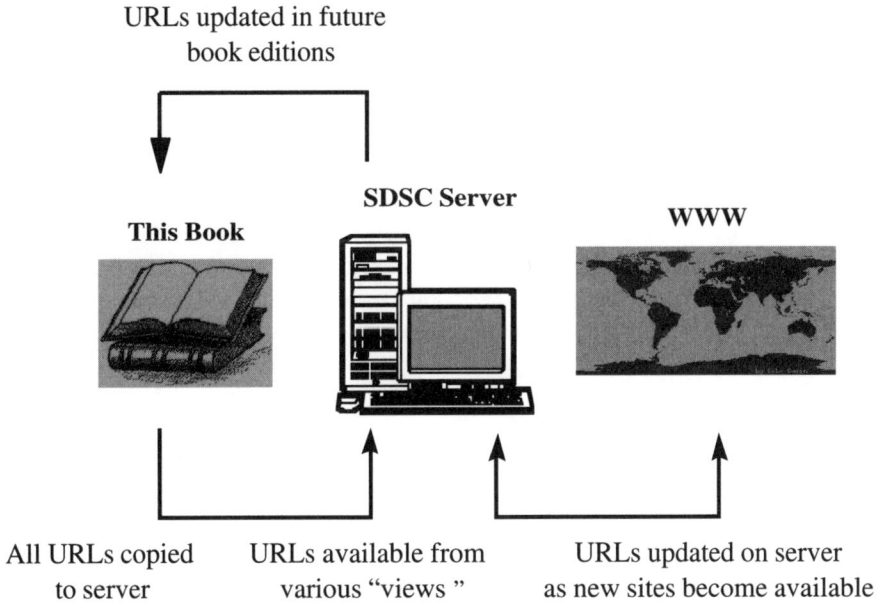

URLs updated in future
book editions

This Book

SDSC Server

WWW

All URLs copied
to server

URLs available from
various "views"

URLs updated on server
as new sites become available

An Internet-Enhanced Book

This book contains a concise summary of lasting information covering why to establish an information server and how to establish and maintain that server. It contains many pointers—that is, *hypertext links*[1] (also called hyperlinks, or just links for short) in the form of *Uniform Resource Locators* (URLs)—to additional sources of information and to software that you will need. Those pointers are available on an Internet server at the San Diego Supercomputer Center (SDSC), a national laboratory for computational science and engineering. This serves two purposes.

First, it is easy to find these pointers without typing them each time you wish to visit a site. All you have to do is remember, or add to the hotlist of your favorite Web browser, a single pointer:

http://www.sdsc.edu/pb/Cookbook/UNIX

From there you can locate the pointer you need. If you do not have Web access, but do have ftp access, you can download all or portions of this information from *ftp://ftp.sdsc.edu/pub/pb/Cookbook/UNIX,*[2] so at least it is easy to retrieve pointers to software or information that is ftp accessible.

Second, and most important, this list of pointers on the SDSC server can be kept current! Thus, while a pointer in this book is considered the best reference at the time of writing, it may not be the best reference at the time of reading. However, the current reference is available to you simply by connecting to the SDSC server. This is important, since Internet technology is changing faster than the time it takes to provide new editions of a book. With the use of an information server current information can be constantly provided as a supplement.

As you read the book, you will frequently see the following symbol, ☞. The symbol is a reminder that up-to-date information can be found on the server and perhaps should be consulted.

Finding current information using the server is easy. The server provides several "views" that you can use. One view is simply the table of contents. By clicking on the section that corresponds to the one you are reading in the book, you will get a list of pointers to current information. Another view is the global recipe, which I introduce in Chapter One, and which gives an overview of the steps you will go through in establishing an information server. Another traditional view is the index. The corresponding electronic view is to search by keyword.

Why don't I put the whole book online and update that? Maybe this will work for future generations, but for now many folks, myself included, like the feel of a book in our hands and are comfortable navigating that medium. If you are reading this in the book-

---

1. Throughout this book the first use of a new term is given in *italics* and is defined in the Glossary.

2. The meaning of an ftp archive given as a URL is discussed under Conventions.

store, or from someone else's copy, at this point you may be thinking: Why buy the book? I'll just jot down the pointer shown above and read what is on the Web site. You are welcome to do that, of course. However, I think the combination of book and Internet server will provide the most useful and usable information.

You may also be thinking: How will he keep all the pointers to pertinent information and software current? In part, the answer is that I will not be keeping it current, you will. There is a *Reader's Corner* accessible on the server for you to report pointers to sites that you think should be included in the Cookbook. I will frequently review these suggestions and, if appropriate, add them first to the server, and later to future editions of this book.

Getting the reader involved in the material he is reading, to the point where he begins to make contributions of his own, seems to me a very good use of the Internet. The Internet has provided a communication channel between reader and author to enhance the quality and longevity of the book. In other words, the book is "Internet-enhanced."

1

The Global Recipe

The order in which the different courses of a meal are served is not something you necessarily find in a traditional cookbook. Eating a sweet dessert after a savory main course seems obvious since it is what we have learned from childhood. The order in which to perform tasks when establishing your information server is far from obvious. You need a global recipe that orders the recipes for each course.

This chapter introduces the steps you need to follow to establish a fully functional Internet information server. Each step is then discussed in one or more chapters of this book. The steps are illustrated in Figure 1–1.

Moving from top to bottom in Fig. 1–1 orders the steps to follow for developing the Internet information server. Each box in the illustration of the global recipe is a specific step in the process. The numbers on the left represent the chapters in which each step is covered. The types of information we will encounter are shown on the left of the boxes and the types of software tools on the right.

This book considers the three most common types of Internet information service in use today—anonymous ftp, *Listservers*, and Web-based services (i.e., those using the *http protocol*). Anonymous ftp is efficient at file transfer and available to a wide audience; a Listserver is a convenient way to broadcast a single mail message to a list of subscribers who may not have any other service; a Web server is a way to deliver text, graphics, and other forms of multimedia as well as support more complex forms of interaction between a user and an information server, for example, have the server perform some complex calculation. Gopher is considered to have been superseded by Web-based services and is not discussed. To reach the widest possible audience you should support all three types of service.

To be successful in installing and maintaining one or more of these services you need to follow the steps in the global recipe in the order given. Let us look at the definition of each of these steps.

- **Planning**—First you have to decide who is your audience, and then what information you are going to provide to this intended audience. Basic ftp requires no

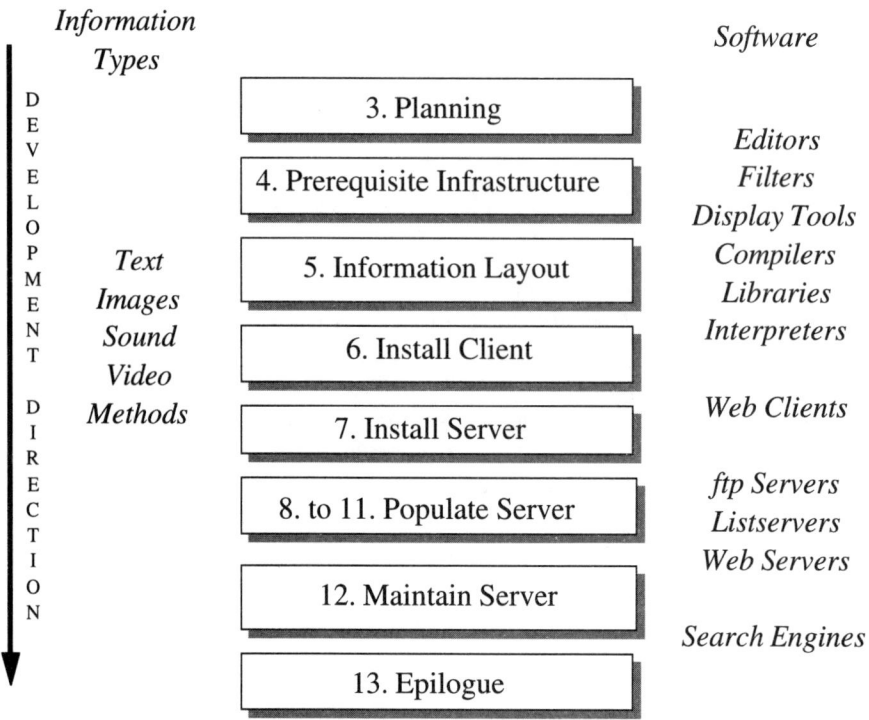

Figure 1–1   The Global Recipe

additional software beyond UNIX and about half an hour to set up correctly. Supporting a Listserver requires that you install and configure one piece of software and takes a couple of hours. Installing a Web-based server can take anything from a couple of hours to months, depending on the complexity of the information being served.

In supporting ftp you have to decide whether to support the basic stock-standard ftp *daemon* or install a security-enhanced ftp server. In supporting a Listserver you have to decide which one and the types of list you will permit. In supporting a Web-based service you have to decide which type of Web server, and the complexity of the information to be supported.

A good server with lots of information provides multiple ways (I call these "entry points") for finding information. I shall explore ways of providing useful entry points. The most direct way is providing the equivalent of an index. You will need to decide (i) whether to provide an index and (ii) what tools to use to generate, maintain, and browse that index. If you are going to provide information and graphics in the form of hypertext, you need to provide tools for preparing information in this form, for example, HTML and graphics editors and format converters to turn existing documents in formats such as *Rich Text Format* (RTF) and *LaTeX* into HTML, and for viewing HTML-based information using Web browsers such as Netscape, Lynx, and HotJava. If you are going to provide sound and/or video you will need tools for producing, editing, and browsing these formats. Certainly support for sound and/or video will place resource demands on the server, which takes us to infrastructure.

- **Prerequisite Infrastructure**—Foremost in providing an Internet server is to have Internet access! I shall consider briefly how to obtain Internet access if you do not already have access, and how to manage it on your UNIX machine once you are connected. Support for an information server places a demand on the computer supporting it that should be considered ahead of time. The most immediate concern is likely to be sufficient disk space to store all the information. If the server is successful, you need to ensure that memory, disk I/O and network bandwidth, and to a lesser extent CPU cycles, don't become rate-limiting. We shall consider what these demands are likely to be and when in the development cycle they are likely to occur. The infrastructure extends beyond the hardware. Further, changes may be required in the configuration of the UNIX operating system, particularly relating to security and to the X/Motif environment. The latter usually relates to X resources and the availability of fonts.

- **Information Layout**—How you organize the various types of information on your server becomes important as the amount of information grows. The tricks are to: (i) avoid duplication; (ii) provide easy file retrieval; and (iii) simplify evolution, that is simplify movement of the information hierarchy to another server or collection of file systems.

- **Install Client**—With the planning done and suitable hardware and software selected you are ready to get started on building your information server. First, you need to install the client components of all the software for which you will provide the server components. You will be the first to use your server to determine whether the server functions as expected and the information is presented the way you want. I briefly discuss installing client software components that you are likely to need. As is true of all discussions in this book, I will make good use of reference material available on the Internet and point you to a myriad of books on Internet clients.

- **Install Server**—Once you can access *ftp archives,* Listservers, and Web pages on remote servers, it is time to download and configure your own information server components. For ftp this requires that you choose between using the ftp program that comes standard with the UNIX operating system, or you install an enhanced ftp server that provides greater security. I will show you how to install and configure *wu-ftpd*, an enhanced ftp program from Washington University. While there are several Listservers to choose from, I will cover Majordomo, the most popular Listserver. I will install and configure two of the most popular Web servers, the National Center for Supercomputer Applications (NCSA) httpd, and wn developed by John Franks. NCSA's server is simpler to install and maintain, but does not have all the security features of wn. Finally, you may also need to provide an index to the information on your server. I will show you how to install and configure the Harvest text indexing system, which includes a gatherer, indexer, and search engine.

- **Populate Server**—This is perhaps the most critical part of the whole book! How you organize the information so it is accessible, readable, useful, and easily maintainable is paramount. Anyone can provide a server with little effort (even if it does not appear so from the previous discussion), but the usability and value to the intended audience of the server requires work. Obviously many of us cannot make the development and maintenance of the server our life's work. I shall dissect information organization on a couple of real and imaginary servers to see what makes them tick. From this you will be able to determine the level of effort required to maintain information servers of different complexity. Servers range from support of a simple text and graphics browser with limited links, to a large server that couples together a hybrid of databases and files containing information in many formats. Users can query this environment through a WWW/forms interface and refine their queries. I will cover the latest in Web server technology, including clickable maps, server side includes, Java applets, and HTML frames.

- **Maintain Server**—Once the server is running there is still more to do. Access statistics need to be gathered and future needs anticipated. Error logs should be monitored. Finally, usage of system resources needs to be monitored and, of course, new information added. I will show you how to download and configure the most popular tools for these tasks.

- **Epilogue**—Internet information servers involve rapidly changing technology and you need to keep abreast of developments that may effect your server. I shall point you to some interesting sources of information on these developments, and, of course, give you some thoughts of my own.

2

Introduction

Ingredients:
- *What is the Internet?*
- *Why Serve?—Internet Statistics*
- *How to Behave—The Canon of Conduct*
- *Internet Backgrounder*
- *Client and Server Defined*
- *Your Basic Tools*

From the global recipe you now have a basic idea of what you will be able to serve using this cookbook. It is now time to get to know your kitchen a little better; a prerequisite to cooking and serving a fine meal.

I begin by introducing you to the Internet. If you have been a client user for sometime, that is, you have been downloading files via ftp, sending mail, or surfing the Web, then much of this may be familiar. At the very least I urge you to read the Canon of Conduct, so that we may all continue to use the Internet in a community-minded way.

2.1. WHAT IS THE INTERNET? ☞

Attempting to answer the question, "What is the Internet?" leads to a variety of detailed discussions, some technical, some philosophical. If you have the time and energy you can find examples of these discussions at the URLs indicated in Table 2–1.

For our purposes, it is enough to know that the Internet is a conglomeration of computer networks. While size, accessibility, management, and so on are all variables within these networks, the one thing they share in common is a common set of protocols, namely the TCP/IP, Transmission Control Protocol/Internet Protocol. Without getting technical, this means these networks all communicate with each other, creating a vast global net-

TABLE 2–1   The History of the Internet

Location	Description
http://www.yahoo.com/-Computers_and_Internet/History/	A definitive list of sites.
http://www.internetvalley.com/-intval.html	A historical description, tracing different roads to Internet development.
http://www.isoc.org/	Detailed discussion of Internet philosophy.
http://www.baylor.edu/baylor/Misc/-timeline	Timeline of Internet history, including growth patterns.

work, and provide the potential to put a user on any Internet computer in contact with the information and resources on your soon-to-be-established Internet server. Worldwide accessibility to vast quantities of information at very low cost has the potential to change the dynamics of most aspects of our society—government, education, commerce, and so on. That change has begun, and you will soon be contributing to that change.

2.2. WHAT IT MEANS TO SERVE THE INTERNET ☞

If you are interested in using and serving the Internet, you are not alone. Consider the following statistics from the past few years and what these statistics imply (indicated in bold).

- Average time between new networks connecting to the Internet: 10 minutes (Aug. 1993).
- Internet users: 7.8 million users using 2.5 million computers (Oct. 1994).
- Number of countries reachable/not reachable by electronic mail: 137/99 (Aug. 1993).
- Number of users with at least e-mail access: 27.5 million (Oct. 1994).
- Growth in number of Web servers: doubling every 51 days (Jan. 1996).
  The growth of the Internet is phenomenal.
- Date of the first known Internet message sent by a head of state: March 2,1993, by President Bill Clinton.
  The Internet has become as much an accepted form of communication as radio and TV.
- Date after which more than half the registered networks on the Internet were commercial: August 1991.

> **The Internet is no longer restricted to universities and other non-profit institutions, but is driven by economic factors and open competition.**

- Round-trip time from Colorado to McMurdo, Antarctica: 640 milliseconds. Number of hops: 18.

  The Internet is an inexpensive, fast, and global form of communication.

These numbers, while not current, illustrate the amazing growth (perhaps faster than anything in history), speed, versatility, and commercial nature of the Internet. If you want current statistics, good sources, including a variety of graphical representations, are given in Table 2–2.

One statistic that the last of these sources provides is that Web[1] usage alone is doubling every 10 weeks and the number of servers as of January 1, 1996 was 1.7 million, or one server for every 3,600 people on the planet. This growth rate is likely to accelerate as telephone companies, cable TV companies, and other communications companies become more active in providing Internet services, and make it easier for the less computer and communications literate to begin serving the Internet. Internet serving will be accessible to everyone.

2.2.1 Canon of Conduct

It is people who make valuable information available on the Internet. The technology is simply the vehicle that makes it happen, hence, the Internet is about people, what they contribute and how they behave. I would be negligent in my duty if I did not discuss the

TABLE 2–2   Sources of Internet Statistics

Source	Description
http://www.yahoo.com/-Computers_and_Internet/Internet/-Statistics_and_Demographics/	The definitive starting point for finding statistical information.
ftp://tic.com/matrix/-growth/internet/	Graphs of Internet usage statistics.
http://www.tic.com/mids/-pressbig.html	Explanation of the above graphs.
http://www.anamorph.com/docs/-stats/stats.html	A fun site that speculates on the number of Web sites at any given point in time.

1. The term Web is used interchangeably with World Wide Web and WWW throughout this book, and implies all sites that communicate using the http protocol.

generally accepted Canon of Conduct for operating an information server. Like most issues relating to the Internet, there is no official canon, just an honest and common sense way to behave that makes sense to a community. There are so-called Acceptable User Policies (AUPs), which can be accessed at *ftp://nic.merit.edu/acceptable.use.policies.* Following is my own interpretation for how to behave and parts may be covered by law in various countries. This interpretation is sure to contain shortcomings and omissions, but does provide the general idea I am trying to get across.

1. Information placed on an Internet information server should be considered a form of publication and should be governed by the same rules that govern good publications—no lies, no misleading statements.

2. Do not make available information and software that are copyrighted by others without their appropriate approval. It is advisable to have written confirmation.

3. Properly protect information you only want accessed by specific groups of people. Do not lead other people into temptation.

4. Do not make available any information that is considered offensive to a subset of the community. If you feel strongly that the information should be available, include a warning before any information is read that the information may be offensive to some people.

5. Do not attempt to profit from the Internet, unless it is clear that this is what you are doing (a fine line). The best analogy I can think of are those bits of junk postal mail which come disguised as checks or bills in an effort to make you open and read them.

6. Strive to make the information the best it can be—comprehensive but easily navigated and understood. Above all, keep it current.

If we all obey these simple rules the Internet will continue to be a wonderful place to work and play.

2.3. INTERNET 101

If you are a user rather that a manager of UNIX computer systems, and/or you are relatively new to accessing the Internet from a UNIX system, this section will be useful. If you are familiar with concepts like IP addresses and name servers, then skip this section.

As stated, the Internet is a conglomeration of individually managed computer networks that share only one feature: They all support the Transmission Control Protocol (TCP) and Internet Protocol (IP). For our purposes, it is enough to know that computers that support TCP/IP (i) are able to communicate, (ii) are potentially able to recognize each other,

(iii) are capable of making decisions about how to route information to each other, and (iv) support other protocols that are used by the Web and other information sharing tools.

2.3.1   Addresses

It is (ii) that requires a little more explanation at this point, since it covers the basics of addresses—the feature that makes each computer unique—and name resolution. Each TCP/IP-based host has a unique address referred to as an IP address. This is of the form nnn.nnn.nnn.nnn where nnn is a single byte of information expressed as an integer in the range 0-255 with certain integers (notably 0 and 255) reserved. In simple terms and with numerous exceptions, the first byte of the four-byte address defines the network, the second byte the institution, the third byte the department or division, and the fourth byte the individual computer. Since it is simpler for a human to remember words rather than numbers (decimal or binary), the number maps to a name contained in the UNIX file */etc/hosts* as shown here.

```
% more /etc/hosts
#
# This file contains the IP address to name mapping
# (both official and aliases) for a small group of
# local computers. The majority of numbers are found
# by a request to the name server.
#
# form:
#   IP number Official hostname Any aliases
#
    127.0.0.1 localhost loopback me
    132.249.40.11 tigerfish.sdsc.edu tigerfish
    132.249.40.16 shark.sdsc.edu shark
    .......
```

Since each computer on the Internet must have a unique address, *you must not arbitrarily assign an address to any machine that is attached to a public network.* Section 3.1.3 discusses how an address should be assigned.

The name is usually defined in the reverse order to the number, that is, of the form:

computer.division.institution.network   or
computer.institution.network

It is possible to maintain the */etc/hosts* file such that it contains mapping of the small number of hosts that you access frequently. It is not possible to maintain the mapping for all the hosts accessed when, for example, surfing the net. How can the mapping of the name to the number be done automatically? Mapping is made transparent to the user through a hierarchy of servers, called domain name servers (DNS), or name servers for short. Name servers maintain tables that map names to numbers. Thus, if you access a host name, for example, using a URL entered to a Web browser, that name is mapped transparently to the appropriate number. If that mapping is not found on the current computer, (which itself may be a name server) the computer will contact a designated name server. If that name server does not have the mapping, it will contact yet another name server higher in the hierarchy until the name is resolved and the information passed back to the requester. How you determine whether the Internet connection of your information server is functioning correctly and that the name server is running correctly is discussed in sections 3.1.6 and 3.1.7, respectively.

How the name server is configured depends on whether you are simply looking up name to number matching or whether your UNIX system is providing name to number matching for other computers. I consider only the simple case here—name resolution using another computer. This is accomplished with a single file */etc/resolv.conf.* A typical example would be

```
% more resolv.conf
domain sdsc.edu
nameserver 198.17.46.33
nameserver 198.17.46.32
nameserver 132.249.40.68
```

which indicates that three name servers are defined to resolve names in the domain sdsc.edu. The first is referred to as the primary name server, the second the secondary, and so on. The primary name server will be use by default. If the primary server is down or not accessible, the secondary server will be used. Further details on the format of this file can be obtained with the UNIX *command* **man resolv.conf.** If you need to set up a name server, then Table 2–3 contains useful sources of information.

Different Internet services use name-based addresses which are extensions to the basic IP address scheme. Table 2–4 summarizes the basic address types by example.

TABLE 2–3   Understanding Domain Name Services

Location	Description
http://oac3.hsc.uth.tmc.edu/staff/-snewton/tcp-tutorial/sec5.html	Brief introduction.
http://www.sidewinder.com/FAQs/-HTML/swdns.html	Frequently asked questions.
http://eeunix.ee.usm.maine.edu/-guides/dns/dns.html	Comprehensive and easy to follow tutorial.

TABLE 2–4 Types of Internet Address

Address	Description
pauline.sdsc.edu	A specific Internet host.
bourne@pauline.sdsc.edu	A user at a specific Internet host.
bourne@sdsc.edu	A user defined uniquely in a sub-domain (the most convenient form of mail address).
http://www.sdsc.edu/	The simplest form of Uniform Resource Locator (URL) for access to a Web page using the http protocol. By default, the Web server at the host *www.sdsc.edu* will try and serve a file called *index.html* from the *document root directory.* If *index.html* is absent, the names of files in the *document root directory* will be returned. The document root directory is discussed in Section 6.3.
http://www.sdsc.edu:70/	As above but on a specific port number, in this instance 70. The default port number is 80.
ftp://rosebud.sdsc.edu/pub/	An ftp archive accessed from a Web browser using a URL.
telnet://info.cern.ch/	A telnet session started from a Web browser.
gopher://gopher.micro.umn.edu/	A *gopher* site accessed from a Web browser.
mailto:bourne@sdsc.edu	A mail address invoked from a Web browser.
news:comp.infosystems.www.-providers	A news group invoked from a Web browser.

As we shall see, the majority of these addresses are used by Web browsers. They serve us humans as a useful guide for recognizing different types of information as it is found on the Internet. In several cases, http, ftp, telnet, and gopher define protocols which are part of, or layered on top of, the *TCP/IP protocol stack.*

2.3.2 The Mechanics of Server Access

The next question to answer is, what happens on the UNIX information server when, for example, a Web browser requests access to information using one of the addresses shown in Table 2–4? Figure 2–1 provides an outline for answering this question.

The program */etc/inetd* is the UNIX Internet daemon that oversees all Internet activity. If this daemon is not running, you are not communicating with the rest of the world (see Section 3.1.6). The *inetd* daemon is started at boot time and should remain active until the system shuts down. How it gets started and where it resides is UNIX operating system-dependent. On many systems, notably derivatives of BSD UNIX, it can be found in the directory */etc* and is started at boot time from the file */etc/rc.local.* On System V derivatives of UNIX it is often found in */usr/etc/inetd* and started from *rc.X* where X is the init state (0 for power down, 1 for single user, and 2 for multi-user). The UNIX command **man inetd** provides the location of *inetd* and a more extensive version

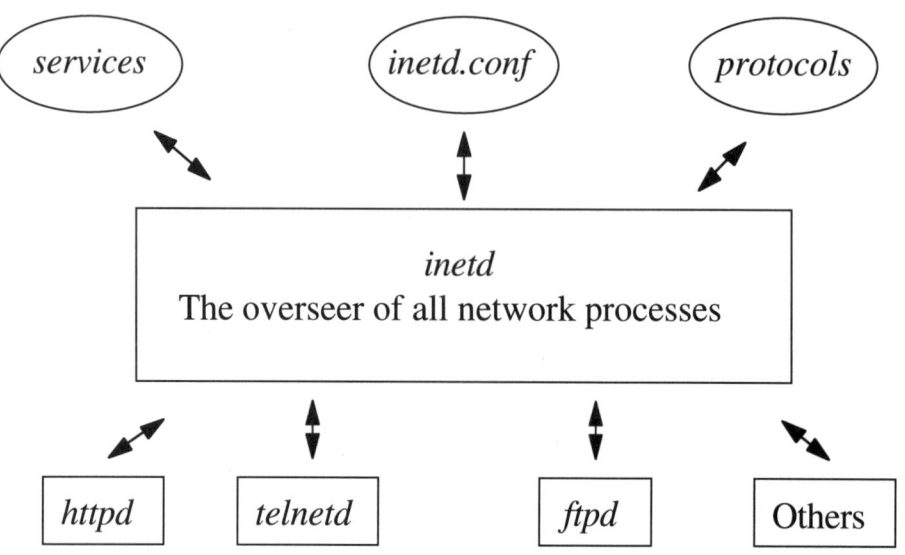

Fig 2–1   UNIX Network Topology

of what is discussed here. Good Internet sources of help on UNIX networking are given in Appendix A.

Here are the basics on UNIX networking:

1. At boot time, the *inetd* program reads the file *inetd.conf* (the *inetd* configuration file), which defines the various Internet services it should oversee, for example, ftp, telnet, and http.

2. *inetd.conf* maps a service (e.g., telnet) to a protocol (e.g., tcp) and a daemon that starts it (e.g., */etc/telnetd*). (The protocols that your UNIX system supports are defined in, for example, the file *protocols.*)

3. The service is mapped to a port number. Port numbers are reserved for the most common services (e.g., 23 for telnet, 80 for http). The mapping is defined in, for example, the file */etc/services.*

4. The *inetd* program listens for connections by these services on the specified ports and starts the appropriate daemon to handle the connection when a service request is made. The UNIX command **ps -aux** or **ps -el** will indicate how many connections exist for each type of service at a given time, since a new copy of the appropriate daemon is started for each request.

This brief discussion of how incoming connections are handled raises a couple of interesting points that we shall come back to later in the book. First, your system has finite resources—there is a limit to how many processes you can support. You may have already encountered how this is controlled by using a client to connect to a popular server and being refused because of the large number of existing connections. If you are lucky enough to have your server become that popular, we will discuss how to control the number of simultaneous requests for a given service.

Second, you can restrict who has access to a service by using a "secret" port number. As was indicated from the addresses given in the previous section, each has the provision for including a port number. If a port number is not given, the default (i.e., commonly recognized number) is used. For example, 80 is the default port number for http, the protocol used by the Web. You could assign alternative port numbers to serve up Web pages to only those users who know the port number. Since it is trivial to try making connections to a large number of port numbers, this is not a secure means of safeguarding who sees what information.

Let us now familiarize ourselves with the contents of each of the UNIX networking files introduced above.

```
% cat /etc/inetd.conf
# inetd.conf Internet daemon configuration database
# fields are:
# Service    Socket      Protocol    Delay    User     Program          Arguments
...
  telnet     stream      tcp         nowait   root     /etc/telnetd     telnetd
...
  wn         stream      tcp         nowait   nobody   /usr/local/wn    wn
```

This file will have an entry for each service, however, for brevity, I include only the services telnet, present on every system and wn, one of the two Web servers we are going to install in Chapter Seven.

All the software described in this book is layered on top of tcp and, therefore, the "Protocol" field will always be *tcp*, already defined as part of the base system. Note that if you add some new protocol you should edit the file *protocols* (resides in *etc* on some systems) and add the new protocol if it does not exist. You will not need to do this for any of the software described in this book.

The "Delay" field will be "nowait" for all the software described in this book. Wait implies only one process can run the service at a time. Obviously, this is not useful for Web servers, telnet, etc., where multiple users are going to want to access the service simultaneously.

The "User" field is critical for security since it defines what user will run the service. You should follow the installation instructions that come with the service software when choosing the owner of the service. For example, having a Web server run by root is not a good idea, since it is a security risk.

"Program" refers to the executable being run when the service is requested, and "Arguments" are any arguments required by that executable.

The service is assigned a port number in the file */etc/services*. Here is an extract.

```
% cat /etc/services
# Service                  Port Number
  ftp                      21
  telnet                   23
...
  http                     80
```

This brief introduction to configuring a UNIX host to accept network connections is all you need to know to set up the various server software components described in this book.

2.3.3 MIME Types

How does a piece of software on the UNIX server recognize the type of information it is receiving? The answer lies in MIME types. MIME (Multipurpose Internet Mail Extensions) is a standardized method of assigning types to documents. It was developed originally for use with mail messages. That is, mailers can recognize specific types of documents embedded in mail messages by their MIME types. This same mechanism has been adopted to assign and detect the format of Internet documents.

The first Web browsers identified the type of a document based on its file extension (similar to the system used on Windows, DOS and other operating systems). Later a MIME Content/Type—ancillary information used to identify the real information being sent—was used. A file extension of a few characters is only helpful if the person or software receiving a file already knows what the extension denotes. MIME provides a standardized, more extended, and human-readable system of identification independent of the filename and contents. As we shall see during Web server installation, this system of identification is distributed with most Web servers.

For a gentle introduction to MIME types refer to the URL http://www.cs.wisc.edu/-docs/mime.html. Further information is given in Section 5.4.

As we configure the various clients and servers described in this book we will encounter MIME types. The basic idea is that when you, as a client, access information on various servers, the appropriate application is run to interpret that information once it is received, e.g., a PostScript viewer to display a PostScript file, a video viewer to view a film clip, a molecule viewer to view a molecule, and so on. If that application is invoked from the Web browser itself we refer to it as a *helper application.* Helper applications extend the functionality of a Web browser since they interpret information provided by the browser; information which could not be interpreted by the browser directly. Helper application as used by the Netscape Navigator browser are discussed in Section 6.3.3.2.2.

Having introduced helper applications, I must also mention *plug-ins*. A helper application appears as a separate window and beyond the initial loading of the file initiated by the Web browser there is no communication between browser and helper. A plug-in is an integral part of the Web browser and appears within the browser window. While not advanced at this point in time, the opportunity exists for a variety of plug-ins to communicate with each other under the control of the browser.

As a general rule it is worth noting that, over time, software has evolved to accommodate a larger variety of MIME types. For example, it may not be necessary to download specific software to handle a MIME type because the standard Web browser can handle it, or the software to handle the MIME type has become part of the standard UNIX operating system, and just needs to be invoked as a helper application, rather than first downloaded from the Internet. We will cover a variety of helper applications in this book.

2.4. CLIENT SERVER 101

Client server computing is a much used and much abused term. At the risk of adding to the abuse let me ask you to consider the simple-minded definition used throughout this book. A client makes a request of a server for a particular resource, which the server dutifully provides to the client subject to any security and resource constraints. That resource could be information or computer resources. The term "client" is used without distinction for the software making the request, such as a Web browser, and the physical computer from which the request was made. The same is true for the term "server."

A simple example is a client running a Web browser requesting information from an information server containing HTML-based documents and running the appropriate server software. Figure 2–2 illustrates the basics of client server access as it relates to this scenario.

The key here is what types of information the server can deliver. As we shall see, server software can variously serve text, images, sound, video, and methods (code to perform specific tasks on the client).

2.4.1 E-mail as an Example

Purists may not consider the sending of e-mail a client server activity, but it does specifically illustrate the interaction between a sender (the server) and the receiver (the client). Besides, given the importance placed on e-mail services in this book, it does not hurt to have some background information on how e-mail functions on a UNIX system. Here is the recipe:

- A program referred to as the Mail User Agent (MUA) is used to compose the message on the server (the computer serving the e-mail message to a remote user). The same MUA is used to read incoming messages (at which time the

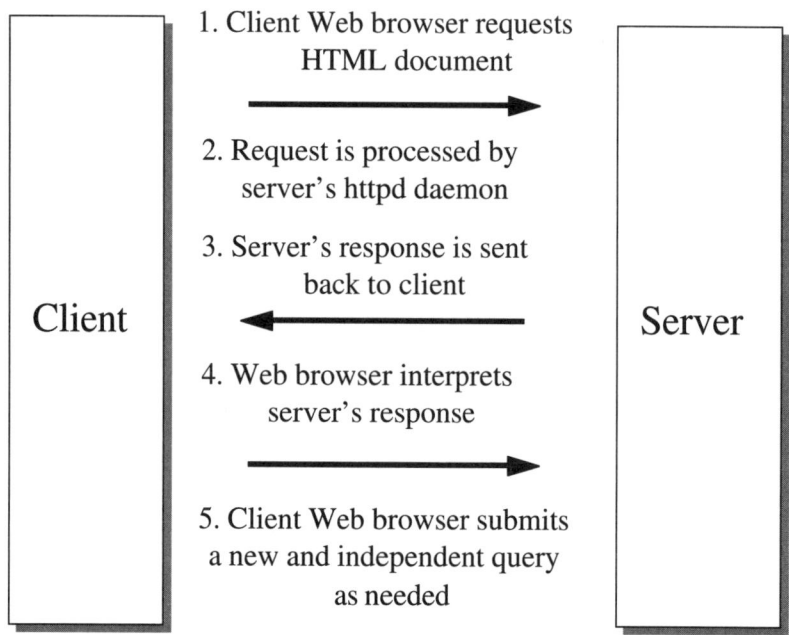

Figure 2–2   Client Server Architecture Made Simple

computer is acting as a client). Typical MUAs are the standard Berkeley UNIX mailer (e.g., */usr/ucb/mail*), and the utility programs *pine* and *elm* (Table 2–5).

- The MUA passes the message and the so-called envelope data (the mail header information containing sender, recipient, etc.) to a Mail Transfer Agent (MTA) on the server. The most common MTA is the UNIX *sendmail* program.
- If the message is to someone on the same server computer the MTA will send it, otherwise it will contact the MTA of the remote client for transfer. The MTA uses port 25 and communicates using the Simple Mail Transfer protocol (SMTP).

TABLE 2–5   Examples of Mail User Agents (MUAs)

Location	Description
ftp://ftp.cac.washington.edu/pine/	Pine mail program distribution. Pine is a line-oriented mail interface.
http://wuarchive.wustl.edu/-packages/mail/elm/	Elm mail program. Elm is a graphically-oriented mail interface.

- Having passed the message to the client MTA the server MTA disconnects. It is then up to the user on the client to read the message, which has been spooled (typically in */usr/spool/mail/login_name*) using their own favorite MUA.
- If the client MTA does not respond, typically you will get a warning message that your server will continue to try and send the message over a period of the next 3-5 days. If after that period the message could still not be delivered, you will get the message back along with a transcript of the session showing the efforts to send the message.

It should be obvious from this discussion of how e-mail works that it is easy to confuse which is the client and which is the server. Often a computer (and a piece of software for that matter) can be both the client and the server. I will try and make the distinction as clear as possible as we work through the recipes in this book. In this particular example, a mail message is being served to a user on a remote client. However, as we shall see in our discussion of Listservers, an e-mail message may be sent to a special server from which it is broadcast to a number of client users.

2.5. INTERNET INFORMATION RELATED TOOLS 101

This section is devoted to a simple introduction to the types of tools I will be discussing throughout this book. These tools can be summarized as follows.

Client tools for accessing an information server
- anonymous ftp
- e-mail
- line-oriented browsers (e.g., gopher and Lynx)
- 2-D graphical browsers (e.g., NCSA Mosaic, Netscape Navigator, and HotJava)
- 3-D graphical browsers (e.g., VRML browser Webview)

Client tools for interpreting information
- sound players (e.g., AudioFile and Xplay)
- video players (e.g., MpegPlay)
- graphics viewers (e.g., xv, Ghostview)

    These tools may be configured as helper applications. Examples of helper applications for the Netscape Web browser can be reviewed at *http://search.netscape.com/assist/helper_apps/-unixhelpers.html*).

Server tools for providing information
- ftp (standard UNIX or enhanced)

- Listservers
- Web servers (e.g., gn, wn, NCSA's httpd, CERN's httpd)

Server tools for preparing information
- text search engines (e.g., WAIS and Harvest)
- sound recorders
- video recorders
- image creation tools (e.g., xv)
- format convertors (e.g., xv, latex2html, rtf2html etc.)
- authoring and editing tools (e.g., htmltext, TkWWW, HoTMetaL, CyberLeaf).
- languages (e.g., Perl, Java)

Maintenance tools

Let me further introduce a subset of these tools.

2.5.1 File Transfer with ftp

File transfer protocol (ftp) is native to all UNIX systems and is used to transfer ASCII and binary files back and forth between client and server. On some UNIX operating systems it may not be installed by default, but it should be available on the distribution media. Ftp is also available native or as a layered product (i.e., at a price) on most other popular non-UNIX operating systems, e.g., DOS, Windows NT, Windows 3.1, Windows 95, OpenVMS, MacOS, and OS/2. Using ftp requires access to both the server computer providing the file(s) and the client computer receiving the file(s). To get files from ftp servers on which you do not have an account, use *anonymous ftp* if it is available. With anonymous ftp, you can log in to the remote machine with a login name of "anonymous" and a password of either "guest", your e-mail address, or some other password specified by the remote anonymous ftp program. The commands associated with ftp (and therefore anonymous ftp) can be found in any good UNIX text. For an online discussion, see

> *http://wsspinfo.cern.ch/file/doc/unixguide/-*
> *subsection2_6_3_1.html#SECTION00631000000000000000*

Section 6.1 provides enough information to permit you to use anonymous ftp successfully.

2.5.1.1 Searching ftp Archives with Archie

Archie is a program that lets you search what amounts to a global table of contents of ftp archives. If you plan to make files available via ftp from your Internet server, you should make sure that those files are registered at an Archie server. We shall see how to do this in Section 7.1.1.2. For now, it is sufficient to know that such a capability exists. Archie communicates with the Archie server(s) by means of a protocol called *Prospero*. Archie makes finding information on ftp servers straightforward. Note that Archie is not made redundant by the search engines accessible from a Web browser since these engines only index sites accessible via the Web (i.e., the http protocol). Many ftp sites do not provide Web access or have their ftp archives separate from their Web documents.

2.5.2 Mail Services

If your goal is to reach a worldwide audience, the value of electronic mail services should not be underestimated, even with the explosion in graphics-oriented information services. This point is underscored in Section 3.2.2 when we plan the services that will be supported on your Internet server. For now, let's consider the two major kinds of mail services:

- Information Service: user A $\Rightarrow$ server $\Rightarrow$ user A
- List Service: user $\Rightarrow$ server $\Rightarrow$ list of subscribers

An *Information Service* lets a user send an e-mail message to the server, whereupon some automated and predefined response is made based on the contents of that e-mail message. This is useful, for example, in automatically distributing information about a specific product or program. A typical scenario might be that a user sends a message containing the one word "HELP." The information server responds by returning an itemized summary of all available information. If one of those items were a program called "Whiz-Bang" then "HELP Whiz-Bang" would return more detailed information on that specific program. Having read the information you wish to try the program, "GET Whiz-Bang" will download the program by sending it as an e-mail message. This works fine for small amounts of ASCII text, but is not the best way to transmit large executable files, graphics images, sound files, and so on.

Another use of an information service is to get files that are accessible by ftp, even when the user does not have access to ftp, but only mail. In this case the body of the mail message contains the ftp commands necessary to connect to the remote ftp site and download the files. This is not discussed further in this book.

A *List Service* is used to send an e-mail message on a specific topic to a Listserver, which then broadcasts that message to anyone who has registered their interest in that topic, that is, people who have subscribed to the list. This service can be automatic or *moderated*. A moderated list means that someone with the appropriate level of access to the Listserver decides whether a particular message should be broadcast to subscribers. This prevents the wide distribution of irrelevant or offensive messages.

2.5.3 Web Browsers

For our purposes, consider a Web browser to be software resident on the client that permits a connection to be made to a Web server and accepts the information returned. Given this simple definition, I identify three classes of browser: line-oriented, graphical, and 3-D. The former requires only a character-based display device, while the latter two require at least a *bit-mapped display.*

2.5.3.1 Line-oriented Web Browsers

Gopher, while now obsolete, was the tool that really opened the eyes of the world to the potential of information serving on the Internet. It was the first methodology that popularized the idea of transparent network links between documents. It is included here simply to illustrate a line-oriented browser. Gopher presents a list of documents as a menu from which the user can choose. The following is the now defunct gopher menu from the San Diego Supercomputer Center (SDSC).

```
% gopher sdsc.edu
  Internet Gopher Information Client 2.0 pl10


        San Diego Supercomputer Center


   1. About SDSC's gopher (README FIRST!).
   2. SUPERCOMPUTING '95 Information/
   3. General Information about SDSC/
   4. Partnerships and Collaborations/
   5. Search the menu titles in the SDSC Index <?>
   6. Internet Resources/
 ->7. Beyond SDSC ( the rest of gopherspace )/
```

Menu items are generally filenames or directories. As you can see, gopher has the advantage of working from a simple line interface, but is restricted in the types of information that it supports. Further, while there is a search capability, there is no possibility of any interaction with the gopher server like that possible with a Web server when invoked through a *Web form.* All graphical Web browsers and lynx (see below) can access remaining Internet gopher servers (most have been converted to Web servers). Therefore, to establish your information server you do not need to install gopher either as a client or as a server. I mention gopher simply to give you the complete picture of the available tools and to indicate its role in the history of Internet information provision. There will be no further discussion of gopher in this book.

Lynx is a full-screen browser for accessing Web-based documents using character cell terminals. Lynx was developed at the University of Kansas. The lynx program uses the arrow keys found on all keyboards to navigate HTML documents. Here is an example of accessing the SDSC home page using lynx.

```
% lynx http://www.sdsc.edu

   San Diego Supercomputer Center (p1 of 3)


   [SDSC Logo]

   Welcome to the San Diego Supercomputer Center. SDSC is a national
   laboratory for computational science and engineering established in
   1985 to advance research and promote U.S. economic competitiveness
   with state-of-the-art computational tools. SDSC is affiliated with the
   University of California, San Diego (UCSD), one of the nation's lead-
   ing research universities, and is administered by General Atomics, a
   high-technology R&D company. SDSC features a variety of collaborative
   research and educational programs, high-performance computational and
   visualization tools, and a nationally recognized staff.
```

Text are contained in square brackets ("[SDSC Logo]" in the above example) indicates that if you using a graphical browser an image would appear at that point. Otherwise the display is much the same as the graphical display with hypertext links to other information sources (i.e., URLs highlighted) which are accessible through the arrow keys rather than the mouse.

To support Lynx on your server you do not have to do anything special. The same Web server software you install to support access via graphical browsers, for example, Netscape Navigator and HotJava (see below) will also work for Lynx. Why install Lynx on your server when it is client software? The first reason is to satisfy users who have login access to the server. To them the same computer is both the client and the server and they need to access Web documents, both on the server and elsewhere. Second, in establishing a Web server you need to see what the information you serve looks like through a text-only browser. I will show you how to install the Lynx browser in Section 6.3.1.

2.5.3.2 Graphical Web Browsers

It is Web browsers that support graphics (not to mention sound, video, and application programs) that have captured our imagination. While line-oriented browsers simply ignore the graphics defined in Web documents, Web browsers display it to dramatic effect. The price you pay as a viewer of the graphics is the time they take to download. I will say much more about this as we begin designing Web documents.

Describing specific graphical Web browsers is hardly worthwhile. Any browser I discuss today will likely be outdated by the time you read this. Therefore, I will consider graphical Web browsers from the point of view of the general features to look for and how those features affect how you design your server.

Browsers are getting smarter and include more features with each release. Ancillary tools that you currently need to access the full range of information services on the Internet are gradually being included in new versions of existing Web browsers and in completely new browsers.

NCSA Mosaic, developed at the National Center for Supercomputing Applications (NCSA), was the first popular graphical Web browser and was responsible for getting the Internet revolution into high gear. Netscape Navigator, from Netscape Communications, Inc., followed and grew to be the dominant Web browser in a few months. From a client user's perspective, Netscape was faster because of the caching mechanism it uses, and had a few desirable features missing from Mosaic, like graphical interfaces to access e-mail, maintain bookmarks, configure helper and plug-in applications, and configure Java support. On the other hand, Mosaic use persists since Mosaic has better multi-language support, Mosaic is free and source code is available. Hence, Mosaic can be compiled and used on platforms for which Netscape is not available. Further, Netscape is a commercial product and requires a license.

In Section 3.4 I will highlight *all* the important features to look for in a browser and where to go on the Internet to find more information, including who is using what browser.

2.5.3.3 3-D Browsers

3-D browsers take the idea of Internet browsing one step, or I should say, one dimension further. While most browsing is "flat," that is, you move up, down, or sideways on the screen, 3-D allows you to zoom into and out of the screen, pick up and move objects, and so on, as if you were actually there. In fact, you are virtually there, and hence this type of environment is given the much abused term of virtual reality. Virtual Reality Modeling Language (VRML) is the language recognized by these browsers, and what they promise is nothing short of astounding. I do not discuss this technology in detail in this book, but I include pointers to more information in Section 6.3.5.

2.5.4 Compute-capable Browsers

Graphical browsers download text and graphics, interpret this information, and display it. "Compute-capable" browsers, (for want of a better term) take these capabilities one step further by also having the ability to download pieces of code from the server to the client and execute them on the client. Java (Chapter 11) is the programming language that provides these pieces of code. In Java terminology, these pieces of code are called *applets*— little applications. The overall effect of this activity is a distribution of the compute load from a single server to multiple clients, but at the price of higher network traffic in downloading application code. It is important at this point to distinguish applets from helper applications and plug-ins. Unlike helper applications and plug-ins, applets reside on the server and are downloaded from the server as needed. Helper applications and plug-ins reside on the client and are invoked as needed.

Applets represent a quantum jump in Internet evolution. To make this point, consider one implication of this development. Instead of downloading an image and displaying it statically in a page, you download the image along with a piece of code that allows you to render that image, that is, rotate it and examine it from all sides. This type of capability greatly increases the power of the Web as an information delivery mechanism. The popular Web browsers, notably Netscape, are now compute-capable. Obviously there are security issues to be considered when using compute-capable browsers. Chapter 11 discusses in more detail the idea of Web-based computing.

2.5.5 Search Engines

As the amount of information on your server grows, however good you are at organizing it, it will still become difficult for users to find what they are looking for. At that point, it is desirable to provide them with a way of searching—based on words or phrases—the contents of all or part of your server. The software available for this purpose is referred to as a search engine. We will explore what are the features to look out for in a search engine, and we will install one so that you get a good idea of how they work. For now, consider a little background on the subject.

The World Area Information Server (WAIS) was arguably the first network-based, information-gathering resource and was developed by Brewster Karle at Thinking Machines Corporation as a client server-based text searching tool. It is this text searching capability, used in conjunction with the more powerful browsing tools, that is popular at the moment. The basic idea in searching arbitrary text is to reduce the time it takes to search for text strings by formatting the text in a way that facilitates searching. In short, indexing the text for quick retrieval of specific words and their location on the information server. There are three basic steps, (i) gathering information, not necessarily just on your information server, but also from related servers, (ii) indexing, and (iii) searching the index.

Section 7.5 discusses how to download, install, configure, and use the Harvest search engine developed at the University of Colorado.

2.5.6 Audio Players

Playing audio on the client is not so much a question of software as hardware support. While many PCs and Macintosh computers support sound, audio support is not so common on UNIX clients. If you plan on supporting sound files on your information server, consider the two types of support. First, passive support, which implies that you act as a simple repository for sound files that you have obtained from elsewhere. Second, active support, which implies you are actually making sound files.

Assuming you and your intended audience have hardware support for sound, what software do you and they need to play sound files? The answer to this question depends on the browser being used to access the sound and the format of the sound file. Chances are that you will need a helper application or a plug-in. The tools that you can use for playing sounds are discussed in Section 3.4.2 and the format of sound files in Section 3.3.5.

2.5.7 Video Players

Like audio players, video players pose challenges with respect to hardware support, format conversion, and the availability of helper applications. Assuming you have hardware audio capability, then you should be able to play movies on the majority of UNIX workstations and PCs running Linux. Most video uses the MPEG format. I will review MPEG viewers which can be used as helper applications in Section 3.4.2.

2.5.8 Image Creation Tools

Creating an Internet information server involves the use of images. While many images can be obtained from the Internet you will most likely wish to create images of your own. Creating images is more the domain of the PC and Macintosh, but there are also good tools for UNIX platforms. I will introduce several such tools, but with emphasis on xv (Section 6.4.2), a beautiful tool for capturing, reformatting, and touching up images.

2.5.9 Format Convertors

The information that you make available through your Internet information server will likely already exist in a variety of formats. It will need to be converted (*filtered*) to a form which can be interpreted by tools on the Internet clients. Section 3.5 introduces a variety of filters.

2.5.10 Authoring and Editing Tools

If the information does not already exist it must be created in a form usable by client tools. This refers primarily to HTML, which is understood by Web browsers. Good tools exist for creating HTML even though it can also be constructed simply using a UNIX text editor. Some of these tools, and places to go to get a current list of tools, are discussed in Section 3.6.

2.5.11 Languages

Sophisticated Internet information servers require that you undertake some programming tasks. While these may be performed in a variety of computer languages, the languages Perl and Java are the most commonly used. Perl because it is good at string manipulation and Java because it was developed specifically for Internet use. String manipulation is important in having the server interpret information that is sent from clients (Chapter 10) and Java is important in developing truly distributed computing (Chapter 11).

By now you should have a sense of scope—all the issues you need to consider in setting up an Internet information server. Purposely, I have not given you a lot of detail, that comes later. We are now ready to progress to the next step in the global recipe, planning what the server will look like to the intended audience.

3

Planning for the Server

Ingredients:

- *Intended Audience*
- *Services to Support*
- *Information Types to Support*
- *Information Management Tools to Support*
- *Available Resources*

Take a liberal amount of your intended audience and the services you think they are likely to need. You can't be too generous here—you will never anticipate everyone's needs and how they will individually gobble up a good supply of information. Choose server software that can provide for this intended audience and add two other major ingredients: software for reading, writing, and filtering all the anticipated information types and sufficient resources, both hardware and human. Mix these ingredients together and you have a good plan in the making, with little chance of ending up with anything half-baked!

3.1. WHO IS THE INTENDED AUDIENCE?

This is the first question you should ask yourself. In our cooking analogy, think of developing an information server in the same way you think about preparing a gourmet meal. There is no point going to the butcher, selecting a choice cut of meat and marinating it for days if your dinner guests are vegetarians! Likewise, there is no point spending months preparing digitized video for your information server audience if 95 percent of them have neither the bandwidth nor the client software needed to play the video.

A good meal naturally leads from one course to another. You start with just enough to whet the appetite and then proceed through just enough of a series of courses to not overwhelm the eater, but to excite all taste buds. So it should be with an information server. Success depends very much on how you organize the information.

Organization of information is covered in Chapter Five. Beyond the basic organization, you need to be aware of special considerations when dealing with hypertext. I will get to these considerations in Section 8.2.5. This chapter is devoted to helping you further distinguish the types of information services that exist, which of them you should provide to your intended audience, what information types are associated with those services, and specifically what tools you need to manage and deliver those information types.

The size of the audience using your information server is a function of the subject material presented, the quality and quantity of that material, how that material is organized and then delivered, and any network and hardware limitations. I cannot help you with the quality or subject matter presented on your information server, but I can help you with organization, delivery, and resource needs. Getting these right requires planning.

3.2. WHAT SERVICES SHOULD I SUPPORT?

As stated previously, this book discusses three basic types of service that you can support on your information server.

- An ftp-based service (file transfer protocol)
- An electronic mail-based service (e-mail)
- A Web-based service

Planning lets you balance the level of service that can be provided against the resources that need to be expended to establish and maintain the information service.

We can no longer talk about an information server in a generic sense. Yes, the server may be a single piece of hardware, but the software, knowledge, and effort required varies when serving e-mail, files via ftp, Web page serving, and Java applets.

A Note on Software Versions

I cannot tell you what version of server software to get for the different types of information you will serve. Whatever I suggest will not be the current version when you read this book. Such is the force of this technology. Instead, I suggest you look at the appropriate README files before downloading any code or executables. *My rule of thumb, since I prefer reliability to being on the cutting edge, is not to take beta releases, but to stick to the last full release of the software.* Bear in mind that software does not always get better with subsequent releases and nearly always requires more resources to run, often in support of new features of no obvious relevance to what you wish to do. Conversely, if you take a very old, but stable version of the software, it may work now, but not when you or your system administrator upgrades the UNIX operating system. You are then forced to repeat the install using the newer version of the software that works with both the new and the old versions of the operating system and that you decided not to install the first time around—twice the work!

In this and subsequent chapters I begin with the simplest types of service: electronic mail and ftp file serving, then move on to more complex Web-based information services incorporating sound, video, and downloadable applications.

After reading this chapter you should be able to decide on the services to provide, the initial level of support to offer for each service, and the particular software to install. Of course, you will add and delete to this list over time, but you will have started on server implementation through some sound planning!

3.2.1 Choice of ftp Servers ☞

The basic UNIX operating system provides the ability to serve information in the form of files to a world of users since *ftp* (file transfer protocol) is an integral part of all UNIX operating systems. Throughout this book I shall refer to the files that you serve to users via ftp as the *ftp archive*.

The directory structure of the ftp archive is as simple or as complex as you wish to make it, and it is the only part of your overall file system that the anonymous ftp user is allowed to see. Once you have archived some files and correctly configured the ftp software (Section 7.1), users can access your ftp archive either using anonymous ftp or a Web browser, since all browsers support the ftp protocol.

Anonymous ftp also provides a mechanism, beyond electronic mail, for users to provide you with information that you might wish to make generally available on your server. That is, you can make a writable directory in your ftp archive writable for anonymous ftp users to use for depositing information. Permitting the uploading of information is discussed in Section 7.1.

The basic ftp program found on most UNIX operating systems is controlled by the *ftpd* daemon (*in.ftpd* on some systems) which handles all ftp requests. The *ftpd* daemon is started at boot time. The standard *ftpd* daemon can be replaced with another that offers enhancements. Why replace the standard *ftpd* and ftp program? Here are some of the available enhancements that might make sense for you:

- You can provide additional instructions and comments when a user accesses the ftp archive and when they access specific directories within the archive.
- The person accessing the archive can be made aware of when files were last modified in the archive.
- You can classify groups of users according to the login id they use to access the ftp archive and from what host or subnet they come from.
- You can restrict how many simultaneous ftp users are allowed to access your system, in total or according to each class that you have defined.
- You can restrict who can upload files to your ftp server.
- The server can uncompress, compress, and tar files automatically as they are transferred.
- You can log who accesses your ftp server and what they do.

- A link between the */etc/shutdown* program and ftpd provides a graceful mechanism for notifying ftp users of an impending shutdown. Using standard ftp, the
  only notification the user gets is a broken connection! The graceful mechanism
  prevents new ftp users from logging on when a shutdown has begun, and warns
  those logged on as the shutdown countdown progresses.

If these points have convinced you that upgrading your standard *ftpd* is a good idea,
Table 3–1 introduces the two best options.

Some of the features highlighted above may already be available with the version
of ftp that comes with your particular UNIX operating system. If a very high level of security is not your major concern, before you consider an alternative to the standard *ftpd* you
should run the ftp archive from the standard *ftpd* for a while and see whether it meets your
needs. If you want to read more about anonymous ftp see *http://iss.net/iss/anonftp.html*.

3.2.2 Mail Services

As was introduced in Section 2.5.2 electronic mail services (hereafter referred to as e-mail
services) are vital if you are trying to reach a wide and diverse audience. Many people
have e-mail access but nothing else. Examples are users in developing countries and those
using the less expensive of the services offered by *Internet Service Providers* (ISPs) like
CompuServe and America Online. This situation will change as more and more people
gain access to more sophisticated services. In the meantime, however, e-mail services are
important and easy to offer because:

- The user of a UNIX system already has the appropriate software installed as
  part of the operating system.
- The user most likely knows how to use e-mail already, so there is no learning
  curve.
- E-mail can provide a great deal of information (see Section 6.2).
- E-mail reaches the widest possible audience (e.g., users located in secure environments may have no other access to the Internet beyond e-mail).
- E-mail services are the most mature of the information services you could provide. Some people believe, therefore, that e-mail is the most secure service. Of

TABLE 3–1 Enhanced ftp Servers

Location	ftp Servers
ftp://gatekeeper.dec.com/-pub/DEC/gwtools/ftpd.tar.Z	DECwrl ftp
http://wuarchive.wustl.edu/-packages/wuarchive-ftpd/	**wu-ftp, Washington University ftp server**[2]

[2]Options in bold are those the author recommneds.

course, breaches, when they occur, affect more people than the other services. The infamous Internet worm which exploited the UNIX **sendmail** program is a case in point. For an excellent discussion of this security breach, written by Charles Schmidt and Tom Darby see

> *http://www.mathcs.carleton.edu/students/darbyt/pages/-*
> *worm.html*

- E-mail services require minimal computing resources.

3.2.2.1 Choice of Mail Information Servers ☞

Recall from Section 2.4.1 that an information server processes a mail message requesting some information. The request is in a form that can be recognized by the standard UNIX e-mail program which, with some additional software, can be made to return a canned response to the e-mail message. For example, that response could include information on a specific product sold by your organization, details of a piece of software you are giving away, or the hypertext framework of this book. Taking this a step further, the response could be a file obtained from an ftp site and sent to the user as part of the e-mail reply. This is exactly what the Ftpmail program does (Table 3–2). Why not just go to the ftp site and get the file directly? As stated earlier, some users will only have e-mail access. If you want them to have access to your ftp archive, you need to install this capability on your server. Ftpmail provides this type of service (Table 3–2).

The canned_reply program (Table 3–2), as the name suggests, provides explicit responses to requests made by mail, so long as the keywords associated with those requests are recognized. The canned_reply program is well documented online and described fully in the excellent book by Cricket Liu, Jerry Peek, Russ Jones, Bryan Buus and Adrian Nye called *Managing Internet Information Services,* which is published by O'Reilly and Associates Inc.

3.2.2.2 Choice of Listservers ☞

A Listserver, as defined in Section 2.5.2, requires additional software beyond basic UNIX mail. Recall that the basic idea of a Listserver is to provide *all* information to *all* users who choose to subscribe to the list. The same piece of software is used to maintain mul-

TABLE 3–2   Mail Information Servers

Mail Information Servers	Location
canned_reply	*ftp://ftp.uu.net/published/oreilly/-* *nutshell/miis/miis.9412.tar.Z*
Ftpmail	*ftp.sterling.com/mail/ftpmail*

tiple lists on the server. Typically, each list deals with a different topic. Subscribers to the list:

- Receive information about that server by sending a message with keyword(s). For example, a list of responses to Frequently Asked Questions (FAQs) or all postings to the list in the last month.
- Post to the Listserver and have that posting broadcast to all subscribers of the list.
- Receive all postings to the list.
- May have a list mediator—someone who monitors what is received and selectively edits what is broadcast to all subscribers.
- Have the option to subscribe or unsubscribe to the list at will.

The major advantage (and potential disadvantage) of a Listserver is that it requires no action on the subscribers' parts beyond subscription to the list. After subscribing, they see everything posted to the list—and I mean everything! They have no control (beyond unsubscribing) over what they receive. This may be good if they read with interest most of the material posted to the list. On the other hand, it can be obtrusive since they may have to deal with a large amount of unwanted information. Contrast this to the information upon demand services like the Web, where consumers go to the information, rather than have it come to them.

If you have decided to run a Listserver, Table 3–3 outlines the major choices.

For a comprehensive discussion of Listservers and a larger list of available software, see:

- *http://www.grfn.org/~topher/listserv.html*
- *http://www.cis.ohiostate.edu/hypertext/faq/usenet/mail/archive-servers/faq/faq.html*

Majordomo, from the Latin *major domus,* is a person who speaks, makes arrangements, or takes charge for another. *This is my recommended starting point, since it is rel-*

TABLE 3–3   Popular Listservers

Location	Listservers
http://www.lsoft.com/listserv.html	LISTSERV™
http://www.cren.net/www/-listproc/description.html	CREN's ListProc
ftp://ftp.greatcircle.com/pub/-majordomo	**Majordomo**
ftp://ftp.informatik.rwth-aachen.de/-pub/packages/procmail/-SmartList.tar.gz	SmartList

atively simple and has the functionality needed by most sites. Majordomo is implemented
in Section 7.2.

As an information provider, typically you establish the Listserver, assign new lists,
and remove old lists as demand dictates. You may also assign moderator(s) to each list. A
moderator is someone who screens incoming postings to the list and then selectively
decides whether they should be discarded, modified before posting, or posted as is. It is
good "netiquette" to indicate to folks when they subscribe to a list whether it is moderated or not. Moderation serves to filter out information that is not appropriate to the list, but
it is a form of censorship.

3.2.2.3 Choice of Miscellaneous Mail-related Tools ☞

The distinction between e-mail services and other forms of service cannot be delineated
completely. For example, you may wish to have the contents of a list (i.e., all messages
posted to the list) available on the Web so users can reference previous discussions. An
example of this is a mail service available through a Web service. This integration requires
a filter to convert UNIX mail messages into HTML so they can be served as Web documents. Examples of these tools are given in Section 3.5.

Consider also whether to support MailServ (*http://iquest.comufitz/www/mailserv/*).
MailServ provides a gateway between the Web and various types of mailing list software.
Written by Patrick Fitzgerald, MailServ simplifies a user's ability to subscribe to various
mailing lists and, therefore, may be of value to your user community. MailServ supports the
ListProc, ListServ, Majordomo, MLP, Manual, and SmartList Listservers. The simplification
comes from not having to know the names of the lists and also from a Web form that helps
the subscriber use the correct syntax for subscribing to the appropriate list. It is not essential
that you install MailServ on your own server; rather you can run it off Patrick's. However, so
as not to rely on someone else's hardware for an important utility, you might do better to
install it locally. Full instructions for doing this can be found at the URL listed above.

3.2.3 Choice of Web (http) Servers ☞

Web servers, that is, those servers that support at least the http protocol used by all Web
browsers, are numerous, and each is varied in its capability. What is worse is a high
turnover rate—what is a very capable Web server today is soon obsolete. The best I can
do is to answer the question, "What features of an http server are important?" and then
give a recommendation. Refer to this book's Web page as one source of the latest recommendations. Here are a few of the more important features:

- *Ability to run from inetd* (see Section 2.3 for a description of *inetd*). This means
  the server is under the control of the standard UNIX network daemons rather
  than running as a separate daemon. As we shall see in Sections 7.3 and 7.4,
  when installing two different servers, which is desirable depends on security and
  the load on the system.

- *Error logging controlled by the UNIX syslog program.* The same issues arise here as arise in the case of *inetd.*

- *Support for CERN/NCSA common log format.* Every event performed by the server is logged to a file. The advantage of using the most common log format is that there are already tools written to summarize this information should you need to do that (Chapter 12 is devoted to this topic). The disadvantage of a common log format is that everyone knows the format and can potentially use it, perhaps for ill-purpose, if they gain access to the log files. *Overall the advantages of a common format outweigh the disadvantages.*

- Support for server-side includes. A server-side include is similar to an include statement in a number of programming languages (Section 9.3). For example, rather than manually insert the date the Web page was last modified into the HTML each time you modify the file you can simply *include* a function that returns the modification date based on the file modification date retained by the UNIX system. In this way you have automated the updating process. Allowing external commands to be invoked through server-side includes, however, represents a security risk. Many servers support this feature, yet optionally allow you to turn it off. *In any but the most secure environments, server-side includes are a must for creating comprehensive and easily managed Web pages.*

- *Limited file access.* Typical for servers supporting this feature, the Web page administrator explicitly specifies what files are accessible. These files are then cached and made available for serving. *Limited file access increases security but requires more effort to maintain.*

- *Access prohibited by IP address.* Only specified remote Internet hosts can access the server.

- *Access prohibited by domain name.* Only specified Internet domains can access the server.

- *Easy Install.* Uses a Graphical User Interface (GUI) to install and configure the server software.

- *Actions based on UNIX file type.* This implies the ability to perform some action on specific types of file, for example CGI scripts (in other words good support for MIME types).

- *Default directory tree.* A directory hierarchy is automatically configured for containing files associated with the Web server and the information being served.

- *Permits access to user directories.* This represents a convenience, since different people with accounts on the server can serve Web pages, however, it also presents a security risk. For example, it is useful to have a URL point to *~fred/.plan,* the finger plan file for user fred, which presumably provides useful demographic information. This same information is then available to Web users and people using the *finger* program. The disadvantage is that you have permitted Web access to a user's directory rather than just the Web document directory tree.

- *Available search engines.* Text search engines require close cooperation with the Web server. Search engines generally only support a subset of the available Web servers. (e.g., Section 7.5).

- *Cost.* Not all servers are free. Whether you buy a server should depend on whether you need support services and not on software quality. The free Web servers are generally of high quality.

If you thought that this is a long list of considerations, note that it is only a partial list. Do not be deterred, however. Table 3–4 provides a list of common http servers, many of which support a significant number of these options.

The URL *http://www.proper.com/www/servers-chart.html* gives a current list of available servers mapped to the desirable options. I recommend you review this list prior to installing a Web server. Other less comprehensive discussions of available servers can be found at the URLs:

- *http://www.yahoo.com/Computers_and_Internet/Internet/-World_Wide_Web/HTTP/Servers/UNIX/*

- *http://www.w3.org/hypertext/WWW/Servers.html*

If this is all too much information, I would recommend you start with httpd from NCSA, if you want a true and tried product without the need for excessive security. If security is a concern, I recommend wn from John Franks.

TABLE 3–4   Popular Web Servers

Location	Web (http) Server
http://www.apache.org/apache	Appache HTTP
http://wsk.eit.com/wsk/doc/	EIT Webmasters Starter Kit
http://hopf.math.nwu.edu/	**gn from John Franks**
http://www.w3.org/hypertext/-WWW/daemon/Status.html	httpd from CERN
ftp://ftp.ncsa.uiuc.edu/Web/httpd *http://hoohoo.ncsa.uiuc.edu/docs*	**httpd from NCSA**
http://www.netscape.com/-comprod/netscape_commun.html	Netscape
http://openmarket.com	Webserver from Open Market
http://www.bsdi.com/server.doc/plexus.html	Plexus from Tony Sanders at BSDI
http://hopf.math.nwu.edu	**wn from John Franks**

A current survey of what Web servers others have recently installed can be found at *http://www.proper.com/www/servers-survey.html.* At the time of writing, NCSA's httpd server has 41 percent of the market.

3.2.4 Emerging Server Technology

Internet server technology is evolving rapidly, with the biggest developments in Web-based servers, rather than mail or ftp servers. Even the definition of what constitutes a Web-based server is undergoing change. This change is occurring on two fronts:

- Hardware specific to Internet information serving and retrieval is becoming available.
- Software with a wider range of capabilities is becoming available.

The term "Web Server" will evolve from referring to a combination of generic hardware and specific software to referring to specific hardware and specific software. Vendors are already selling hardware made from basic components but customized for information serving, notably database servers (see, for example, *http://www.chensys.com/*), which optimize such features as text searching and handling many simultaneous network connections.

Further, with languages like Java (Chapter 11) the idea of a Web server as a single piece of software handling http requests is disappearing. In Java, it is easy (a few lines of code) to open a TCP/IP-based socket connection to a server, which can then be used to communicate with a server-side application that has no reliance on the http protocol. This lends credence to the idea of a "global computer," since computation and information lookup are easily distributed. We will return to this notion in Chapter 11.

3.3. WHAT INFORMATION TYPES WILL I ENCOUNTER?

Running an information server brings you in contact with a wild variety of wonderful information types. Knowing something about these information types is a prerequisite to the information server planning process and is discussed in some detail in this section.

The good news is that there are only four basic types of information: text (including source code of applications), graphics, sound, and movies (which are a combination of the first three). The bad news is that they come in a variety of formats. These formats each represent some kind of *de facto* standard, since they are recognized by commonly used software, rather than being defined as a standard by some standards organization. The really important software is, of course, that which recognizes one information format and writes another; this type of software is called a *filter.* Filters are vital items in the information server manager's bag of tricks. A typical example is the manager's need to convert some existing document into HTML for Web access. Table 3–5 considers the most common information types.

TABLE 3–5   Common Information Types

Information Type	Description	Typical UNIX File Extensions
Text	Any ASCII characters	.txt, .doc, .java, .c
Tar	Files and (optionally) directories of files represented as a single file created with the UNIX **tar** command	.tar
Compressed	Any file which has been compressed, typically with the UNIX **compress** and **gzip** commands	.Z (compress) .gz (gzip)
Binary	Bit-based data representation; may be architecture specific or neutral	.obj, .exe, .class
Sound	Contains digitized sound	.snd, .au, .wav
Images and graphics	Pixel-based representation	.gif, .tif, .jpg, .pict, .pcx
Movies	A series of images	.mpeg, .mov, .moo
HyperText Markup Language	Text containing markup recognized by Web browsers	.html, .htm, .shtml
TeX	Text containing markup recognized by the TeX or LaTeX programs	.tex
TeX	Intermediate file processed by Tex or LaTex	.dvi
PostScript	Text and/or graphics in Adobe PostScript format	.ps, .eps
Rich Text Format (RTF)	Text interchange format developed by Microsoft	.rtf
Mail files	Files recognized by the UNIX mailer; may have been uuencoded	
man pages (troff/roff/nroff)	UNIX manual pages recognized by the UNIX **troff, nroff,** and **roff** commands	1, .2, .3 etc.

Let us look at each of these information types. Remember that the UNIX command **file** can be used to identify at least some file types if it is not obvious from the *file extension.*

```
% file *.*
urls.txt        ascii text
zen.ps          PostScript
bin             directory
form            English text
prog.java       ascii text
page.html       ascii tex
myfile.dat      data
prog            executable
```

In the above example, file has not made a distinction between Java code and HTML, but has at least recognized both as ASCII text.

3.3.1 Text Files

What constitutes a text file is somewhat arbitrary, however, for reasons of simplicity let's define it as any file containing just those characters conforming to the ASCII character set, as shown in

> *http://www.w3.org/hypertext/WWW/Protocols/rfc1341/-*
> *7_1_Text.html*

That is, here I consider ASCII characters to be those that can be read by humans. This classification, though, is somewhat arbitrary. PostScript files or RTF files (see below) are types of text files, since they are also made up of ASCII characters, but there are not many people who curl up in bed with a PostScript file that has not been suitably interpreted by a printer. In other words, PostScript and RTF files, among others, are a special form of text file. Text files are the most common information format that you will encounter and wish to serve.

3.3.2 Tar Files

Tar files, written with the UNIX **tar** command, are often found in ftp archives, since they offer a convenient way of grouping files together and distributing them. The files can be maintained as a single tar file, which internally maintains a directory structure that can be recreated on the client. A tar file is typically created with a command such as

```
% tar cvf /tmp/export.tar .
```

This command creates (c option) a single file */tmp/export.tar* (f option indicates a file argument follows) that contains the contents of the current directory and any subdirectories (indicated by the period), which are typically directories like *src* (source files), *bin* (binary executable files), *man* (any manual pages associated with the distribution), and *doc* (documentation). The v option (verbose) lists files as they are loaded into the tar file. The tar file simplifies the distribution process by sending a single file with ftp (in binary mode) while still maintaining the directory structure vital to the operation of many free software distributions. As we shall see in Section 3.3.3, the tar file may be compressed to shorten the transmission time and conserve disk space on the information server.

　　Note: this example produces a relative distribution—a collection of files referenced relative to the current directory. The receiver then recreates the directory structure relative to the current directory on his or her client.

The alternative is an absolute distribution which would start at the root directory, for example */usr/local/bin. The creation of an absolute tar file should be avoided since it offers the receiver no flexibility (without significant effort and knowledge) as to where the files must reside.*

When you have made or obtained a tar file and wish to check its contents, use a command like:

```
% tar tf /tmp/export.tar
```

This command lists the contents of the tar file (t option) on standard output (*stdout*—usually the terminal), but it could redirect the output to a file or printer. Again, the f option indicates that a tar file argument, in this instance */tmp/export.tar,* follows.

To recreate the files and directory structure from a tar file use the general form of the command:

```
% cd desired_directory
% tar xvf export.tar
```

The second command extracts the individual files (x option) and maintains the directory structure stored in the file (f option) *export.tar.* The v option (verbose) reports on each file as it is written from the tar file to a separate disk file.

This use of tar is introductory UNIX 101, but I chose to include it, since it is of great importance when building an information server. Much of the software you will install in establishing your server comes as tar files. If you need further information on tar and other basic UNIX commands refer to Appendix B, which provides a list of useful sources of UNIX tutorial material.

3.3.3 Compressed Files

Compressed files are useful for conserving disk space and simplifying distribution, since it takes less time for transmission over the Internet. There are various compression algorithms and software that implements them. If you are compressing files, use compression software that you know the receiver of the compressed file will have, or provide (assuming it does not infringe copyright) the decompression software as a separate uncompressed file.

Three common commands are used to compress files on UNIX systems: **uuencode, compress** (standard UNIX commands), and **gzip** (from the Free Software Foundation), **uuencode** is used to compress information for transmission by electronic mail and **compress** and **gzip** are used to compress and uncompress UNIX files. Since **uuencode** and the corresponding **uudecode** are used by one user transferring information to another user, rather from a server to group of client users, it is not discussed further in this book. The man page does an adequate job of describing how to use **uuencode**. There is also a nice recipe at *http://taipan.nmsu.edu/aght/soils/soil_physics/tutorials/int_lit/step_by.html*

You may find other compression programs on your UNIX system with commands like **man -k compress**. For example, the **pack** command will be present on some systems, however, **compress** and **gzip** are suitable for most purposes. There are also compression programs specific to different types of image formats. These are not discussed here, refer to *http://www.aber.ac.uk/~dcswww/Public/Research/Telematics/EIUF/new_eiuf/subsection3_7_2.html* for details.

The major difference between compression programs is how much they compress a file. The degree of compression is file type-dependent as you can see from Table 3–6, which shows compression ratios for different types of files—larger numbers indicate better compression. For example, a PostScript file compressed with the **compress** command is compressed to16 percent of its original size, whereas a binary file is only compressed to 34 percent of its original size.

The **gzip** program performs better compression than **compress,** but takes longer to compress the file. However, on the average UNIX workstation, this time difference is so little for files of several megabytes or smaller as to be irrelevant. The advantage of **compress** is that it comes distributed with most versions of UNIX, whereas **gzip** must be downloaded from, for example, *http://mathssun5.lancs.ac.uk:2080/-~maa036/GNU/GNUWeb/gzip.html*

```
% compress export.tar
```

This command will compress the file *export.tar* into a file called *export.tar.Z.* Note: you must have enough free disk space to contain both *export.tar* and *export.tar.Z.* Once the compression is complete, export.tar is deleted, leaving only the compressed file. If there is not enough disk space, compression fails and *export.tar* is left unchanged. To decompress a file use the following command:

```
% uncompress export.tar.z
```

Decompression requires that you have enough disk space to hold both *export.tar.Z* and *export.tar.* If not enough disk space is available for both compressed and uncom-

TABLE 3–6   Compression Ratios for **compress** and **gzip** Given Various File Types

File Type	compress	gzip
Postscript file	6.25	9.55
binary file	2.93	4.25
tar file	2.87	3.78

pressed file, decompression fails and only the compressed file remains. After successful decompression, the compressed file is deleted.

The **gzip** program is used in much the same way except that it produces a compressed file with the extension of *.gz*. You use it as follows:

```
% gzip myfile
% ls
myfile.gz
% gunzip myfile.gz
% ls
myfile
```

*I recommend that you install the **gzip** program since you will encounter software you need that requires **gzip** to uncompress it, and besides it provides the best compression ratios for every file type.*

3.3.4 Binary

In this book "binary files" means any files that produce indecipherable output when displayed with a UNIX command like **more** or **cat**. This includes not only programs processed by a compiler or loader, but also some of the other information types described here. Thus, text and binary formats are supersets encompassing a variety of other information formats.

3.3.5 Sound

Sound files are binary files with built-in compression applied by the software that produced the sound file. Common sound formats are listed in Table 3–7.

Not all formats shown in Table 3–7 are produced by UNIX systems. It is easier and less expensive to produce sounds on a PC or Macintosh platform. For a more detailed discussion of sound formats, see *http://www.cis.ohiostate.edu/hypertext/faq/usenet/audio-fmts/part1/faq.html.*

TABLE 3–7   Common Sound Formats

Name	File Extension	Description
AIFF	.aif, .aiff	Silicon Graphics IRIX produced
	.voc	SoundBlaster produced
HCOM	none	Macintosh produced
IFF/8SVX	.iff	Amiga produced
	.mod, .nst	Another Amiga format
WAVE	.wav	Microsoft Windows produced
μlaw	.au, .snd	NeXT and Sun produced
none	.snd	Macintosh produced

3.3.6 Images (Including Graphics)

A plethora of graphics formats exist; I consider only the most popular here.

GIF (Graphics Interchange Format) files are the most common. This is the format recognized by all Web browsers, and information providers tend to make their images available as GIFs. These files have filenames with the extension *.gif*. This format was developed in 1987 by CompuServe, the large, well-known Internet provider. The major drawback of this format is that it only supports 256 colors for use with 8-bit color displays, which may be insufficient to provide the richness needed for some images. There have been extensions to this standard, notably GIF89A, which includes support for more colors available on 24-bit color displays. Some Web browsers recognize the enhancements offered by GIF89A. This is noticeable through the support of transparent images, which give the effect of an image and the browser background being the same, so that the image appears to be floating on the page. You can read more about transparent images at the URL *http://www.cowan.edu.au/ecawa/mbooka/giftrans.txt.*

TIFF (Tagged Image File Format) was designed by Microsoft and Aldus Inc. and is the format produced by most scanners.

JPEG (Joint Photographic Expert Group) is not used as commonly as the others, partly because the early Web browsers did not support it. This is changing though, since Web browsers do support it now and it supports higher resolution images. MPEG (see below) is derived from JPEG.

For further details on these and other graphics formats, see:

http://www.cis.ohio-state.edu/hypertext/faq/-
usenet/graphics/utilities-faq/faq.html

http://www.cis.ohio-
state.edu/hypertext/faq/usenet/graphics/faq/faq.html

The major trade-off in comparing graphics formats is size of the image file versus resolution. We will be dealing primarily with standard GIF files, since these provide a compromise between quality and size and are suitable for most Web-based applications.

3.3.7 Movies

MPEG (Motion Picture Expert Group) is a binary compressed format for video and the most common movie format. I discuss players for this format in Sections 3.4.2 and 6.6.

AVI is used by Microsoft Windows, but not popular on UNIX platforms.

For further information on movie formats, see:

http://www.det.mun.ca/staff/gporter/mmfaq.htm

3.3.8 Hypertext Markup Language (HTML)

HTML is the so-called "language of the Web" and the format with which you likely will have the most contact. It is a markup language used to "tag" standard text, which causes a program (e.g., a Web Browser) to present that text in a certain way.

HTML is popular because it is relatively simple to use, although as HTML evolves to support tables, special characters, etc., it is by necessity becoming more complex. As with all markup languages, you only need to use a subset of its features. The major attraction of HTML is, of course, the links it allows you to create to other documents anywhere in the world. Chapters 8-10 cover HTML in detail.

HTML was developed by the folks at Conseil Européen pour la Réherche Nucleaire (CERN), now known as the European Laboratory for Particle Physics, and is based upon Standard Generalized Markup Language (SGML). SGML has been around for a long time and used extensively in the publishing industry.

3.3.9 TeX

- TeX and its derivatives, for example LaTeX, are, like HTML, also markup languages. TeX was developed by Donald Knuth at Stanford University and has a large following, particularly in the publishing, physics, computer science, and mathematics communities. The marked up file is processed by the TeX program producing a DVI (DeVice Independent TeX) file. The DVI file is an intermediate format that can be processed into a variety of other formats including PostScript and HTML. DVI files can be viewed directly with certain viewers, notably *xdvi*. For details see

    http://www.cis.ohio-state.edu/hypertext/faq/usenet/-
    tex-faq/faq.html.

3.3.10 PostScript

PostScript was developed by Adobe Systems Inc. as a device-independent text representation, and is now recognized by most printers. Encapsulated PostScript is an integral part of the PostScript language that supports the imbedding of images. For details see

    http://www.cis.ohio-state.edu/hypertext/faq/-
    usenet/postscript-faq/part1-4/faq.html.

3.3.11 Rich Text Format

RTF (Rich Text Format) was developed by Microsoft as an interchange format and, because of the popularity of the Microsoft Word word processing software, is now a standard interchange format. It is one of the easiest ways to convert documents written using Word, WordPerfect, and other popular PC word processing programs into HTML for use on your information server. For details, see

    http://www.lib.ox.ac.uk/internet/news/-faq/archive/text-faq.html

It does not work well for complex documents including equations and imbedded graphics images.

3.3.12 troff/nroff/roff

roff (run-off) was the original UNIX text formatter; it was replaced by **troff** (text run-off) and finally by **nroff** (new run-off). None is used much these days, except by UNIX diehards and UNIX system administrators preparing man (manual pages), since the UNIX **man** command will invoke some version of **nroff** to create the formatted man page from an unformatted nroff file. As we shall see in the following section, it is possible to convert nroff formatted documents into HTML for Web browsing. For details see *http://www.cs.pdx.edu/~trent/nu/groff/index.html.*

3.3.13 Mail Files

UNIX supports a standard mail format (the story is really more complex than this), which is text-based. As a result, mail messages can be treated like any other files. There are converters that convert UNIX mail formatted files into various other formats, notably HTML. We will see examples of this in the following section.

3.4. WHAT BROWSERS, VIEWERS, AND PLAYERS WILL I NEED?

The distinction between a browser, viewer and player is somewhat arbitrary, but maintaining the distinction may help clarify your particular needs. In this book, a browser is software to browse a combination of text and graphics, a viewer is software to display and possibly edit a graphics image, and a player plays sound or video.

3.4.1 Browsers

If you are going to support Web access to your Internet information server, you need a Web browser, also called the Web client. In theory you do not require a browser to view your own documents before serving them on the Web, but in practice it is foolhardy to serve something you have not viewed yourself! HTML is a simple markup language to use and Web page markup is therefore not too difficult, but it is rare that you get a reasonably sized page right the first time unless you are using a What-You-See-Is-What-You-Get Editor (*WYSIWIG*) (Section 3.6). Another reason for the browser is it represents the simplest mode of access to the various pieces of Internet server software you will need to download to establish the Internet server described in this book.

One arbitrary classification of browsers divides them into 2-dimensional browsers capable of reading HMTL, versus 3-dimensional browsers capable of reading Virtual Reality Modeling Language (VRML). The implications of VRML are profound, since they bring information access via the Internet closer to the way we traditionally get information. For example, rather than click our way through highlighted text on the electronic page, VRML lets us "walk" into a virtual library, take a virtual book off the virtual shelf, open it, and browse. At the time of writing, the hardware resources needed to use VRML effectively on a UNIX workstation have so far precluded its wide use. Further, while extensive libraries of scene information are emerging that can be used to make your scenes, you must still do a lot of work to develop the necessary pages. For these reasons, VRML is not covered in depth in this book; however, I do provide you with adequate pointers to all the information you need to get started (Section 3.4.1.2).

3.4.1.1 2-D

There are many choices of 2-D browsers. There is a Catch-22 here. To select the browser that best suits your needs you need to refer to the Web for information and reviews of the latest releases. To refer to the Web requires a browser! To solve this dilemma I suggest you install one of the recommended browsers. If later you find there are inadequacies with the browser you have chosen, refer to the following to help you make another selection.

http://www.ski.mskcc.org/browserwatch/browsers.html

http://www.browserwatch.com/

The second entry has a test page that you can view with the browser you are currently using, see what it looks like and then see what that same page looks like when viewed with other browsers. Since the HTML specification is constantly changing, the test indicates how many of the current features of HTML are recognized by a particular browser (*very useful*). *This discussion should be telling you to update your browser regularly.*

Consider also whether the browser should be Java-ready, that is capable of downloading, interpreting, and executing Java applets (Chapter 11).

Table 3–8 lists some of the more popular Web Browsers.

If you are a novice and unsure how to proceed, I would suggest you follow the crowd, as defined by the URLs:

http://www.gakit.caltech.edu/~ta/browsers/browsers.html

http://www.netaxs.com/~jayfar/sursays.html

These sites contain statistics for which browsers were used to select random heavily-accessed Web pages. Based on these statistics—*at the time of writing Netscape should be your first choice since it has 59% of the UNIX market share. NCSA's Mosaic is second with 30.8% and Lynx third with 8.6%. Install Netscape (see Section 6.3.3) and if you like it there is no need to look further. If you are looking for different features, try some of the others on the list.*

Netscape supports the majority of features you likely will need (including Java applet support) and does so in a relatively secure way.

TABLE 3–8   Popular Web Browsers

Location	HTML Browsers
ftp://moose.cs.indiana.edu/pub/elisp/w3/	Emacs WWW Browser
http://www.spyglass.com/index.html	Enhanced Mosaic
http://java.sun.com/	**HotJava**
ftp://ftp2.cc.ukans.edu/pub/lynx	**Lynx**
http://www-midas.slac.stanford.edu/midasv22/-introduction.html	MidasWWW
ftp://ftp.ncsa.uiuc.edu/Mosaic	**Mosaic**
http://www.netscape.com.home/welcome.html	**Netscape Navigator**
ftp://info.cern.ch/pub/www/bin/next/	NeXT
ftp://archive.cis.ohio-state.edu/pub/w3browser/	perlWWW
http://www.commerce.net/software.-Smosaic	Secure Mosaic
http://info.cern.ch/hypertext/-WWW/TkWWW/Status.html	TkWWW Browser Editor
ftp://ftp.ora.com/pub/www/viola/	ViolaWWW

If you need to access the Web from a device without a bit-mapped display, or from a slow connection, you will need a line-oriented browser. Recall from Section 2.5.3.1 that Lynx is a line-oriented browser, and the one I recommend.

3.4.1.2 3-D

To find the currently available VRML browsers, refer to the locations in Table 3–9.

I have not used any of these browsers enough to make a recommendation and good comparative reviews could not be found. However, each location has a brief synopsis of each browser.

TABLE 3–9   VRML Browsers

Location	Description
http://www.lightside.com/~dani/cgi/VRML-index.html#browsers	Browsers arranged by hardware platform and version of UNIX.
http://www.sdsc.edu/SDSC/-Partners/vrml/software/browsers.html	Comprehensive list of browsers with a summary of features and version compliance information.

TABLE 3–10   Common Graphics Viewers, Editors, and Players

Location	Viewers, Editors and Players
	DVI Viewers
ftp://export.lcs.mit.edu/contrib/	**xdvi**
http://gopher.awis.auburn.edu:70/-1/monthly/gifviewers/	**GIF Viewers**
file://ftp.cis.upenn.edu/pub/xv	**xv**
http://www.cis.ohio-state.edu/hypertext/faq/usenet/jpeg-faq/part2/faq-doc-3.html	**JPEG Viewers**
ftp://ftp.x.org/contrib/-applications/ImageMagick/-ImageMagick-3.7.1.tar.gz	Image Magick
ftp://ftp.uu.net.graphics/jpeg/-jpegsrc.v5b.tar.gz	JPEG Player
ftp://ftp.cs.umn.edu/packages/-X11/R5contrib/	xloadimage
file://ftp.cis.upenn.edu/pub/xv	**xv**
	Postscript Viewers
ftp://ftp.cs.wisc.edu/pub/ghost	**Ghostscript**
ftp://ftp.cis.upenn.edu/pub/xv	**xv**
http://www.cs.brown.edu/fun/bawp/-sound_utilities.html#unix	**Audio Players**
http://www.btg.com/FedWeb/archives.htm	XPlayGizmo
	MPEG Players
ftp://ftp.cs.columbia.edu/archives/-X11R6/contrib/applications	MpegPlay
ftp://ftp.iuma.com/audio_utils/	Variety of MPEG players.
http://www.geom.umn.edu/docs/-mpeg_play/mpeg_play.html	Mpeg Player/MI
http://www-dsed.llnl.gov/documents/tests/tiff.html	**TIFF Viewers**
ftp://ftp.cs.umn.edu/packages/-X11/R5contrib/	xloadimage
ftp://ftp.cis.upenn.edu/pub/xv	**xv**
ftp://ftp.cs.umn.edu/packages/-X11/R5contrib/	**xpaint**

3.4.2 Viewers, Editors, and Players

Since you will need to view, edit, and play a variety of non-HTML information types, Table 3–10 lists locations for some of the more popular viewers, editors, and players.

The right hand column of Table 3–10 indicates a class of tool followed by representative examples. The corresponding location is a URL locating a review on the class of tool, or the location of each individual tool, respectively. We will touch upon some of these tools as we progress through the steps necessary to establish your information server. However, it is beyond the scope of this book to discuss each tool in detail. Notice that the xv program appears multiple times. The xv program was written by John Bradley and is so versatile as to deserve special mention.

The xv program reads images in a variety of image formats. Images may then be edited in a variety of ways—cropped, color maps changed, annotated, expanded, contracted, rotated, and so on. The edited image can then be output in a variety of formats.

I recommend that you install xv, since you will almost certainly need it, and then turn to other tools as you come across important information types not supported by xv.

If you would prefer to make your own decisions regarding viewers, editors and players, Table 3–11 provides locations where reviews of multimedia tools may be found.

3.5. WHAT FILTERS WILL I NEED?

There are a large number of forever changing filters available via the Internet. The trick is to not download those filters that you think you might need, but to wait until you need

TABLE 3–11   Reviews of Viewers, Editors, and Players

Location	Description
http://-cwsapps.cu-online.com/video.html	Review of the major multimedia players.
http://www2.ncsu.edu/bae/people/-faculty/walker/hotlist/graphics.html	Comprehensive list with pointers to related information such as descriptions of graphics formats.
http://documents.cfar.umd.edu/-imageproc/improc.html	Includes pointers to some image processing tools not indicated at the other locations.

TABLE 3–12   Lists of HTML-based Filters

Location	Description
http://www.w3.org/hypertext/WWW/-Tools/Filters.html.	List of HTML-based filters.
http://www.yahoo.com/-Computers_and_Internet/Internet/-World_Wide_Web/HTML_Converters/-Shareware_Freeware/	List of HTML-based filters.

a filter and then download it. This way you get the most capable version when you need it. Table 3–12 provides sites where current lists of available filters for converting various formats to and from HTML are maintained.

Table 3–13 provides a list of the more common, general purpose text and graphics filters. Filters are characterized by whether they filter with word processing documents, computer code, mail files, graphics, or other types of textual information.

The word-processing options presented in Table 3–13 filter by starting not with the native word processing format, but with an intermediate format (like RTF) which you convert (in most cases to HTML). Microsoft Word templates are an exception, since they permit you to write HTML directly. I consider this an example of an editor. Editors are introduced in the following section.

TABLE 3–13   Common Text and Graphics Filters

Location	Information Type/Filter
	Word Processing
http://www.seas.upenn.edu/~meng-wong/txt2html	ASCII TEXT to HTML
http://www.research.att.com/biblio.html *ftp://gaia.cs.umass.edu/pub/hgshulz/-windex-1.2.tar.Z*	BibTeX to HTML
ftp://ftp.cranfield.ac.uk/source/info-tools/WWW/decw2html	DECwrite to HTML
http://goya.ucs.ed.ac.uk/General/epoch.html	Emacs to HTML
ftp://ftp.nta.no/pub/	Frame2html
http://info.cern.ch/hypertext/-WWW/Tools/il2html.html *http://info.cern.ch/hypertext/-WWW/Tools/interleaf.html*	Interleaf to HTML
http://cb1.leeds.ac.uk/nikos/-tex2html/doc/latex2html/latex2html.html	**LaTeX to HTML**
http://stasi.bradley.edu/ftp/pub/-ps2html/ps2html-v2.html	PostScript to HTML
ftp://ftp:.cray.com/src/WWWstuff/RTF/rtftohtml_overview.html	RTF to HTML
ftp://skye.aiai.ed.ac.uk/pub/tex2rtf	TeX to RTF
http://asis01.cern.ch/infohtml/texi2html.html	Texinfo to HTML
http://cui_www.unige.ch/ftp/-PUBLIC/oscar/scripts/ms2html	Troff to HTML
http://www.research.digital.com/-nsl/publications/TN-12.html	Scribe to HTML
http://207.68.137.43:80/msword/internet/ia/	Word to HTML (Internet Assistant)

continued

TABLE 3–13   (Continued)

Location	Information Type/Filter
	Computer Languages
http://www.w3.org/hypertext/-WWW/Tools/ctohtml.txt	C to HTML
http://www.atd.ucar.edu/jva/c++2html.html	C++ to HTML
http://vscrna.cern.ch/floppy/contents.html	Fortran to HTML
http://www.cs.purdue.edu/homes/-young/software/src2www.html	Source to HTML
	UNIX Mail Files to HTML
http://www.connect.org.uk/-techwatch/archive/unix/WWW/MHonArc-1.0.jpg.html	**MHonArc**
ftp://ftp.uci.edu/pub/dtd2html	Mail to HTML
	Miscellaneous Text
ftp://ftp.uci.edu/pub/dtd2html	Hotlist to HTML
http://www.tile.net/tile/info/index.html	Lotus Notes to HTML
http://www.stuff.com/~bcutter/-home/programs/bbc_man2html.html	man pages to HTML
	Graphics
file://ftp.cis.upenn.edu/pub/xv	xv

3.6. WHAT EDITORS WILL I NEED?

Here I do not mean basic text editors, for example, *ex, vi,* and *emacs,* but editors that facilitate the preparation of information you are going to offer on your server. This really boils down to editors to produce HTML and editors to produce graphical images.

3.6.1 HTML Editors

As we shall see in Chapter 8, writing HTML is relatively straightforward using a standard UNIX editor. However, a WYSIWYG HTML editor that works like a word processor and does the coding in the background, while presenting you with a final view of the document (in this case a Web page), definitely speeds up the markup process and simplifies debugging of more complex documents. There are a number of approaches for editing HTML:

- You can download a free HTML editor.
- You can buy a commercial HTML editor.
- You can use an extension to an existing word processing package that produces HTML as an export format.
- You can use a free or commercial filter to convert an existing format to HTML as described above (Section 3.5).

When making a choice it is worth noting the following:

- Documents produced using an HTML editor nearly always look better than those written directly in HTML, simply because most people do not remember all the syntax necessary to produce a high quality document.
- Editors are WYSIWYG, anything else involves a two step process—writing and viewing.
- The evolution of HTML is occurring faster than the editors that write it. Thus, features supported by HTML may not be available using your editor.
- A native HTML editor will shorten the development cycle.
- HTML produced by editors may be difficult or impossible to maintain and edit by hand.

Table 3–14 provides the locations of current lists of HTML editors.

Note that, in general, more sophisticated editors are available for Macintosh and PC platforms than UNIX platforms. You may choose to edit your HTML on one of these platforms and then copy it to the UNIX platform where it will be served.

Among this list I see no clear first choices, therefore I would suggest you read the surveys presented in Table 3–15 in making a choice of HTML editor.

TABLE 3–14   Lists of HTML Editors

Location	Description
http://204.91.49.11/hteds.htm	Contains a brief review of each editor with good features and shortcoming indicated.
http://www.ccs.org/htmledit/-index.html#Overview	Contains scores for each editor and a feature table.
http://sdg.ncsa.uiuc.edu/~mag/work/-HTMLEditors/unixlist.html	Useful list of UNIX editors.

TABLE 3–15   Common HTML Editors

Location	HTML Editors
ftp://ftp.cs.rpi.edu/pub/puninj/-ASHE/README.html	Ashe
cwerner@ileaf.com	Cyberleaf
ftp://ftp.ncsa.uiuc.edu/Web/html/-elisp/htmp-mode.el	Emacs (in HTML mode)
http://info.cern.ch/hypertext/-WWW/Frame/ *http://ww1.cern.ch/Webmaker/-WEBMAKER.html* *ftp://bang.nta.no/pub* ftp://ftp.alumni.caltech.edu/pub/-mcbeath/web/miftran	FrameMaker templates
http://www.tools.gnn.com/press/index.html	GNNpress
http://web.cs.city.ac.uk/homes/-njw/htmltext/htmltext.html	htmltext
ftp://ftp.ncsa.uiuc.edu/Web/html/hotmetal	HoTMetaL
ftp://space.mit.edu/pub/davis/jed/	jed
http://www.bsd.uchicago.edu/ftp/-pub/phoenix/README.html	Phoenix
http://www.griff/fr/	Symposia
http://sdg.ncsa.uiuc.edu/~mag/-work/HTMLEditors/unixlist.html	tkHTML
http://www.math.fuberlin.de/~guckes/vim/	Vim

3.7. WHAT SEARCH ENGINES WILL I NEED?

This section introduces software (Table 3–16) that you can use to gather, index and search all or parts of the information you are providing on the Internet. This is not a discussion of the various search engines (e.g. Alta Vista, Lycos, Webcrawler) you can use when you browse the Internet. A very informative paper on those can be found at *http://www.indi-ana.edu/~librcsd/search/*.

The situation is complicated since gatherers, indexers, and search engines can be mixed and matched. For example, a set of documents gathered and indexed by WAISindex may be searched by both WAIS and Harvest. A comparison of these tools, from a Harvest perspective, can be found at

http://harvest.cs.colorado.edu/harvest/-FAQ.html#what-is-harvest

TABLE 3–16   Common Search Tools

Location	Search Tools
http://harvest.cs.colorado.edu/	Harvest
http://glimpse.cs.arizona.edu:1994/	Glimpse
ftp://ftp.cnidr.org/pub/NIDR.tools/freeWA IS-0.202.tar.Z	WAIS distribution WAIS overview
ftp://think.com/wais/wais-corporate-paper.text	

These tools can be further contrasted to robots which, for the purposes of this brief introduction, follow the detailed definition found in *http://info.webcrawler.com/mak/projects/robots/faq.html*. A robot actively searches the whole Web by requesting documents and then placing them in an index. While the principle is the same, a robot generally uses some heuristic to determine when to stop gathering documents. Here we are being more specific, restricting ourselves to searches of the information at your site and possibly explicitly defined hyperlinks elsewhere. Harvest and WAIS will serve you well. I will show you how to install and maintain Harvest in Section 7.5.

3.8. WHAT OTHER TOOLS WILL I NEED?

To complete your kitchen and be ready to begin cooking, you will need the following additional appliances.

- Compilers—If you have a less popular hardware and/or UNIX-based operating system, you may need to compile some of the software described in this book as opposed to simply downloading and running the executables. The majority of code will require either a C or C++ compiler, but there may be instances requiring Basic, Pascal, or Fortran.
- Interpreters—You will absolutely need Perl (*http://www.perl.com/perl/index. html*); some software will need to be interpreted by Perl v5.0 or later. Perl comes standard with most UNIX operating systems these days. Chapter 10 goes into more detail on the use of Perl to interpret information provided on Web forms, and includes pointers to further sources of information specific to Internet serving and to basic Perl tutorials. You may also require Tcl (*http://www.neosoft.com/tcl/*), which is not part of the standard UNIX operating system.
- Image editors—This category refers to paint programs and the like, used to create or annotate graphics images that you will include in your Web documents.

- Clickable map builders—Tools that assist in building clickable maps. As we shall see in Section 9.4, these are tools that produce the map file that relates a point on an image to a URL. In other words, when you mouse click on a clickable image that point on the image is mapped to a specific URL which is downloaded to your browser. A clickable map builder helps in defining the relationship between the point on the image and the URL, One noteworthy package for the creation of clickable maps is Tgif (see the *URL http://bourbon.cs.ucla.edu:8001/tgif/*).

A great source for compilers and interpreters is the Free Software foundation; see the URL *ftp://prep.ai.mit.edu/pub/gnu/DESCRIPTIONS*. Good, easy to use, image editors for UNIX are hard to obtain, this is really the domain of the PC and the Macintosh. An extended list of PC and MAC options can be found at *http://www.xnet.com/~blatura/-linapps.shtml#graphics*. For a review of these and some commercial products see *http://www.tc.cornell.edu/Visualization/software.evaluation.study*. For UNIX *xfig*, a drawing package for X11 releases 4 and 5, is available from *ftp://ftp.x.org/contrib/applications/drawing_tools/xfig*. A filter, transfig, will convert a number of graphics formats for use in *xfig* and is located at the same site as *ftp://ftp.x.org/contrib/applications/drawing_tools/transfig/*.

3.9. WHAT NON-SOFTWARE RESOURCES WILL I NEED?

This section explores the hardware and human resources that are needed to create a successful information server.

3.9.1 Hardware

Hardware refers to the resources, both computer and network, needed to have the information server operate efficiently. This is a difficult issue to address. First, the information server is usually also used for other compute tasks. Second, the demands for information on each server can be quite different. For example, the number of hits made on the server is a function of the generality of the information—the NCSA "What's New" Web page gets millions of hits each week, while my molecular biology page gets a few thousand. Then again, the number of hits is not necessarily indicative of server load, since the amount of information transferred by a single hit can vary dramatically. Further, a Web forms interface may permit users to perform a database lookup or a complex calculation, both requiring significant hardware resources.

Here I make a general recommendation on what hardware is required initially. Once your server is established you should monitor activity very closely and try to have the resources (money and personnel) available to quickly respond to the need for a new disk drive, more memory, etc. I appreciate that this is a poor recommendation, but information server growth is very difficult to predict. Let us consider each of the major potential problem areas separately.

3.9.1.1 Network Bandwidth

The required bandwidth is a function of the services you are supporting. The rules of thumb are:

- Whatever services you provide beyond mail require a dedicated (i.e., 24-hours-per-day, seven-days-per-week) connection.
- For mail and ftp support only, you might get by with a 28.8 kilobaud type connection supporting the SLIP or PPP protocols (see Section 4.1.2).
- For Web access you need at least an ISDN (128 kilobaud) connection, or better still an Ethernet connection (10 megabits per second). T1, T2, T3, or ATM connections will be required for very high bandwidth.

What you need to do to create these levels of service is introduced in Chapter 4.

3.9.1.2 Disk Space

Before we get to the rules of thumb, we need to cover Disk Space 101. You can never have enough disk space. In a multi-user environment, without disk quotas, all available space always gets consumed. What varies is the amount of time it takes to consume that space. Here are some basic rules to follow:

- If possible, keep the information you are serving separate from other data on the server. This calls for separate partitions, if not separate disks.
- If possible, spread the information across various disks connected to separate disk controllers to minimize I/O load.
- If you permit users to write to the server through, for example, uploading files via ftp, you need to monitor disk space usage more carefully than would otherwise be the case.
- Providing index files to facilitate searching can double disk space requirements since the index files (depending on the indexer used) can be as large as the original files.
- Graphics, sound and audio files are large even in a compressed state—be prepared with extra disk space.
- To be secure may require that you keep multiple copies of information available for each service you are offering.

These rules become particularly important when we look at examples of interacting with the server through, for example, *CGI scripts* (Section 10.3). Often these scripts write temporary files on the server and will fail if the file system is full, frustrating the user.

3.9.1.3 Memory Requirements

As a general rule, this would seem a non-issue on most of today's UNIX platforms since they typically come with a minimum of 16 MB of memory, and most likely 64 MB of memory or more. You are unlikely to see *swapping* on a computer dedicated to basic information serving with 16 MB of memory or more, regardless of what type of information is being served. The key words to note in this statement though are "dedicated" and "basic." If you have other memory-intensive applications running (i.e., the server is not dedicated) and non-system processes running information serving functions get swapped out, interactive response will be hampered. Similarly, if you permit memory intensive applications to be run via the information server, and those applications get run a lot, you will also have problems.

3.9.1.4 CPU Requirements

What is true for memory is true for CPU—other applications on a non-dedicated server are more likely to kill you than information-serving applications. The possible exception is a lot of gathering, index generation and searching, which can be CPU, memory and I/O intensive.

3.9.2 Human

The nuts and bolts (i.e., the hardware) resources pale by comparison to the human resources required to maintain a good server. Nuts and bolts are relatively inexpensive when compared to labor costs. Setting up and maintaining a good server takes people's time.

How do you measure the time required to maintain a server? This is a question that is difficult to answer without knowing how complex a server will be. Here are a couple of observations from my own experience:

- An organization of 10 people serving a minimal amount of information requires 10 hours per week of someone's time to set up and maintain the server in the first year.
- An organization with 20 people with information serving a vital part of their operation requires a full-time employee, to set up and maintain the server in the first year.

From these observations you can attempt to assess your own needs. Determining what human resources are required is not simple, since it is generally *more than* one person providing information on a successful information server. It may be one person managing the information server, but the information supply should come from the source, that is, everyone in the organization. That cost is hard to determine.

You have now been introduced to all the ingredients you will need to cook up a great information server. We can now move on to the basic utensils needed to begin cooking.

4

Prerequisite Infrastructure

Ingredients:

- *Internet Service Providers*
- *A physical network connection*
- *An IP address*
- *Network software to use the physical connection*
- *A name server*
- *A correctly configured and secure server*

Before you can begin cooking you need a well-equipped kitchen. This equipment consists of the appropriate kitchen appliances and utensils.

Chapters Two and Three introduced the types of information we can make available from our information server, the services we can provide for disseminating that information, and the software components necessary to provide those services. You should also have determined from the discussion of resource requirements in Chapter Three that the UNIX server(s) you have will be able to support the anticipated information flow. The next step is to make sure you have the prerequisite network infrastructure within your organization or home to provide the desired level of service.

If the computer you will use as the information server is already connected to the Internet and operating satisfactorily, that is, allows you to send and receive mail, telnet to other hosts, and use ftp, you can skip to Section 4.2. If you have yet to get connected to the Internet and are contemplating how best to do this, read on.

4.1. INTERNET ACCESS

There are four requirements for providing Internet access from your server.

- A physical network connection

* An Internet Protocol (IP) address
* Appropriate networking software
* Name resolution using a name server

Once these requirements have been addressed you need to test the connection. Both the requirements and testing are considered in this section.

4.1.1 A Note on Internet Service Providers (ISPs) ☞

Internet Service Providers (ISPs) provide services that (at a price) make part or all of this book unnecessary, depending on the level of service they provide. Here are some examples of the types and levels of services they offer:

* A *complete package*—The ISP provides hardware, software, Internet access, and information serving via ftp, mail servers, and Web pages. You simply provide them with the information and how you want to see that information presented. They format, organize and present that information *at their site*.
* A *network provider*—The ISP provides hardware, software, and Internet access *at their site*, but you organize and format the information.
* A *turnkey system*—Hardware, software, services, and maintenance are provided by the ISP as a package for installation *at your site*. You format, organize, and present the information.
* A *consultant service*—The ISP helps you set up your server *at your site* and ensure that it is operational, and it formats and organizes your information. There is the option for ongoing maintenance.
* A *basic connection*—The ISP provides you with an IP address and a connection to the Internet, otherwise you are on our own.

Unless you have Internet access through your place of work, you will need an ISP to gain access to the Internet. How much you pay defines the level of service you will get. *Which ISP you use and the level of service you purchase should be considered carefully.*

If you are going to use an ISP, the first step is to get a list of providers in your region. From there, you can examine the services offered by each one. I appreciate that getting this list from the Internet is putting the cart before the horse: How can you determine, from the Internet, details of Internet provision when you do not yet have an Internet connection? I suggest you visit a cyber café or work with a friend who is connected. Table 4–1 provides the locations of lists of ISPs.

What you will discover from this information is that you need to know more about the type of connection and services that are offered to make an informed decision, in which case, read on. If you are using an ISP's hardware, you need to consider not only the

TABLE 4–1 Lists of Internet Service Providers

Location	Lists of ISPs
http://www.primus.com/providers/	A list of US providers arranged by telephone number area code.
http://sensemedia.com/crisp/crisp	A list of providers covering the U.S., Asia, and Australia.
http://www.celestin.com/pocia/index.html	A list of 885 providers (Feb. 1996) in the U.S., Canada, and many other countries.
http://www.panix.com/sea/providr.html	A list of providers in New York and the northeastern U.S., but with many pointers to other lists.
http://akebono.stanford.edu/yahoo/-Business/Corporations/-Internet_Access_Providers/	Comprehensive list from Yahoo.

type of connection that exists from the ISP's information server to the rest of the Internet, but also the type of connection from your system to the ISP's server.

4.1.2 A Physical Network Connection

If it is your hardware which will run the Internet information server, you must consider the physical connection to the Internet. In simple terms, the physical Internet connection can be characterized in one of two ways: *dedicated* and *non-dedicated*.

As the names suggest, a dedicated connection has a single function: It continuously listens for packets (chunks of information) destined for your information server and broadcasts packets as required. A dedicated connection typically uses a copper cable (thin coax, thick coax, twisted pair, etc.) or optical fiber (FDDI) cable. These physical media are already found in most large organizations and starting to appear in some suburban communities. Dedicated connections are generally fast in transmitting data, fast at establishing the connection, and automatic, that is they require no human intervention to make the connection. The physical wire over which this connection runs may belong to and be maintained by the organization, or it may be leased from and maintained by a telephone company or other carrier.

A non-dedicated connection, on the other hand, is used for purposes in addition to the Internet connection, usually as a voice line. Typically, this is a telephone line attached to a regular telephone exchange. These non-dedicated connections are generally slower and require start-up time to establish the connection, for instance, one modem dialing another to make the connection. The dialing action may be automatic or invoked manually.

The distinction between dedicated and non-dedicated connections has become less relevant since the widespread adoption of ISDN (Integrated Services Digital Network) lines. An ISDN line can multiplex, that is, carry both voice and data at the same time. ISDN lines are reasonably fast and, while not necessarily dedicated, connect very fast and without any user intervention. ISDN lines are maintained by the telephone companies, and you pay as you would for a voice line, albeit at a different rate. Those rates are regional and expected to rise as the telephone companies realize what a valuable service ISDN provides.

Table 4–2 summarizes the characteristics of each type of connection.

A networking expert will tell you that the information in Table 4–2 is misleading because, for example, you never reach peak speeds, compression changes these numbers, ATM (Asynchronous Transfer Mode) can be run over ISDN, and so on. These are valid criticisms. My goal here is simply to put each service into perspective, so that you can decide which service(s) to investigate further.

The type of connection to the Internet determines the kind of server you can operate. If you want users to have continuous access to your server, a dedicated or ISDN line is a must. *Since the majority of UNIX servers operate through dedicated lines, I will concentrate on this type of infrastructure.*

Here are some rules of thumb for the type of Internet access needed to support different server loads:

- *A small business.* A few Web hits per hour downloading text and images plus the occasional ftp archive access—ISDN.
- *A medium-sized business.* Thousands of Web hits per hour downloading text, images, sound, video, plus tens to hundreds of downloads from the ftp archive per hour—T1 and above.

TABLE 4–2   Types and Characteristics of Internet Connections

Connection Type	Peak Speed (1000's of bits per second - Kbps)	Type of Connection	Payment Structure
Non-dedicated			
Modem	1.2- 28.8	Manual	Usage Based
ISDN	56 - 128	Automatic	Usage Based
Dedicated			
T1	1,500	Automatic	Flat Fee
Ethernet	10,000	Automatic	Flat Fee
T3	45,000	Automatic	Flat Fee
FDDI	100,000	Automatic	Flat Fee
ATM	155,000	Automatic	Flat Fee

- *A large business.* Hundreds of thousands of Web hits per hour and thousands of ftp downloads—T3 and above.

Obviously, this is just a gentle introduction to getting connected to the Internet. Table 4–3 provides locations of more detailed information.

4.1.3 Getting an IP Address ☞

Once your information server is physically connected to the Internet, it needs to have a unique address so that clients on the Internet can locate it. I discussed the format of that unique address, the Internet Protocol (IP) address, in Section 2.3.1. The most likely ways you can get assigned an IP address are:

- from the network manager of your organization
- from an ISP
- from the Network Information Center (NIC)

The first two options require little work on your part, and the second and third options will cost you money. The third assumes that you or your organization has no form of Internet access already and requires that you register yourself or your organization. Table 4–4 indicates how to register online for an IP address.

TABLE 4–3   Further Reading on Internet Connectivity

Location	Topic
http://www.msic.com/enet_info.html	Ethernet Information.
http://www.psi.com/orgservices/demand/	The view from a typical Internet provider.
http://www.eff.org/pub/GII_NII/ISDN/	ISDN information, including a tutorial.
http://www.isdn.ocn.com/	Comprehensive site discussing ISDN.
http://www.bsdi.com/- white-papers/- becoming-an-isp-kolstad.html	Becoming a service provider and an overview of the business.
http://web.cnam.fr/Network/- Internet-access/how_to_select.html	How to select an Internet provider.

TABLE 4–4   Where to Register for IP Addresses

Where to Register	Location of Internet Server
http://rs.internic.net/rs-internic.html	US
http://www.apnic.net/	Asian Pacific region
http://www.ripe.net/	Europe

These days you are strongly encouraged to work through an ISP rather than apply for addresses directly from the NIC. Either way the result should be an assignment of a group of IP addresses pertinent to the size of your organization. Table 4–5 provides further information on IP addressing.

4.1.4 Network Protocols

Beyond the details of the physical connection are the network protocols that use that connection. Remember that the term Internet implies at least support of the TCP/IP protocols. Typically, a dedicated server runs the TCP/IP protocols directly, thereby supporting such standard services as ftp and telnet. Additional services such as http can be thought of as being layered on top of TCP/IP.

A non-dedicated line requiring access to TCP/IP services requires additional protocols and, hence, software. The most common protocols for use on modem lines are SLIP (Serial Line Internet Protocol) or PPP (Point-to-Point Protocol). TCP/IP runs on top of either SLIP or PPP.

To use a non-dedicated line through a telephone exchange, first dial another machine already attached to the Internet and establish a connection with either SLIP or PPP. Then start TCP/IP, and run ftp, telnet, http, etc. When your client starts SLIP or PPP, a temporary IP address is assigned from a pool of available addresses. Your Internet server, which is going to have clients connecting in this manner, needs to have modems accessible that can accept SLIP and PPP connections and it must be running the SLIP and PPP protocols. Support for these protocols is distributed with most versions of the UNIX operating system. However, they may not be installed by default. Table 4–6 provides pointers to additional information on the PPP and SLIP protocols.

4.1.5 Configuring the Network Software

This topic falls under UNIX Administration 101, which this book does not propose to cover in any detail. Most versions of UNIX now have tools to help you configure your hardware so that it can communicate with the Internet. For a simple connection (i.e., your system will not route other traffic or be a name server) there are really only three things you need to know, and I summarize them here. If you use this information, plus that which

TABLE 4–5   Further Reading on IP Addressing

Location	Description
http://www.wcmh.com/uworld/-archives/95/tutorial/001.html	A tutorial on IP addressing.
http://www.shiva.com/prod/tips/-SHIVA13.TIP.html#HDR3	Another perspective on IP addressing.

TABLE 4–6   Further Reading on the PPP and SLIP Protocols

Location	Description
http://www.stokely.com/stokely/-unix.serial.port.resources/-ppp.slip.html#ppp.link	Pointers to software supporting PPP and further information.
http://www.cis.ohio-state.edu/-htbin/rfc/rfc1661.html	The official definition of PPP.
http://www.cis.ohio-state.edu/-htbin/rfc/rfc1055.html	The official definition of SLIP.

comes with your UNIX operating system, and have read Section 2.3 on Internet basics, you should not have any problems in configuring your network software.

The three things you need to know are the following:

- *IP Address*—This is the address of the form nnn.nnn.nnn.nnn (e.g., 128.59.98.1) assigned in one of the ways described above.
- *Subnet Mask*—This number defines how a network segment may be divided further into subnets. The value depends on the size of your network. For D class networks configured to support 256 hosts (2^8), this is usually set to 255.255.255.0. For C class networks configured to support 65536 (2^{16}) hosts, this is usually set to 255.255.0.0.
- *Default Gateway*—This is where to direct network traffic so that it may be sent correctly. Usually a computer will be designated by the network administrator as a default gateway and is configured with the UNIX **route** command.

If you do not have a simple interface to which you can plug in these values, you should seek help, and/or refer to the additional sources of information given at the end of this chapter. By way of getting you started I should say that reading the man pages on the following UNIX commands may be helpful:

- **ifconfig**—interface configuration. Used at boot time to configure the network interface.
- **netstat**—network status. Used to analyze the state of the network connection.
- **route**—manipulate the routing tables. Used to set a default gateway.

4.1.6 Testing the Connection

If you think you have the appropriate physical connection and software configured to begin serving information, here are a couple of simple tests to check whether your server is working correctly.

Entering the command **telnet 127.0.0.1** allows you to connect to your own system.

```
% telnet 127.0.0.1                        # or telnet localhost
Trying 127.0.0.1...
Connected to 127.0.0.1.
Escape character is '^]'.


OSF/1 (pauline) (ttyp3)


login: bourne
Password:
```

This connection does not use the network at all, but makes a loop internal to the operating system. If you get no response or an error, your networking software is not installed, or is installed and configured incorrectly. In short, *inetd,* the daemon overseeing all network processes is most likely not running (Section 2.3.2). You can check this with a command like **ps -aux |grep inetd** (or **ps -el|grep inetd** on some systems).

If your networking software is functioning correctly you can move on to test the physical connection with the **ping** command.

```
% ping 132.249.40.68
PING 132.249.40.68 (132.249.40.68): 56 data bytes
64 bytes from 132.249.40.68: icmp_seq=0 ttl=255 time=1 ms
64 bytes from 132.249.40.68: icmp_seq=1 ttl=255 time=0 ms
 <ctrl> C
----132.249.40.68 PING Statistics----
2 packets transmitted, 2 packets received, 0% packet loss
round-trip (ms) min/avg/max = 0/0/1 ms
```

The **ping** command attempts to bounce network packets off a remote computer, in this example a computer with the IP address 132.249.40.68. Typing *<ctrl>c* terminates **ping** and returns the minimum, maximum, and average transfer rate for the packets sent and subsequently echoed back. If you are communicating, but there is a very slow transfer rate (in the seconds) or a significant packet loss, you probably have a software configuration problem or, less likely, a hardware problem. The most likely scenario is that you are using an IP address assigned to someone else. If you think this may be the problem you should *immediately* disconnect yourself from the network until you resolve this problem.

Note: in using **ping** we used the computer's numeric address rather than its name. The reason is that if the name is not recognized, the problem may be elsewhere related to name serving.

4.1.7 Name Serving

Once the physical connection and the networking software are functioning properly, you are ready for the next step: name serving. Recall from Section 2.3.1 that name serving (also referred to as Domain Name Service (DNS) and Berkeley Internet Name Domain (BIND) is the ability to resolve the IP address in the form 123.123.123.123 from a name of the form *pauline.sdsc.edu.*

For clients to access your information server they must resolve the names; name resolution may or may not be a function of your information server. Remember, as you are using the URLs listed in this book to look up information, you are acting as a client. You are resolving the names to locate the various items you need on a variety of servers. Thus, it is important that you understand how names are resolved.

In simple terms, the name-to-number mapping is needed since humans work better with names, but computers work better with numbers. All your information serving tools can use the names—the majority of the URLs in this book are names—and these must be resolved (converted to a number) if the server is to provide routing to the destination.

Section 2.3.1 discussed simple name serving. For more complex cases in which you intend to serve names rather than being a passive listener, refer to the additional reading list in Section 4.1.8.

If you are unsure if name serving is functioning correctly, try connecting to a machine for which you know the name and IP number using the name. If you get a response, your name server is running and your information server tools should function. If you get a message "network unreachable" then either you have no physical connection or the network software is not configured correctly. If you can connect using the number, but not the name, then the problem lies in the configuration of the name server.

As a final test, you can try the UNIX command **nslookup,** which queries the name server directly in an attempt to resolve a name, for example:

```
% /usr/bin/nslookup pauline.sdsc.edu
Server: dns1.sdsc.edu
Address: 198.17.46.33


Name: pauline.sdsc.edu
Addresses: 132.249.40.68, 132.249.20.68, 132.249.200.68
```

This reports the name server used to resolve the request (*dns1.sdsc.edu*) and then the IP address associated with *pauline.sdsc.edu.*

4.1.8 Further Reading ☞

Further information about physically getting a UNIX Internet connection up and running is given in Table 4–7.

TABLE 4–7   Further Reading on Internet Connectivity

Location	Description
http://www.lanl.gov/-general-information	General information about the Internet.
http://www.racal.com/internet.html	Starting point for getting Internet documentation.
http://www-neteng.uchicago.edu/Docs/terms.html	Glossary of Internet-related terms.
http://www-neteng.uchicago.edu/Docs/terms.html	Overview of TCP/IP.
gopher://ss1.racal.com/00/-Networking/TCP%20IP%20Admin.txt	Guide to setting up an Internet connection (free).
http://www.sunquest.com/-netsvc/net_eval.html	A randomly selected commercial Internet service consultant.
http://oac3.hsc.uth.tmc.edu/staff/-snewton/tcp-tutorial/sec5.html	A brief tutorial on name serving.
http://titus.is.co.za/dnsrd/	A comprehensive guide to DNS.

Books	Description
UNIX System Administration Handbook, Second Edition Authors: Evi Nemeth, Garth Snyder, Scott Seebass, Trent R. Hein Published: 1995 Publisher: Prentice Hall ISBN: 0-13-151051-7	The "how to" gospel of UNIX administration.
TCP/IP Network Administration Author: Craig Hunt Published: 1992 Publisher: O'Reilly & Associates ISBN: 0-937175-82-X	A complete guide to the TCP/IP protocol stack.
DNS and BIND Author: Paul Ablates & Cricket IL Published: 1992 Publisher: O'Reilly & Associates ISBN: 1-56592-010-4	A complete guide to DNS and BIND.

4.2. CONFIGURATION

Your information server should now be ready for you to begin loading software and information to be served. However, it is very important that you configure it appropriately from the start by considering global configuration issues. These are distinct from the configuration of each individual software component, which can be found as part of the discussion of each component.

4.2.1 Naming the Server

The key here is to plan ahead. While you may be running an ftp archive or serving Web pages from a computer called, for example, *rosebud.sdsc.edu* today, next year you might be serving information from *thorn.sdsc.edu*. The reason for the change could relate to efficiency (the popularity of the server required a more powerful computer), reorganization (the original computer was assigned to a new project), and so on. Your goal is to hide this underlying turmoil from users accessing your system, irrespective of which information service they are using. It is traditional practice (if one to two years can be considered long enough to establish a tradition) to provide the following aliases for an information server:

- *ftp.organization.domain* for the organization's ftp site
  (e.g., *ftp.sdsc.edu*)
- *listserv@organization.domain* for the organization's Listserver (e.g.,
  listserv@sdsc.edu)
- *www.organization.domain* for the organization's Web site
  (e.g., *www.sdsc.edu*)

These names could refer to the same computer or different computers. The point is the computer can change without requiring the name to change. Therefore, users of your information server who have added *http://www.sdsc.edu/* to their Web browser hotlists would not be disappointed when they visit the site in the future, since the URL will remain valid even though you have changed the computer.

This approach is also useful for users who do not know which specific computer in an organization they want to access, even though they know the IP address of the organization. For example, if I know Digital Equipment Corp. has some nifty software on their ftp server (and they do), my first guess in trying to locate their ftp archive would be *ftp.digital.com* or *http://www.digital.com*. This scheme can be extended in larger more diverse organizations. So, *ftp.dept.organization.com,* for example, works just as well to locate a departmental ftp server in a large organization.

However, this approach only works if there is only one server providing this service in the domain or subdomain. If there were two ftp servers for *sdsc.edu* they must be consolidated (the best choice) or there should be a designated primary (called ftp) and secondary (called ftp1 or some such name) server.

To establish a generic domain name for an information service, do one of the following

- If you are not responsible for maintaining the name server database, ask your network administrator to add the alias.

- If you are responsible for maintaining the name server database, add the alias to the primary name server database file for your type of UNIX system (the specific file depends on the version of UNIX). For ftp, this would appear as follows:

    ftp   IN   CNAME official.domain.name

    The official domain name is the part specified by you.

4.2.2 Mail Aliases

Mail aliases are used for the same reasons that server aliases are used, but because the person changes, not because the computer changes. The person who is the Webmaster and/or the ftp archive administrator today may not be the same person next year. Using a mail alias assures that the mail always gets to the correct person at any point in time. There are two ways to establish a mail alias:

- Define separate accounts for the aliases, typical login names are webmaster and ftp-admin, e.g., *webmaster@sdsc.edu.*
- Define an alias for an existing mail account, changing the alias when someone new takes over the job responsibility.

Option 1 separates information server-related mail from your regular mail, since you must log in to the webmaster or ftp-admin accounts to read it. This may be an advantage or a disadvantage depending on your personal preferences. Implementing option 1 simply requires that you establish the appropriate accounts, or have your UNIX administrator create the appropriate accounts.

Option 2 causes the mail to show up in your regular account. Whether you choose option 1 or 2 depends on how quickly you wish to see and have the opportunity to respond to information server-related mail, that is, how important this mail is relative to other mail you receive. To implement option 2, review **man aliases** on your UNIX server. The basic steps are as follows:

1. Edit */etc/aliases* (or */usr/lib/aliases* on some UNIX systems)
2. Add a line similar to
    webmaster: bourne@sdsc.edu
3. Execute the UNIX command **newaliases** (or, if not found, the command **sendmail -bi)**

In this example you have defined an alias named webmaster, allowing mail to webmaster to be forwarded to *bourne@sdsc.edu.* Since the **sendmail** program does not use this ASCII representation found in */etc/aliases* (or */usr/lib/aliases),* but a binary file, the **newaliases** or **sendmail -bf** commands will update that binary file from the changes made to the ASCII file.

4.2.3 UNIX

To make life easier, standard UNIX supports a number of practices you should adopt to help manage your information server. These are checklisted here as a reminder. If you are fairly new to UNIX, refer to Appendix B, which has a number of pointers to additional information on basic UNIX.

- Include aliases in your shell configuration file (e.g., *.cshrc*) or your login file (*.login*) to create shortcuts to commonly visited directories. For example:

  alias wwwroot "cd /usr/local/bin/httpd/docs"
  alias ftproot "cd /misc/ftp/pub"
- Alternatively, use environment variables. For example:

  setenv WWWROOT '/usr/local/bin/httpd/docs'
  then **cd $WWWROOT/levels1** can be used to change directories.
- Include commonly executed programs in the path variable for the shell. For example:

  set path = ($path /usr/local/bin /usr/apps/bin)

4.2.4 X/Motif

X/Motif is the window system software running on the majority of UNIX clients and servers. OpenWindows from Sun Microsystems is the other major window system in-use on UNIX platforms. This distinction has become less important, since the recent OpenWindows distribution contains parts of the X Window System. In any event, OpenWindows is not considered further here; for additional information see

  http://www.cs.indiana.edu/faq/OpenLook/front_page.html

  http://wmwap1.math.uni-wuppertal.de/pub/Mosaic/OWconfiguration/contents.html

There are two features of X/Motif that you may wish to customize:

1. The information server-based applications that appear on the desktop when you start an X session (for example, Web browser, HTML editor, and graphics editor).
2. X resources—usually done at the application level.

The first feature is very dependent on the hardware vendor's particular implementation of UNIX and hence X, since each has additional tools that give you control over which applications appear at the start of a session. For example, DEC UNIX uses the DEC session manager, and SGI IRIX uses the desktop manager to add and remove applications. At the most basic level, this is controlled by the window manager startup file. For individual users, that file is *~/.mwmrc*

Any good X/Motif application will run on your server without modification to X resources. However, you may wish to customize that application as indicated by item 2 above. An amazing feature of the X Window System is the variety of things you can customize. For our needs, it is necessary to modify no more than the file *~/.Xdefaults*—your own personal customization file—which gets invoked each time you start the X Window System. The URL *http://www.iscs.nus.sg/~chinyees/x.html* provides a good description of the contents of this file. In summary, it consists of name-value pairs. The name is the attribute and the value is what it is set to. An attribute is then broken down further into an *application*name,* which is the name of the attribute for a specific application. This is illustrated below for part of the additions to the *.Xdefaults* file used to customize the *Xmosaic* Web browser.

```
% more ~/.Xdefaults

!!! Example .Xdefaults file for NCSA Mosaic
!!! This text could be appended to your existing .Xdefaults file.
!!! Lines beginning with ! are comments.

!!! Color Resources

Mosaic*Foreground:         black
Mosaic*Background:         lightgrey
Mosaic*anchorColor:        blue
Mosaic*visitedAnchorColor: darkviolet

!!! Font Resources

Mosaic*font: \
-adobe-times-medium-r-normal-*-17-*-*-*-*-*-iso8859-1
Mosaic*italicFont: \
-adobe-times-medium-i-normal-*-17-*-*-*-*-*-iso8859-1.
```

As you see, this part of the *~/.Xdefaults* file can be modified to vary colors and fonts to be displayed by *Xmosaic.*

4.3. Security

Each software component comprising your information server comes with its own set of security considerations. The security of these individual components is discussed when I show you how to implement each individual component. Here I provide a brief summary of the overall security features you should consider, not just for an UNIX information server, but for any UNIX system.

4.3.1 Checklist

This list consists of information provided by David Curry in the document *http://geminga.dartmouth.edu/security.html* with additions from my own experience (which includes mistakes and subsequent break-ins). Those marked with *** should be of particular concern to maintainers of an information server. If some of the terminology is unfamiliar consult one of the suggested texts on UNIX administration.

Account Security

- A password policy should be developed and distributed to all users with accounts.
- All password selections should be checked against obvious choices, like children's and spouse's names.
- Expiration dates should be set on all accounts.
- No unused guest accounts should be permitted.
- All accounts should have passwords or an asterisk (*) in the password field of */etc/passwd* or the appropriate file.
- No group accounts should be permitted.
- "+" lines in */etc/passwd* and */etc/group* should be set appropriately.

Network Security

- The */etc/hosts.equiv* file should contain only local hosts, and no "+".
- No *.rhosts* files should be permitted in users' home directories.
- Only local hosts should be permitted in root's *.rhosts* file.
- Only "console" should be labeled as "secure" in */etc/ttytab* (or equivalent file).
- No NFS file systems should be exported to the world. ***
- Recent versions of *ftpd* and *finger* should be used, since they likely contain the latest security patches. ***
- No "decode" alias should be used in the aliases file. ***
- No "wizard" passwords should be used in *sendmail.cf.* ***
- No "debug" command should be used in *sendmail.* ***
- Modems and terminal servers should hang up correctly. ***

File Security

- No setuid or setgid bits should be set on shell scripts or executables accessible via the server. Check setuid and setgid on all "nonstandard" programs, irrespective of whether they are accessible via the server. ***
- The Setuid bit should be removed from */usr/etc/restore.*
- Sticky bits should not be set on world-writable directories.
- The proper umask value should be set on the root account. ***
- The proper modes should be set on device special files in */dev.*

• Level 0 dumps should be performed at least monthly. Incremental dumps should be performed with a frequency that balances resource demands against the value of the information.

4.3.2 Further Reading ☞

Table 4–8 contains sources of additional information on UNIX security.

We are now ready, well almost ready, to begin loading information serving software and the information itself onto our information server. But first we need to consider the short, but important, subject of how the software and information should be organized. This is covered in the next chapter.

TABLE 4–8   Further Reading on UNIX Security

Location	Description
http://geminga.dartmouth.edu/-security.html	Site and UNIX security by the author of "UNIX System Security - A Guide for Users and Administrators" (see below).
http://www.yahoo.com/-Computers_and_Internet/-Operating_Systems/Unix/Security/	Good pointers to other places.
ftp://cert.org/pub/info/-security-doc.txt	Site maintained by the Computer Emergency Response Team (CERT), the U.S. organization responsible for overseeing computer security issues.

Location	Books
http://pantheon.yale.edu/-~danu/ce91b.html (review)	Title: Practical Unix Security Authors: Simson Garfinkel and Gene Spafford Edition: 1991 Publisher: O'Reilly ISBN: 0-937175-72-2
http://aw.com/devpress/titles/-57030.html (publishers description)	Title: Unix System Security Author: Rik Farrow Edition: 1991 Publisher: Addison Wesley ISBN: 0-201-57030-0
http://www.aw.com/cp/curry.html (publishers description)	Title: Unix System Security - A Guide for Users and System Administrators Author: David Curry Edition: 1992 Publisher: Addison Wesley ISBN: 0-201-56327-4

5

Information Layout

Good cooking requires efficiency. Delicate dishes will easily be overcooked while you hunt around for the right dish or pan, so be sure to organize your kitchen.

5.1. INTRODUCTION

By now you should have a basic understanding of the services you can provide, the tools you need to install to make these services available to a community of information seekers, and how to get connected to the Internet. In short, you are *almost* ready to begin building your information server.

First, however, you need to focus on the content and organization of the information you wish to serve. An *ad hoc* approach now will cost you dearly in the future. It takes a great deal of time to reorganize a large amount of poorly organized information and it could disrupt the services you are providing.

This chapter makes you consider how to map your virtual information world (organized by content) onto the physical world of disks, UNIX file systems, directories, and files. Your goals should include:

- Making it easy to find a specific file of information or program when you need to modify or reference it.
- Maximizing maintainability, which, in turn implies:

    Easing the burden of moving information to new file systems and disks.

    Minimizing the number of copies of redundant information.

    Facilitating file backup and recovery.

    Providing a suitable growth path as the amount of information grows.
- Maximizing efficiency of access.
- Making it straightforward to navigate your complete information hierarchy should that be desirable for indexing or other purposes.

• Facilitating the maintenance of your information by *mirror sites* (should that be desirable).

Do not confuse this topic on the general principles of information layout with the specific topic of hypertext document organization. What is discussed here applies to all types of information. Organizing hypertext documents is discussed in Section 8.2.6 as part of the general discussion of hypertext navigation.

5.2. TYPES OF INFORMATION TO ORGANIZE

One way to organize the types and locations of information that will be found on your server is by service type, as follows.

Mail Services

• Incoming mail to */usr/spool/mail/xxx,* where *xxx* is the login name of the user receiving the mail
• Mail messages converted to HTML for Web access
• Log files

ftp Services

• Standard ftp directories *~ftp/bin, ~ftp/pub, ~ftp/etc, ~ftp/import,* and so on (Section 7.1)
• Text, images, and compressed tar files organized by subject areas
• Log files

Web Services

• HTML documents
• Images
• Video clips
• Sound bytes
• Configuration files
• Log files
• cgi scripts and other programs executed or downloaded through the information server

The above is not necessarily a recommendation for how to separate your information, merely a way to think about the various information types you will be faced with and how they *might* be arranged. The division is more complicated than the simple classification shown above, as there are various subcategories of information. For example, you can think of subcategories of images associated with Web documents rather than grouping them as a single category. One subcategory is images used by many documents, for example, horizontal bars, arrows, and other basic icons seen in HTML documents. Another subcategory is those used in a specific group of Web documents, for example, a logo for a particular product. Finally, there are those images that will likely only appear on a single Web page. Organizing these subcategories of images should aim to minimize redundancy and make it easy to reference these images (if needed) as you add new pages.

There are some constraints imposed by either the UNIX operating system or the software you are installing on how you organize your information. These constraints can be overridden, but doing so may not be advisable.

Do not change the default (i.e., recommended) directory and file layout of software you are installing, unless there is a compelling reason to do so. Making changes can lead to a more significant installation and maintenance effort.

These changes do not include making symbolic links, which are often necessary. For example, I serve the same Web pages off different servers using a shared file system. This requires a change to the directory structure from the default Web server organization, which is effected by a symbolic link (Section 5.3.1). Symbolic links maintain the virtual directory hierarchy, while giving you variability in the physical layout.

5.3. DIRECTORY HIERARCHY

How you organize your information will be based on the types of information you support and the complexity of that information. However, it is worth describing one possible scenario since it highlights the issues to consider.

Let's assume you are going to be maintaining a Listserver, a Web server, and an ftp server. Access to your ftp files is going to be via anonymous ftp and the Web. Other sites will mirror parts of your ftp archive and some Web documents. One possible directory hierarchy you might employ is shown in Figure 5–1.

The directory names shown in a standard (i.e., non-italic) font are physical directories defined by the UNIX operating system or the application software, whereas those in italics are what I call "virtual directories." A virtual directory is a placeholder for an actual directory whose name is assigned by you and exists in the hierarchy relative to an actual directory. That is, a virtual directory's location is determined relative to a physical directory. So for example, *info_root* is somewhere in your directory hierarchy and assigned by you based on disk space availability, efficiency of access, and so on, whereas /usr/spool/mail is a specific location defined by the UNIX operating system. Similarly, wherever *ServerRoot* is located, it contains directories *conf* (configuration), *logs* (log files), and so on located relative to *ServerRoot,* which is defined as part of the Web server software installation (Section 7.3 and 7.4).

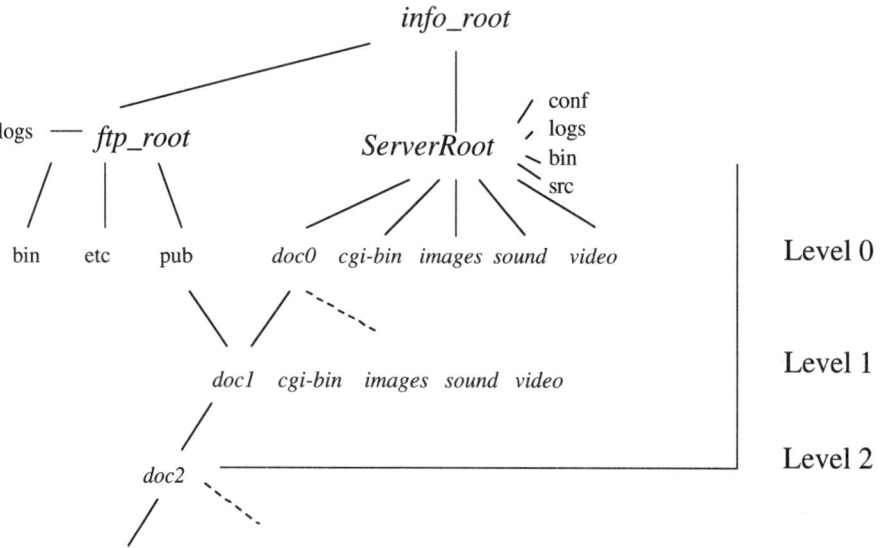

Fig. 5–1   An Example of a Directory Structure to Support an Information Hierarchy

This server is arranged with information at different levels based on how general it is. A recommended practice is to organize your information from most general to most specific. At level 0 of the hierarchy is a set of Web pages (doc0) and any associated information used by those pages or any pages lower in the hierarchy. Typically, the home page (the single document that introduces the information hierarchy) is placed here, as well as any images and cgi scripts used by the home page or any of the pages below it. Thus, as I discussed earlier, images of icons used by many pages should be placed in the *ServerRoot/doc0/images* directory and be referenced by all documents lower in the tree by way of a relative path name in the file description. The relative path name maintains the virtual relationship even when the physical relationship changes. We shall see this more clearly when we discuss hypertext documents and embedding images in hypertext pages (Section 8.2.2). Following these guidelines will allow you to move the whole document tree without having to change references to other Web pages or images.

At Level 1, the ftp files and the Web files share a directory structure in this example hierarchy. This might be useful for a couple of reasons. First, if you have users who access your information server by ftp only, and others who access it via the Web, you can maintain a single file, for example, a README file, rather than have one accessible via the Web and one accessible to ftp only users. Second, if your server is successful, there may be sites who wish to mirror all or parts of your Web-accessible information hierarchy. Many mirror programs mirror ftp-based directory hierarchies, since anonymous ftp is the method they use to gain access to the site they are mirroring and compare their local copy of the files with the remote copy.

Mirroring implies maintaining a current copy of the information on another information server. This could be used within an organization to provide a redundant copy of information. In the event that one system failed, the information would still be available from the other. Alternatively, mirroring could be on a global scale. In a perfect Internet world, global mirroring would not be necessary as all links would be instantaneous. However, in reality, links are often slow. Consider how slow the transatlantic link can be. It is useful for European sites to get information from a site in Europe even though the source of information is a U.S. site. Conversely, if the source of information is in Europe, it is useful for U.S. users of that information to get it from a mirror site in the U.S. The European mirror means there is one transfer to the European site and subsequently many continental accesses, which are fast, rather than frustrated attempts at many transatlantic downloads, which are slow.

A secure method for setting up a mirror is to have file transfer via anonymous ftp, and free software is available to do this from these locations:

ftp://src.doc.ic.ac.uk/pub/computing/archiving/mirror
(United Kingdom)

ftp://ftp.th-darmstadt.de/pub/networking/mirror
(Germany)

ftp://ftp.sun.ac.za/pub/packages/mirror
(South Africa)

These are mirror copies of the same software, not different software programs performing a similar task.

The mirror software functions as follows. The information server needs to do nothing apart from make the information available via anonymous ftp, hence the suggestion of the directory structure at Level 1 (Figure 5–1). The client or mirror site at predetermined times, usually based on how rapidly the information on the server changes, makes a connection via anonymous ftp. The client checks its mirror, that is, its directory structure and file contents (based on modification date) against the server and downloads from the server the files and directories it does not have, or that have been updated since it last received files. The software optionally also deletes the files on the client that are now missing on the server.

Returning to Figure 5–1, at Level 2 in our example information hierarchy we take files posted to the Listserver, convert them to HTML and make them available via the Web. Section 3.5 highlighted filters for doing this conversion. An example using the MHonArc software can be seen at

http://www.sdsc.edu/projects/pb/wpdb/threads.html

5.3.1 A Note on Symbolic Links

Symbolic links are used to maintain a virtual information hierarchy while distributing the information across a variety of physical locations. This is useful for distributing the I/O across a variety of file systems and physical devices, which is important for large information servers. If you are familiar with symbolic links skip to the next section; otherwise here is symbolic links 101. Consider this example (see Figure 5–2):

```
% cd doc1
% ln -s /misc/apps/app1 app1
```

I used a symbolic link (the **ln -s** command) to graft a directory */misc/apps/app1* to my information tree via *doc1*. Thus, if my present working directory is *./doc1* and I enter the command cd app1, my present working directory will, in reality, become */misc/apps/app1,* even though it appears I have a single directory structure under which my documents appear. In other words, *./doc1/app1* becomes merely a pointer to the actual location of the information.

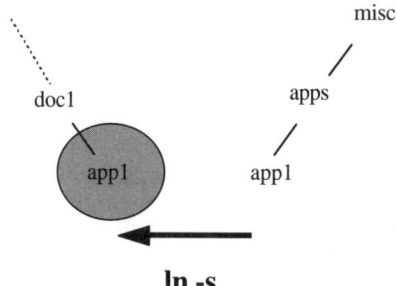

ln -s

Fig. 5–2   A Symbolic Link

5.4. FILE NAMING

Consistent file naming is an important aspect of information layout for three reasons.

1. It helps <u>you</u> recognize the information content of files.
2. It helps <u>other people</u> recognize the contents of your files.
3. It helps <u>applications</u> recognize the correct files upon which to act and, subsequently, how to act.

This latter reason brings us back to MIME types, which were introduced in Section 2.3.3. Recall that a MIME type is a specification for particular types of files that are universally recognized by programmers and, hence, applications. Thus, *image/gif* is a registered MIME type for a graphics image in GIF format. This GIF file has associated with it an extension of *.gif.* The MIME specification registers the type of file and the file extension that is used by convention. Hence, Web browsers and Web servers understand the mapping of a file with an extension of *.gif* to the GIF MIME type and respond accordingly.

Building on our initial discussion of MIME types in Section 2.3.3, Table 5–1 provides useful pointers to further information on MIME types and file extensions.

The last entry in this table provides an example of the MIME types and associated file extensions recognized by the Xmosaic Web browser. Table 5–2 lists common file

TABLE 5–1   Further Reading on MIME Types

Location	Types of Information
http://www.cs.wisc.edu/docs/mime.html	Good introduction
http://www.w3.org/hypertext/-WWW/Protocols/rfc1341/-0_TableOfContents.html	Hypertext MIME specification
http://www.cis.ohio-state.edu/text/faq/usenet/mail/-mime-faq/top.html	MIME FAQ
http://www.ncsa.uiuc.edu/SDG/-Software/XMosaic/extension-map.html	Filetype-to-file-extension mapping used by the Xmosaic Web browser

TABLE 5–2   Common File Extensions

File Extension	MIME Specification
.mime	message/rfc822
.ps	application/postscript
.html	text/html
.c	text/plain
.cc	text/plain
.c++	text/plain
.h	text/plain
.text	text/plain
.tex	text/plain
.pl	text/plain
.txt	text/plain
.nd	audio/basic
.au	audio/basic
.aiff	audio/x-aiff
.aifc	audio/x-aiff

continued

TABLE 5–2   (Continued)

File Extension	MIME Specification
.tar	application/octet-stream
.uu	application/octet-stream
.saveme	application/octet-stream
.dump	application/octet-stream
.bin	application/octet-stream
.gif	image/gif
.tif	image/x-tiff
.tiff	image/x-tiff
.jpg	image/jpeg
.jpeg	image/jpeg
.mpg	video/mpeg
.mpeg	video/mpeg
.hdf	application/x-hdf
.cdf	application/x-netcdf
.nc	application/x-netcdf
.dvi	application/x-dvi
.xwd	image/x-xwd
.rgb	image/x-rgb
.rtf	application/x-rtf
.pdf	application/x-pdf
.src	application/x-wais-source
.wsrc	application/x-wais-source

extensions that I suggest you adopt to be consistent. We met many of these file extensions in Chapter 3.

Those MIME types marked as x-, for example, application/x-wais-source, are not yet official but are in common use.

You should now have some idea how to organize your information. We are now ready to install client software, so that you can see this information as your users will see it.

6

Clients

Ingredients:
- *Using ftp*
- *Using a Listserver*
- *Using traditional Web browsers*
- *Using the newer Web browsers*
- *Helper applications*

It is now time to learn how to make appetizers—the first batch of recipes in this book. A good appetizer is both a culinary delight in itself and also prepares the palette for the forthcoming joys of the main course. Here are recipes for a variety of appetizers.

Knowing how to use the basic information-based clients that come with the UNIX operating system (i.e., mail and ftp), and how to install and use Web clients (i.e., browsers) is a prerequisite to installing an information server since you need a client to download server software and test the functioning of the server. The great majority of information about the Internet, both in books and online, covers clients. In this chapter I filter this vast supply of information, present you with a concise summary of installing and using client software, and point you to the best sources of additional information.

We begin simply with a discussion of how to effectively use ftp and a Listserver. Then, using ftp, we download, install, and configure a couple of the most popular Web browsers. Your client needs still will not be fully satisfied. Recall from Section 3.4 and 3.5 that ancillary tools will be necessary if you wish to support external graphics viewers, sound players and video clips. Recall that a subset of these tools are often invoked directly from a Web browser, and are referred to as helper applications and plug-ins. I end this chapter with examples of how to install the most popular ancillary software tools.

The order in which tools are installed here and the tools themselves are recommended. I will justify these recommendations as we proceed.

6.1. USING FTP

As described in Section 2.5.1, ftp provides the simplest mechanism for gaining access to files on a remote server connected to the Internet. No fancy graphics display devices are needed; ftp is already available with most versions of UNIX, and files can be transferred across slow communication lines typical of modem connections. What follows is ftp 101. *Using ftp is so central to developing a successful server, I consider it in some detail.* If you already use ftp regularly, skip to the next section. The steps in using ftp are:

1. Invoke ftp.
2. Open the connection to the remote ftp server.
3. Log on to the remote ftp server with a login name of "anonymous" and a password of your full email address.
4. Determine what files you wish to download (or possibly upload) by moving to the appropriate directory.
5. Make sure the modes (i.e., **binary** or **ascii**) are set correctly for the file(s) to be transferred.
6. Download or upload the file(s).
7. Close the connection.

Ftp provides a bidirectional connection and is a useful way for users to upload files to your information server, should that be desirable. This requires that you maintain a world-writable directory; I discuss the security implications of maintaining a world-writable directory in Section 7.1.1.1. A subset of ftp commands for completing the steps above are given in Table 6–1. This subset of ftp commands are all I have ever used. Entering the command **help** or **?** at the ftp prompt will provide the complete list of commands, should you need it.

6.1.1 Downloading—An Example

The use of some of these commands is illustrated with an annotated example for downloading the **lynx** Web browser, which is subsequently installed in Section 6.3.1. *This is the only example in this book of a complete ftp download.* User input is in **bold**, responses are in normal type, and annotations are preceded by a hash (#) and terminated by an end-of-line.
There are many "live" examples like this in the book and I suggest you follow them and read the annotations carefully if you wish to understand what is happening.

```
# Invoke ftp
% ftp
# Open a connection to a remote host.
ftp> open ftp2.cc.ukans.edu
Connected to ukanaix.cc.ukans.edu.
```

TABLE 6–1   Common ftp Commands

Step	Command	Function
2.	**open {host}**	Open a connection to *host*
4.	**!**	Escape to the client UNIX shell and issue a command.
	cd	Change the current directory on the server.
	dir (or **ls**)	List contents of a server directory.
	lcd	Change the current directory on the client.
	pwd	Show the current directory on the server.
	size	Show the size of a file resident on the server.
5.	**ascii**	Transfer the file as ASCII characters.
	binary	Transfer the file as binary.
	prompt	Toggle on/off the prompting for each file as it is copied.
	newer	Get the file from the server if the file is newer than the client file.
	rstatus/status	Show current settings on the server/client.
6.	**append**	Append to an existing file.
	get/recv	Get/receive a file.
	mget	Get multiple files (see **prompt**).
	mput	Send multiple files (see **prompt**).
	put/send	Put/send a single file.
7.	**bye** (or **quit**)	Terminate an ftp session and exit.
	close (or **disconnect**)	Terminate an ftp session but do not exit ftp.

```
220 ukanaix.cc.ukans.edu FTP server (Version 4.14 Fri
Aug 5 13:39:22 CDT 1994) ready.
# Login as anonymous and use your e-mail address as
# a password.
Name (ftp2.cc.ukans.edu:bourne): anonymous
331 Guest login ok, send ident as password.
Password:name@address [not echoed]
230 Guest login ok, access restrictions apply.
Remote system type is UNIX.
Using binary mode to transfer files.

ftp> cd /pub/WWW/lynx    # Move to appropriate dir.
ftp> get README          # Get the instructions.
200 PORT command successful.
150 Opening data connection for README (992 bytes).
226 Transfer complete.
992 bytes received in 0.32 seconds (3 Kbytes/s)
```

```
# Escape to the shell and read the instructions from
# the file now on the client.

ftp> !more README
If you grab a pre-compiled binary you may also wish to
pick up a copy of the "lynx.cfg", "mailcap", and
"mime.types" files. These files provide system wide
configuration of Lynx. Make sure you use "binary" mode
when downloading the executables. Use "lynx.cfg" and
"lynx.man" from the same directory you download your
binary from as these files differ between versions.

On UNIX systems after you have got a Lynx Executable
use: "uncompress [Name of the Executable]" and
then:"chmod 755 [Name of the Executable]" to make it
runnable.

The UNIX executables here have been compiled with
debugging information. If you wish a smaller binary, run
the UNIX utility 'strip' on the uncompressed executable.
("strip EXECUTABLE_NAME")

The files lynx_help_files.tar.Z and lynx_help_files.zip
contain the default help files for Lynx. They are not
required unless you wish to have a local copy of the
Lynx documentation.

Craig Lavender
lynx-help@ukanaix.cc.ukans.edu
lynx-bug@ukanaix.cc.ukans.edu


# Set binary mode for file transfers
ftp> binary
200 Type set to I.


# Get the compressed tar file containing the help
# information.
ftp> get lynx_help_files.tar.Z
200 PORT command successful.
150 Opening data connection for lynx_help_files.tar.Z
(64823 bytes).

# Move to the directory containing the binaries
ftp> cd lynx2-4-2
250 CWD command successful.
```

```
# List what binaries are available.
ftp> ls
200 PORT command successful.

150 Opening data connection for ..
lynx2-4-2.zip
lynx2-4-2.tar.Z
README
unzip
INSTALLATION
lynx.cfg
lynx.man
lynx2-4-2.aix32.exe.Z
lynx2-4-2.tar.gz
lynx2-4-2.linux.exe.Z
lynx2-4-2.osf.exe.Z
lynx2-4-2.sun4.exe.Z
lynx2-4-2.ultrix.exe.Z
mailcap
mime.types
226 Transfer complete.

# Get the README file and name it differently on the
# client.
ftp> get README README.2-4-2
200 PORT command successful.
150 Opening data connection for README (1288 bytes).
226 Transfer complete.
1288 bytes received in 0.22 seconds (5.6 Kbytes/s)

# Read the file on the client
ftp> !more README.2-4-2
Lynx Distribution Site at ftp2.cc.ukans.edu

This is the primary distribution site of the Lynx WWW
browser. To download Lynx look for available pre-com-
piled version of Lynx for your system, or download the
source code distribution and compile Lynx on your
site.

Pre-compiled versions:
        lynx<version>.<system>.exe.Z, or
        lynx<version>.<system>.exe.zip

Instructions to install the pre-compiled versions are
given in the INSTALLATION file.
```

Note: pre-compiled versions will be limited to those
systems used at the University of Kansas (at least,
those I can get access to) and any that are contributed
by the Lynx community.

Source code distributions:
      lynx<version>.tar.Z, or
      lynx<version>.zip

Note: VMS version will contain the source distribution
along with object files as these may need to be re-
linked on your system.

All zip files have been successfully unzipped using
UNZIP v.5.12. If you have problems unzipping any of our
files with a different version of UNZIP, we have
included source code for UNZIP v5.12 in the
pub/lynx/unzip directory.

Once you have downloaded the source code for Lynx, read
the file called INSTALLATIONS for instructions on compiling, configuring, and installing
Lynx.

```
# Get the installation instructions

ftp> get INSTALLATION
200 PORT command successful.
150 Opening data connection for INSTALLATION (2676
bytes).
226 Transfer complete.
2676 bytes received in 0.49 seconds (5.3 Kbytes/s)

# Get the executable for DEC UNIX

ftp> get lynx2-4-2.osf.exe.Z
200 PORT command successful.
150 Opening data connection for lynx2-4-2.osf.exe.Z
(447667 bytes).
226 Transfer complete.

# Get the configuration file

ftp> get lynx.cfg
200 PORT command successful.
150 Opening data connection for lynx.cfg (27364 bytes).
```

```
226 Transfer complete.
27364 bytes received in 4.5 seconds (6 Kbytes/s)

# Get the man page

ftp> get lynx.man
200 PORT command successful.
150 Opening data connection for lynx.man (8450 bytes).
226 Transfer complete.
8450 bytes received in 0.83 seconds (10 Kbytes/s)

# get the mailcap file

ftp> get mailcap
200 PORT command successful.
150 Opening data connection for mailcap (4156 bytes).
226 Transfer complete.
4156 bytes received in 0.7 seconds (5.8 Kbytes/s)

# Get the MIME types file

ftp> get mime.types
200 PORT command successful.
150 Opening data connection for mime.types (1057 bytes).
226 Transfer complete.
1057 bytes received in 0.34 seconds (3 Kbytes/s)

# Terminate the connection

ftp> bye
221 Goodbye.
```

This annotated ftp session raises a number of points regarding ftp and ftp-accessible software distributions.

- Many information providers go to considerable trouble to ensure that access to information in their *ftp archives* is straightforward. You should endeavor to do the same.
- If you do not already have access to a Web browser, ftp provides an efficient means of getting one.
- The root of an ftp directory tree is usually */pub,* but when you login the directory is usually */.*
- ASCII files will be transferred successfully in binary mode between UNIX systems, albeit at a slower rate. Binary files will NOT be transferred successfully in ASCII mode.

- If you are operating from a display that does not support multiple terminal windows, the escape to the shell mechanism (!) to issue commands on the client is useful.

Not shown in the example (but a useful point to note) is the procedure for downloading multiple files.

```
ftp> prompt
Interactive mode off.
ftp> mget *
```

The **mget** ftp command will download (get) multiple files from the server. The **mput** command will upload (put) multiple files on the server. The ftp **prompt** command toggles on and off whether to prompt for each of multiple files before copying. Prompting is on by default. Issuing the **prompt** command will turn prompting off, and multiple files will be copied without further intervention. Issuing the **prompt** command again will turn prompting back on.

6.1.2 Installing archie ☞

Recall from Section 2.5.1.1 that archie is a resource to assist you in finding information in ftp archives around the world.

There are three ways to access archie.

1. Via telnet to an archie database site.
2. Via email to an archie database site.
3. Using the archie program, which can be downloaded from any archie database site via ftp or a Web browser.

The URL *http://www.earn.net/gnrt/archie.html* provides a list of all the archie database sites.

If you are going to use archie frequently, option 3 above is recommended. Versions of the archie software are available for both command line execution and via an X Window interface.

6.1.2.1 Software Snapshot

The URL (Table 6–2) that provides documentation on archie fully describes the system and there is no purpose repeating that information here. The distributions available as source can be downloaded via ftp as compressed tar files, uncompressed, and compiled into a working executable in several minutes. How to perform the identical steps for lynx is given in Section 6.3.1.2.

TABLE 6–2   Archie Software Snapshot

Location	*ftp://ftp.sura.net/pub/archie/clients/*
Binaries	No
Source	Yes in C, Perl, and Bourne shell
Documentation	*http://www.cobleskill.edu/faculty/rileje/-comp195/archie.txt* *http://www.earn.net/gnrt/archie.html*

6.1.3 Using archie

Once compiled, the *archie* executable file is ready to be invoked. Here is an example of searching ftp archives for a string "rasmol," which happens to be the name of a popular molecular graphics program.

```
% archie rasmol

Host plaza.aarnet.edu.au

 Location: /graphics/graphics/packages
   DIRECTORY drwxr-xr-x           512 Mar 7 1995 rasmol

Host forte.mathematik.uni-bremen.de

 Location: /pub/unix/visualization
   DIRECTORY drwxrwxr-x           512 Jul 2 1995 rasmol

Host colonsay.dcs.ed.ac.uk

 Location: /export
   DIRECTORY drwxr-xr-x 512       Nov 30 1994 rasmol
```

This search of the archie server returned 3 hits. You would be wise to download the most recent version, that is, the one at the ftp site *forte.mathematik.uni-bremen.de.* The above example illustrates the simplest of all searches. As the archie help display shows, you can search using regular expressions and force different display options.

```
% archie -help
Usage: archie [-acelorstvLV] [-m hits] [-N level] string
      -a : list matches as Alex filenames
      -c : case sensitive substring search
```

```
         i-e : exact string match (default)
         i-r : regular expression search
         i-s : case insensitive substring search
         i-l : list one match per line
         i-t : sort inverted by date
    -m hits : specifies maximum number of hits to return (default 95)
-o filename : specifies file to store results in
    -h host : specifies server host
         -L : list known servers and current default
   -N level : specifies query niceness level (0-35765)
```

What happens when you issue an archie command?

```
% archie -L
Known archie servers:
    archie.ans.net (USA [NY])
    archie.rutgers.edu (USA [NJ])
    archie.sura.net (USA [MD])
    archie.unl.edu (USA [NE])
    archie.mcgill.ca (Canada)
    archie.funet.fi (Finland/Mainland Europe)
    archie.au (Australia)
    archie.doc.ic.ac.uk (Great Britain/Ireland)
    archie.wide.ad.jp (Japan)
    archie.ncu.edu.tw (Taiwan)
* archie.sura.net is the default Archie server.
For the most up-to-date list, write to an Archie server and give it
the command `servers'.
```

The -L option lists known archie servers. Our request to find rasmol was served by the archie server *archie.sura.net.* If that server had not been available, the request would have been met by one of the other servers.

Archie was introduced in Section 2.5.1.1 and we will see how to register your own ftp archives for inclusion in the archie database in Section 7.1.1.2.

6.2. Using a Listserver

Most likely, your first use of a Listserver is based upon instructions received by e-mail or read from the Web. These instructions describe how to subscribe to a specific list. Let us take a step back from that scenario, for a moment, to understand how a Listserver operates. As I discussed in Section 3.2.2.2, the same Listserver software maintains multiple lists, where each list relates to a specific topic of interest to a community of users. To learn about the commands that can be sent to a Listserver, send e-mail to *listserv@mailserver.sdsc.edu* with no subject line and a message body that contains the single word, "help." What is returned is shown below and provides all the information needed to use a Listserver; read it carefully.

```
From Listserv@sdsc.edu Thu Jan 18 09:02:53 1996
Date: Thu, 18 Jan 1996 08:55:51 -0800
From: Mailing List Processor <Listserv@sdsc.edu>
To: bourne@hercules.sdsc.edu
Subject: Re: your LISTSERV request "help"


WHAT IS LISTSERV ?
------------------


    The listserv package allows you to communicate with
selected interest group through an automated electronic
mailing list system.

    You can subscribe or unsubscribe to any of the
various SDSC mailing lists and the local redistribution
of global mailing lists. You can also submit email
messages to any of the SDSC mailing lists to which you
subscribe.

    This enables you to send email to an entire list of
people by simply addressing mail to the name of a sin-
gle distribution list name.

    SUBSCRIPTION AND INFORMATION REQUESTS
    -------------------------------------


    To subscribe to, unsubscribe from, or request
additional information, send E-mail to
"listserv@mailserver.sdsc.edu". The subject line of
messages sent to listserv are ignored, but the body of
your message should contain one or more commands
understood by the listserv program:

    HELP
        lists this file. This is also sent whenever a
message to listserv is received from which no valid
command could be parsed.
```

HELP groupname
> lists a brief description of the group requested.

INDEX
> lists all the groups available for subscription.

LONGINDEX
> lists all the groups and their descriptions.

ADD listname
DELETE listname

ADD address listname
DELETE address listname
> adds or deletes the given address to or from the list specified. Mail is sent to the address given to confirm the add or delete operation. We strongly recommend that you use your SDSC registered mailname when subscribing (i.e., use the second form of the command which includes a specification of the address). If you omit the 'address' the command will assume the mailbox that is in the From: line of the message. Note that SUBSCRIBE is a synonym for ADD; UNSUBSCRIBE for DELETE.

DELETE-ALL
UNSUBSCRIBE-ALL

DELETE-ALL address
UNSUBSCRIBE-ALL address
> unsubscribes given address from all mailing lists. Mail is sent to the address given to confirm the deletions. If you omit the 'address' the command will assume the mailbox that is in the From: line of the message.

LIST

LIST address
> lists all mailing lists to which the given address is subscribed. If you omit the 'address' the command will assume the mailbox is in the from line.

FAQ
FAQ listname
> sends a list of "Frequently Asked Questions" for

```
the appropriate mailing list. The command "FAQ" by itself
sends an index of available FAQ's.

    INFO

    INFO filename1 filename2 ... filenameN
    GET filename1 filename2 ... filenameN
        sends a copy of the appropriate information sheet
associated with each file name. The command "INFO" by
itself will send an index of available info sheets.


    NOTES ABOUT COMMANDS
    --------------------


    A command must be the first word on each line in the
message. Lines which do not start with a command word
are ignored. If no commands were found in the entire
message body, this help file will be returned to you.
    A single message may contain multiple commands; a
separate response will be sent for each.
```

Notice we sent mail to *listserv* which happens to be one of several available Listserver packages; another is Majordomo, which we will meet subsequently. Each Listserver has slightly different commands, but the principle is the same. Knowing how to use listserv is ample training for using Majordomo.

Once you have made contact with a Listserver, if you do not know the name of the list you are interested in, the next step is to determine what lists are maintained on that particular server. As indicated by the **HELP** command above, the commands **INDEX** and **LONGINDEX** provide you with details of the available lists. Here is an abbreviated example using the same SDSC Listserver.

```
From Listserv@sdsc.edu Thu Jan 18 09:07:12 1996
Date: Thu, 18 Jan 1996 09:04:37 -0800
From: Mailing List Processor <Listserv@sdsc.edu>
To: fred@chem.harvard.edu
Subject: Re: your LISTSERV request "index"

Index of mailing lists
admin
afarmers
afsusers
agua_leaders
....
```

```
vistech
vrml-behaviors
vrml-modeling
vtc_wg
vtcsupport
webster
websupport
workgang
www_ug
```

The **INDEX** command returns an index of the lists available at this site. This statement is not strictly true, since there are actually more lists at this site, some of which are for internal use only. To see internal lists you would have to be accessing the Listserver from the same Internet domain (i.e., *sdsc.edu* in this example). As you can see, some of the names are not very meaningful (*when you create lists on your Listserver give them meaningful names*). The **LONGINDEX** command can be used to provide more detail.

```
Date: Tue, 27 Feb 1996 10:01:58 -0800
From: Mailing List Processor <Listserv@sdsc.edu>
To: fred@chem.harvard.edu
Subject: Re: your LISTSERV request "longindex"

Index of mailing lists
admin

        ADMIN

        The SDSC administration information mailing
list.
    ..
    vissoft
        vissoft:
    Information about the VisSoft mailing list.

        VisSoft is a forum for discussion between
members of the NSF Supercomputer Centers and the
Visualization community at large. The main topic of
discussion is Visualization Software Infrastructure.
    ..........
```

After obtaining an index of the lists available on the Listserver, you might again send e-mail to the Listserver, this time relating to a specific list with one or more of the following annotated sample commands as the body of the message. Note that Listserver commands are case insensitive:

```
# Add yourself to a list called hpcwire.
add hpcwire      # or subscribe hpcwire

# Add someone else to a list by giving their
# email address (requires their verification).
add immee@podunk.edu sdsc_discuss_applications

# Remove yourself from a list called hpcwire.
delete hpcwire  # or unsubscribe hpcwire

# Remove someone else (wombat) from a list
(requires their verification).
delete wombat@cyberpunk.sdsc.edu sdsc_important

# Find out more about a specific list called
# sdsc_important_workstations.
help sdsc_important_workstations
```

Using listserv to mail submissions to an SDSC mailing list to which you are a subscriber, you would address mail to the desired mailing list with the suffix *@mailserver.sdsc.edu*. For example,

```
% mail etec@mailserver.sdsc.edu
```

would broadcast the contents of your message to everyone subscribing to the *etec* list, assuming it was an unmoderated list. If it were a moderated list, the message would be sent to the list moderator, who would then decide whether it should be posted.

Using these simple examples as templates you should now be able to subscribe, unsubscribe and post to a list. If you need more information refer to

http://www.clark.net/pub/lschank/explore/lists.html

6.3. Web Browsers (Clients)

In this section I cover how to obtain, install, and if necessary configure, three of the most popular Web browsers—lynx, NCSA's Mosaic, and Network Navigator from Netscape Communications Corp. Making a choice of Web browser was covered in Section 2.5.3. I have chosen lynx since it is the best line-oriented browser; I have chosen Mosaic since it can be compiled from source and is, therefore, effectively available on all UNIX platforms; and I have chosen Netscape, since it is by far the most popular browser used on UNIX platforms at the time of writing, if you happen to be using a platform for which a binary is available.

6.3.1 lynx

Recall from Section 2.5.3.1 that lynx is a Web browser that can be run on character-only display devices. That is, it converts complex HTML documents into something decipherable when viewed on a character cell terminal. We shall see later (Chapters 8 and 9) that you should organize your information so that character-only browsers can make good use of it. Typically, you would install a lynx Web browser on a UNIX client when

- The connection of that UNIX client to the Internet is via a slow connection and image downloading is not practical. This is not a compelling argument, since most Web browsers permit you to turn off image downloading.
- The display on the UNIX client does not support graphics.

6.3.1.1 Software Snapshot ☞

TABLE 6–3   Lynx Software Snapshot

Location	*ftp://ftp2.cc.ukans.edu/pub/lynx*
Binaries	AIX, DEC UNIX, SunOS, Linux, Ultrix
Source	Yes
Questions	*lynx-help@ukanaix.cc.ukanas.edu*
Bugs	*lynx-bug@ukanaix.cc.ukanas.edu*
Features	Runs on character displays
	Supports direct posting to newsgroups

6.3.1.2 Installing and Configuring Lynx—A Template for all Software Installations

This is the only complete example in this book of uncompressing a compressed tar file; there is no point repeating it for every piece of software, since the steps are the same.

The steps shown in the following example are taken from an installation on a DEC UNIX system, but apply to all versions of UNIX.

1. Uncompress the executable and the help tar file.
2. Use the **install** command to perform a global install (optional, since it can be run locally).
3. Although step 2 failed because the DEC UNIX version of **install** did not recognize the options, it was easy to work around the problem, since it only required that files be copied to the appropriate directories and the protections set.
4. Define any configuration parameters in the file *lynx.cfg*.
5. Install the man pages.

Here is the complete annotated dialog; read it carefully.

```
% uncompress lynx2-4-2.osf.exe.Z \
  lynx_help_files.tar.Z

# The INSTALLATION is easy to follow and only
# specific items to be considered carefully
# are discussed here. In other words read this after
# you read the file INSTALLATION and before you do the
# install!
# lynx can be run locally i.e. by an individual or
# globally by having it accessible from a directory in
# every users path variable. Here we install it
# globally

% install -c -s -m 555 lynx2-4-2.osf.exe -
  /usr/local/bin/lynx
install: The -c, -f, -n options each require a directory
following!
The -m, -u, -g options require mode, owner or group
following!

# The install command operates differently on
# different Unix operating systems. Since all it does
# is move the executable to the appropriate directory
# and set the protection, we can do this by hand.

% mv lynx2-4-2.osf.exe /usr/local/bin/lynx
% chmod 755 /usr/local/bin/lynx

# The next step is to modify the file lynx.cfg
# (configuration file) to suit your particular site.
# This file is well documented. Here are a list of the
# items I modified.
#
# STARTFILE: - The page which lynx displays when
# invoked. Typically this would be your or your
# organizations home page.
# DEFAULT_INDEX_FILE: - File retrieved using the lynx
# I command. Usually a file with interesting URLs
# VI_KEYS_ALWAYS_ON: - Default for use of vi keys. Can
# also be set in .lynxrc (individual user)
# EMACS_KEYS_ALWAYS_ON: - As above but for the Emacs
# editor.
```

```
# DEFAULT_EDITOR: - Path to the editor used by most
# users.
# PRINTER: - Default printer. The format is well
# described.
# DOWNLOADER: - Used to define a default protocol for
# downloading files to your host, typically over
# serial lines. Again well documented
# UPLOADER: - As above, but for uploading files to a
# remote computer.
# SUFFIX: - File extensions to be defined for MIME
# types.
# VIEWER: - Viewer capable of responding to specific
# MIME types.
# KEYMAP: - Key remapping if desired.


# Make the configuration file globally accessible

% mv lynx.cfg /usr/local/lib/lynx.cfg
% chmod 644 /usr/local/lib/lynx.cfg


# Make the MIME types and mail configuration globally
# accessible

% mv mime.types /usr/local/lib/mosaic/mime.types
% chmod 644 /usr/local/lib/mosaic/mime.types


% mv mailcap /usr/local/lib/mosaic/mailcap
% chmod 644 /usr/local/lib/mosaic/mailcap


# Install the man page

% cp lynx.man /usr/man/man1/lynx.1
% chmod 444 /usr/man/man1/lynx.1


# Remake the whatis database for use by the man -k (or
# appropos) command.
% makewhatis
```

6.3.1.3 Using lynx

The following is an example of a Web page viewed with lynx on a character cell terminal. Images are omitted, but the text associated with the ALT HTML attribute is displayed (Section 8.2.2.3). The hyperlinks do not highlight, but as indicated, using the up and down arrow keys will move you from one link to the next, and the left and right arrow keys move you backward and forward to pages represented by the links.

```
% lynx
```

                                                    SDSC (p1 of 2)

[Home page for text based browsers]
[Image of the Week]

Welcome to the SDSC (San Diego Supercomputer Center) home page. SDSC is a national laboratory for computational science and engineering that was established in 1985 by the National Science Foundation. Its mission is to advance research in the computational sciences, develop the underlying enabling computational technologies, and help industries adapt state-of-the-art computational tools to their design and engineering processes.

   For information about SDSC, its staff, affiliates, industrial partnerships, employment opportunities and more, see the General Information page. For specific information use the navigational buttons below.

[Navigational Tool Bar]
— press space for next page —
Arrow keys: Up and Down to move. Right to follow a link; Left to go back.
O)ther cmds H)elp K)eymap G)oto P)rint M)ain screen o)ptions Q)uit

6.3.2 Mosaic

The Mosaic Web browser from The National Center for Supercomputing Applications (NCSA) fueled the Web revolution. While it was Tim Berners-Lee at CERN who developed the idea of distributed documents accessible via the network, it was the Mosaic browser that popularized the notion. However, as we saw in Section 2.5.3, at the time of writing Mosaic is not the most popular Web browser. It is included in this book as an example of a *free* browser for which source code is available and has multi-language support. We shall compile and configure this browser from source code. This could be important to you if:

- an executable for a more popular browser is not available for the UNIX client on which you are working
- the more popular browsers are not available free to your organization

6.3.2.1 Software Snapshot ☞

TABLE 6–4   Mosaic Software Snapshot

Location	*ftp://ftp.ncsa.uiuc.edu/Mosaic*
Binaries	AIX, DEC UNIX, Irix, HP/UX, Linux, Solaris, SunOS, Ultrix

continued

TABLE 6–4   (Continued)

Source	Yes
Questions	*mosaic-x@ncsa.uiuc.edu*
Bugs	*mosaic-x@ncsa.uiuc.edu*
Best Source of Information	*http://www.ncsa.uiuc.edu/SDG/Software/Xmosaic/*

6.3.2.2 Compiling—An Example

Here are the steps to follow in compiling Mosaic. They can be used as a general guide for compiling all software in this book. *These guidelines on compilation will not be repeated for each subsequent software tool discussed in this book.*

1. Carefully read the README, INSTALLATION, or any other file associated with the installation before attempting the installation.
2. Modify the files indicated in step 1 to suit your particular needs. At the very least this will likely be a *"makefile"* to set compiler options, hardware type, directory paths, and so on, for use by the *make* program. Some software uses the *imake* utility which determines your hardware type and compiles and builds an executable accordingly. In short, *make* and *imake* simplify the compile and link phases. If you are not familiar with *make* and *imake* Table 6–5 has some pointers to additional information I have found useful. The first two are online tutorials and the last two useful books which are summarized online.

The software installations described in this book require no more that a cursory knowledge of *make*.

3. Run *make* or *imake* as instructed. This will create the executables and install them in the correct locations as defined by you. Sometimes this is a multi-step

TABLE 6–5   Further Reading on the *make* Utility

Location	**Description**
http://physics.ucsc.edu/tutor/make.html	Introductory tutorial
http://www.cs.montana.edu/people/- starkey/PEXbook/imake.html	Tutorial associated with PEXlib, but useful for learning *make*
http://www.ora.com/gnn/bus/ora/- item/make2.html	Managing Projects with *make* A. Oram & S. Talbot (1991) O'Reilly & Associates
http://www.ora.com/gnn/bus/ora/- item/imake.html	Software Portability with *imake* P. DuBois (1993) O'Reilly & Associates

process defined by commands like **make** (compile only), **make install** (install the compiled code), **make all** (compile and install), and **make clean** (remove object code). "Install," "all," and "clean" are entry points defined by the writer of the *makefile,* and therefore not universal, but certainly in common use.

4. Test the executable file produced in step 3.

Let us apply these general rules to compiling Mosaic. Here is the README file:

```
NCSA Mosaic for the X Window System Version 2.5
===============================================

Welcome to NCSA Mosaic for the X Window System 2.5!

This README details installation steps.

More complete information and documentation on NCSA Mosaic is
available online, via NCSA Mosaic.

Binaries
--------
NCSA Mosaic is known to compile on the following platforms:
   SGI (IRIX 4.0.x and 5.x)
   IBM (AIX 3.2.4)
   Sun (SunOS 4.1.3 and 5.3 (Solaris))
   DECstation 5000-200 (Ultrix 4.x)
   DEC Alpha (OSF/1 1.3 and 3.0)
   Hewlett Packard (HP/UX 7.x, 8.x, 9.x)
   Pentium (Linux 1.1.94)

Binaries for these platforms (and possibly others) are
available on ftp.ncsa.uiuc.edu in /Mosaic/Unix/binaries/

If you have to make nontrivial changes to NCSA Mosaic to get
it to compile on a particular platform, please send a set
of context diffs (e.g., 'diff -c oldfile newfile') to
mosaic-x@ncsa.uiuc.edu.

Installation Instructions
-------------------------
Simply examine the toplevel Makefile, change the appropriate
customizable options, and type 'make'.

The final result is a single independent executable, src/Mosaic.
```

(The *Makefile.*[*sun,dec,ibm,alpha,*etc.] files are the *Makefiles*
we use locally for compilation on various platforms; they
will almost certainly NOT WORK for you without modification.
We recommend you start with the stock *Makefile* and
make modifications as necessary to avoid confusion.)

There is one tricky thing:

-- You have the option of compiling in support for NCSA HDF, a
platform-independent hierarchical scientific data format,
and NCSA DTM, a network-based message-passing protocol useful
for exchanging scientific data between applications. If
you compile one of them in, you should compile both of them in.
If you don't already know what HDF and DTM are and want
to compile Mosaic quickly, forget about them for the time
being you can always recompile later.

   The DTM library is in subdirectory *libdtm*. The HDF
library must be obtained separately from *ftp.ncsa.uiuc.edu*
in */HDF*; get version 3.3r1 or later. Set the various options
in the Makefile to point to all the right places, and you
should be set.

After You Have Compiled

  If you do not normally run Motif on your system (e.g., if
you run Sun OpenWindows instead), then you may get a whole
bunch of run-time errors about translations when you
start Mosaic.

If this happens, copy the file *XKeysymDB* (included in
this directory) to */usr/lib/X11*. (If you compile
Mosaic yourself, you may need to place this file
elsewhere, depending on your X configuration.) See
the FAQ list online for more information.

X Defaults

NCSA Mosaic includes sets of fallback X resources that provide
reasonable screen display properties for three configurations:
color, monochrome, and color SGI. (Color SGI has its
own configuration since SGI systems commonly use a
gamma correction factor of 1.7, which makes their
screens brighter than usual.)

```
If you compile NCSA Mosaic out of the box, or if you download
a binary from ftp.ncsa.uiuc.edu, the default resources will
be for a color display (or, if you compile on an SGI, the
default will be for color SGI). See the Makefile for
information on how to have monochrome resources by default.
On the command line, the flags '-mono' and
'-color' allow you to switch resource configurations at runtime.

For your convenience, three corresponding X app-defaults
files are included in this distribution: app-defaults.color,
app-defaults.color-sgi, and app-defaults.mono.


Bug Reports and Comments
------------------------
 Bug reports and other comments can be sent to
 mosaic-x@ncsa.uiuc.edu.

If you find NCSA Mosaic useful or particularly interesting,
please also send us a note—continued development of
this project partially depends on user feedback and support.
--
Dave Thompson <davet@ncsa.uiuc.edu>
Alan Braverman <alanb@ncsa.uiuc.edu>
Scott Powers <spowers@ncsa.uiuc.edu>
Software Development Group
National Center for Supercomputing Applications
```

As you see, this is a well written and clear description of what needs to be done. Here is the *Makefile* with modifications annotated and flagged with "# ****" to distinguish them from the comments provided by NCSA. Look it over carefully.

```
 # Toplevel Makefile for NCSA Mosaic.

# You shouldn't need to touch any of the Makefiles in the various
# subdirectories if you configure this Makefile correctly.

# If you need to make serious changes to get Mosaic to compile on your
# platform, send context diffs to mosaic-x@ncsa.uiuc.edu.
```

```
# -------------CUSTOMIZABLE OPTIONS-------------

RANLIB = /bin/true
#### On non-SGI's, this should be ranlib.
RANLIB = ranlib          # **** This is the one I need therefore no
# **** change is necessary since the new definition will supersede the
# **** original definition
CC = cc
#### On Sun's, this should be gcc (ANSI required).
CC = gcc # **** This is the one I need


#### For a few files in the source, some compilers may need to be
#### kicked into K&R mode. E.g., on SGI's, -cckr does this.
knrflag = -cckr
#### On most systems, no flag is needed.
knrflag =           # **** This is the one I need


#### Random system configuration flags.
#### -> *** For Motif 1.2 ON ANY PLATFORM, do -DMOTIF1_2 *** <-
#### For IBM AIX 3.2, do -D_BSD
#### For NeXT, do -DNEXT
#### For HP/UX, do -Aa -D_HPUX_SOURCE
#### For Dell SVR4, do -DSVR4
#### For Solaris, do -DSVR4
#### For Esix 4.0.4 and Solaris x86 2.1, do -DSVR4
#### For Convex whatever, do -DCONVEX
#### For SCO ODT 3.0, do -DSCO -DSVR4 -DMOTIF1_2
#### For Motorola SVR4, do -DSVR4 -DMOTOROLA -DMOTIF1_2
sysconfigflags =
# **** I am installing on SunOS therefore I do nothing


#### System libraries.
syslibs = -lPW -lsun -lmalloc
#### For AIX 3.2
# syslibs = -lPW -lbsd
#### For most other Motif platforms:
# syslibs = -lPW
#### For Sun's and Ultrix and HP and BSD/386:
syslibs =           # **** This will work
#### For Sun's with no DNS:
# syslibs = -lresolv
```

```
#### For SCO ODT:
# syslibs = -lPW -lsocket -lmalloc
#### For Dell SVR4:
# syslibs = -lnsl -lsocket -lc -lucb
#### For Solaris (?)
# syslibs = -lnsl -lsocket -lgen
#### For Motorola SVR4:
# syslibs = -lnsl -lsocket -lgen


#### X include file locations--if your platform puts the X include
#### files in a strange place, set this variable appropriately. Else
#### don't worry about it.
#### HP X11R4 version:
# xinc = -I/usr/include/Motif1.1 -I/usr/include/X11R4
#### HP X11R5 version:
# xinc = -I/usr/include/Motif1.2 -I/usr/local/X11R5/include
#### NeXT version:
# xinc = -I/usr/include/X11
#### BSD/386
# xinc = -I/usr/X11/include


#### X library locations.
xlibs = -lXm_s -lXmu -lXt_s -lX11_s
#### For Sun's (at least running stock X/Motif as installed on our
     machines):
#### **** This needed changing in our special case
#**** xlibs = /usr/lib/libXm.a /usr/lib/libXmu.a
/usr/lib/libXt.a/usr/lib/libXe
xt.a /usr/lib/libX11.a -lm
xlibs = /usr/local/lib/libXm.a /usr/local/lib/libXmu.a
/usr/local/lib/libXt.a
/usr/local/lib/libXext.a /usr/local/lib/libX11.a -lm
#### For HP-UX 8.00:
# xlibs = -L/usr/lib/Motif1.1 -lXm -L/usr/lib/X11R4 -lXmu -lXt -lX11
#### For HP-UX 9.01: The X11R5 libraries are here on our systems
# xlibs = -L/usr/lib/Motif1.2 -lXm -L/usr/lib/X11R5 -L/usr/lib/X11R4 -
lXmu -lXt
-lX11
#### For NeXT:
# xlibs = -L/usr/lib/X11 -lXm -lXmu -lXt -lX11
#### For Dell SVR4:
# xlibs = -L/usr/X5/lib -lXm -lXmu -lXt -lXext -lX11
#### For Solaris (?)
# xlibs = -lXm -lXmu -lXt -lXext -lX11 -lm
```

```
#### For SCO ODT 3.0 (I'm told that -1XtXm_s is *not* a typo :-):
# xlibs = -1XtXm_s -1Xmu -1X11_s
#### For nearly everyone else:
# xlibs = -1Xm -1Xmu -1Xt -1X11
#### For BSD/386:
# xlibs = -L/usr/X11/lib -1Xm -1Xmu -1Xt -1X11
#### For Motorola SVR4:
# xlibs = -1Xm -1Xmu -1Xt -1Xext -1X11 -1m


#### DTM AND HDF SUPPORT; READ CAREFULLY

#### If you want to compile with DTM and HDF support, you should leave
#### the following lines uncommented and make sure you have a copy of
#### HDF 3.3 (r1 or later) installed and ready. You can find HDF on
#### ftp.ncsa.uiuc.edu in /HDF.

#### If you do not want to compile with DTM and HDF support, comment
#### the following lines out. (If you are compiling from source for
#### the first time, you should probably not bother with HDF and DTM
#### support.)

#### dtmmachtype needs to be set to one of the following:
#### sun, sgi, dec, ibm, next, cray, convex
#### If your platform is not one of the above, then either do not
#### compile with HDF/DTM support or try hacking libdtm/makefile.

#dtmmachtype = sun
#dtmdirs = libdtm libnet
#dtmlibs = ../libnet/libnet.a ../libdtm/libdtm.a
#dtmflags = -DHAVE_DTM -I.. -I../libnet
#### **** No HDF support included
#**** hdfdir = /hdf2/scratch/sxu/4.0b1_SunOS
#**** hdflibs = $(hdfdir)/lib/libnetcdf.a $(hdfdir)/lib/libdf.a
#**** hdfflags = -DHAVE_HDF -DHDF -I$(hdfdir)/include


#### JPEG SUPPORT
#### For inline JPEG support, the following should be defined:
#### The library used is Independent JPEG Group (IJG's) 5.0a.
#### **** Not supported at this time
#**** jpegdir = /X11/mosaic/libjpeg/sun4
#**** jpeglibs = $(jpegdir)/libjpeg.a
#**** jpegflags = -I$(jpegdir) -DHAVE_JPEG
```

DIRECT WAIS SUPPORT

```
#### If you want to have Mosaic be able to communicate directly with
#### WAIS servers, do set the following flags appropriately. We
#### recommend linking with CNIDR's freeWAIS 0.1 distribution; other
#### WAIS distributions may work but we have not tested them with
#### Mosaic. freeWAIS 0.1 can be found on sunsite.unc.edu in
#### /pub/wais.

#### If you do not wish to link to the WAIS libraries, then comment
#### the following lines out. Mosaic will then communicate with WAIS
#### servers via a HTTP gateway.

#### -lm is required for freeWAIS 0.1, as ceil() is used.
# **** we will communicate via http
#**** waisroot = /X11/mosaic/freeWAIS-0.202-sun
#**** waisflags = -DDIRECT_WAIS -I$(waisroot)/ir
#**** waislibdir = $(waisroot)/bin
#**** waislibs = $(waislibdir)/inv.a $(waislibdir)/wais.a\
#**** $(waislibdir)/libftw.a
 -lm


#### PEM/PGP SUPPORT
####
#### PEM stands for Privacy Enhanced Mail.
#### PGP stands for Pretty Good Privacy.
####
#### PGP and PEM are programs to allow you and a second party to
#### communicate in a way which does not allow third parties to read
#### them, and which certify that the person who sent the message is
#### really who they claim they are.
####
#### PGP and PEM both use RSA encryption. The U.S. government has
#### strict export controls over foreign use of this technology, so
#### people outside the U.S. may have a difficult time finding
#### programs which perform the encryption.
####
#### If you have a way to encrypt/decrypt with PEM or PGP, and will be
#### communicating with a server (or servers) which also uses PEM or
#### PGP you will want to set this flag when you compile.
```

```
# PEM_FLAG = -DPEM_AUTH

#**** Not supported at this time
#### Customization flags:
#### . If you want Mosaic to come up with monochrome colors by
#### default, use -DMONO_DEFAULT
#### . If you want to define the default Mosaic home page, set
#### -DHOME_PAGE_DEFAULT=\\\"url\\\"
#### . If you want to define the default Mosaic documentation
####      directory (should be a URL),
####      set -DDOCS_DIRECTORY_DEFAULT=\\\"url\\\"
#### . Other things you can define are spelled out in src/mosaic.h.
customflags =
```

Note the changes I made relate to:

- which options to install
- non-standard paths for system libraries and include files
- the level of security to provide

The *make* command can now be used to create the Mosaic executable (not shown). Mosaic can then be run to produce the familiar Web browser.

6.3.2.3 Installation Notes

When you start Mosaic for the first time, you will not see the Web page shown above, but the Mosaic home page at NCSA. This is just one of the items you may wish to customize, so that the Web browser initially points to your most logical starting point for Web access. Refer to

http://www.ncsa.uiuc.edu/SDG/Software/XMosaic/
mosaic-docs.html

for details of how to customize this and other options.

6.3.3 Netscape Navigator

Netscape Navigator[1] is currently the most popular of the Web browsers, and the browser recommended if a binary exists for your hardware and operating system, and the licensing suits your organization. There is no source code available for Netscape Navigator.

1. Netscape Navigator is one product from Netscape Communications Inc. As the most popular product, it is frequently and incorrectly referred to as simply Netscape.

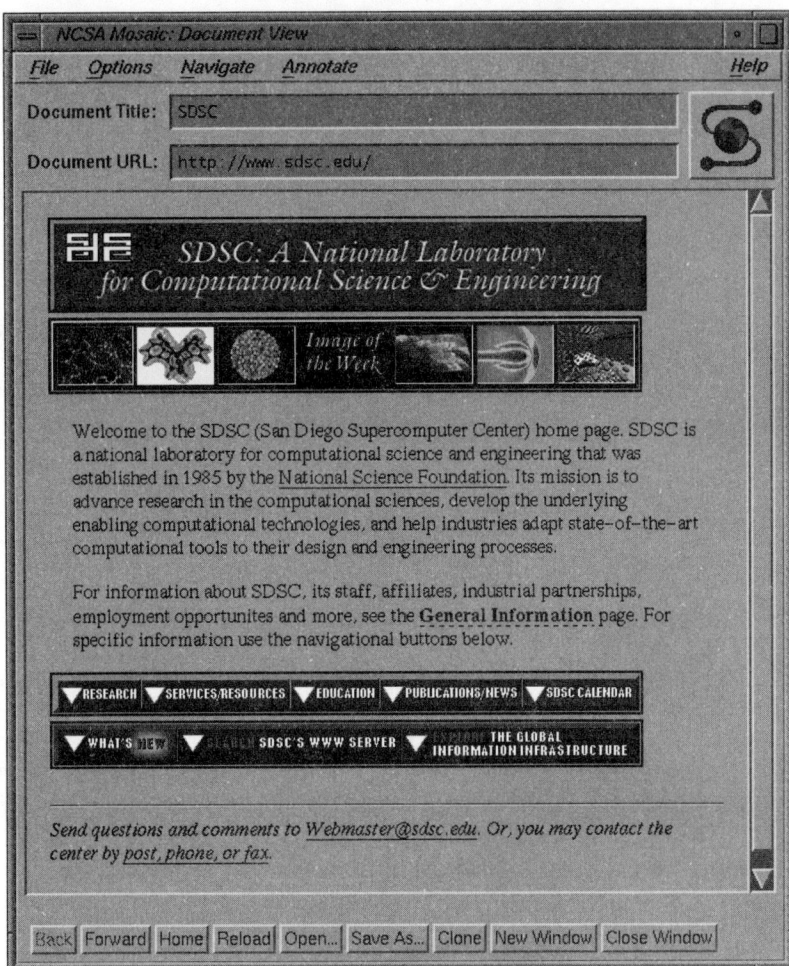

Fig 6–1   View of the Mosaic Browser Showing the SDSC Home Page

6.3.3.1 Software Snapshot ☞

TABLE 6–6   Netscape Navigator Software Snapshot

Location (via Web)	*http://home.netscape.com/comprod/mirror/index.html*
(via ftp - 7 sites)	*ftp://ftp2.netscape.com - ftp://ftp8.netscape.com*
Binaries	AIX, OSF/1, SunOS, Linux, Ultrix, Solaris, NetBSD, FreeBSD, Mips platforms, HP/UX
Source	No

continued

TABLE 6–6   (Continued)

Questions (after subscribing)	*http://home.netscape.com/comprod/upgrades/-index.html#details*
Best Features	Good functionality, current *de facto* standard, widely used and therefore familiar, includes Java support. Supports network proxies for secure environments

6.3.3.2 Installation Notes

Once downloaded and uncompressed the software may be used immediately. All configuration is done from the "preferences" options of the options pull-down menu. There is a myriad of items that can be configured, here are the four most important to consider:

- the cache
- helper applications
- mail and newsgroups
- security

I consider each option separately.

6.3.3.2.1 The Cache.   When a Web page is fetched from a server and displayed on the client, that page is cached on the client. Thus, if that page is revisited it can be retrieved from the cache rather than again having to be retrieved from the server, a much slower operation. There is a memory cache, active while Netscape is active, and a disk cache which gets written periodically. In principle, caching is a good idea, but the size of the caches is dependent on the hardware resources available on the client. Netscape allows you to set the size of the memory cache and the disk cache. The defaults are adequate for most situations. *It is important to remember caching when modifying Web pages.* After a page is modified, if you wish to see those changes, that page should be reloaded. Otherwise, it may be the unmodified page still stored in the cache that is displayed. Caching with Netscape is not always predictable, varying from version to version, and while editing Web pages I have found myself frequently flushing the memory and disk caches to force a reload of a Web page. This, like all cache-based operations, is easily done from the cache preferences menu.

6.3.3.2.2 Helper Applications.   Recall from Section 2.2.3 that a helper application is a separate application that can be called by a Web browser to handle a particular MIME type. For this to work the MIME type must be mapped to one or more file extensions. This mapping is illustrated in Figure 6–2.

There is a system-wide mapping so that the browser running on your information server will call up a specific helper application when that file type is encountered. This may be overridden by each individual user if they prefer an application of their choosing to handle specific file types. How does this work? This question is best answered by look-

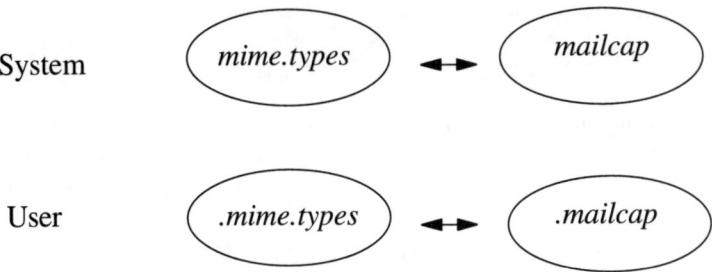

Fig. 6–2 MIME Type Mapping to Applications

ing at the specific files involved. Here is a sample *mime.types* file. Note the URL in the file; this provides you with more information on the details of this file should you need it.

```
# example mime.types file.
# see the NCSA X Mosaic documentation at
# http://www.ncsa.uiuc.edu/SDG/Software/Mosaic/-
# Docs/extension-map.html
# for more details

application/postscript         ai eps ps
application/rtf                rtf
application/x-tex              tex
application/x-texinfo          texinfo texi
application/x-troff            t tr roff
audio/basic                    au snd
audio/x-aiff                   aif aiff aifc
audio/x-wav                    wav
image/gif                      gif
image/ief                      ief
image/jpeg                     jpeg jpg jpe
image/tiff                     tiff tif
image/x-xwindowdump            xwd
text/html                      html
text/plain                     txt c cc h
video/mpeg                     mpeg mpg mpe
video/quicktime                qt mov
video/x-msvideo                avi
video/x-sgi-movie              movie
```

So, for example, an *image/gif* MIME type is mapped to the file extension *gif*. Now consider a related entry from the system-wide *mailcap* file:

```
image/gif; xv %s; ; test=test -n "$DISPLAY"
```

Thus, any *image/gif* MIME type (which implies any file with the *.gif* file extension) will be executed by the *xv* program, provided the DISPLAY variable is correctly set. You can use wild cards in the MIME specification so that *image/** would mean all image MIME types would be interpreted by *xv*.

The UNIX version of Netscape Navigator allows you to define the directory locations of the system-wide and user-defined files shown in Figure 6–2, as well as the specific values in the user-defined files.

6.3.3.2.3 Mail and Newsgroups.   If you wish to send mail directly from Netscape in response to a mailto: HTML tag (see Section 8.2.5.1) you will need to configure mail preferences to provide a valid "return to" address. Similarly, to read newsgroups directly from a news: HTML tag, this must be configured from the Netscape menu. These features are adequately described in the Netscape Handbook, which is a URL accessible from the browser help menu, and not repeated here.

6.3.3.2.4 Security.   Netscape has a security preferences menu that currently (v2.0) covers security issues associated with Java (see HotJava below) and the setting of warning messages when potentially insecure events are about to occur. The defaults are adequate for most sites.

6.3.4 HotJava

The HotJava™ browser does not have all the functionality of Netscape or Mosaic (e.g., an edit pull-down menu for cutting and pasting, or a hierarchical storage manager for hotlists), but it does have full support for Java applets (as does the AppletViewer that comes with the Java Developers Kit). Note the distinction between partial support provided by Netscape (if turned on) and full support. For example, Netscape will not download an applet and permit that applet to write to the disk on the client, HotJava will. In short, HotJava unleashes the full power of Java, while Netscape is more cautious for security reasons.

6.3.4.1 Software Snapshot ☞

TABLE 6–7   HotJava Software Snapshot

Location	*http://java.sun.com/*
	ftp.javasoft.com
Binaries	Solaris
Source	No
Questions (after subscribing)	*http://java.sun.com/faq2.html*
	http://java.sun.com/doc.html
Features	Full support of Java, but not all the features of Netscape

6.3.5   VRML Browsers

VRML is a markup language and subject to display using a variety of VRML client browsers (Section 3.4.1.2). Since VRML places emphasis on graphics, on UNIX platforms it has tended to be somewhat synonymous with Silicon Graphics hardware, OpenGL, and the Irix operating system. However, there are also versions for other UNIX operating systems. Rather than provide the specifics for various browsers, I point you to sites which summarize and compare what is available. Additional information on VRML browsers was given in Table 3–9.

6.3.5.1 Software Snapshot ☞

TABLE 6–8   VRML Browsers Software Snapshot

Location	*http://www.sdsc.edu/SDSC/Partners/vrml/ software/browsers.html* *ftp://ftp.sdsc.edu/pub/vrml/software/browsers*
Binaries	Solaris, AIX, DEC UNIX, SunOS, Irix, Ultrix, Linux, HP/UX
Source	Some

6.4. GRAPHICS VIEWERS

Table 3–10 summarized popular graphics viewers. Here I provide further details on the two I recommend since I use them frequently, Ghostview and xv.

6.4.1 Ghostview

Ghostview is a viewer written by Tim Theisen that uses the Ghostscript software package to interpret and display a PostScript™ file according to the Adobe document structuring conventions. Without Ghostview you can use Ghostscript but commands to show pages are given from the command line rather than a graphical interface. Ghostview is recommended.

6.4.1.1 Software Snapshot ☞

TABLE 6–9   Ghostview Software Snapshot

Location	*http://www.cs.wisc.edu/~ghost/ghostview/index.html* *ftp://ftp.cs.wisc.edu/ghost/gnu/ghostview*
Binaries	FreeBSD, HP/UX, Ultrix, AIX, Irix, SunOS
Source	yes
Documentation	*http://www.cs.wisc.edu/~ghost/ghostview/man.html*
Questions	Newsgroup: *gnu.ghostscript.bug*

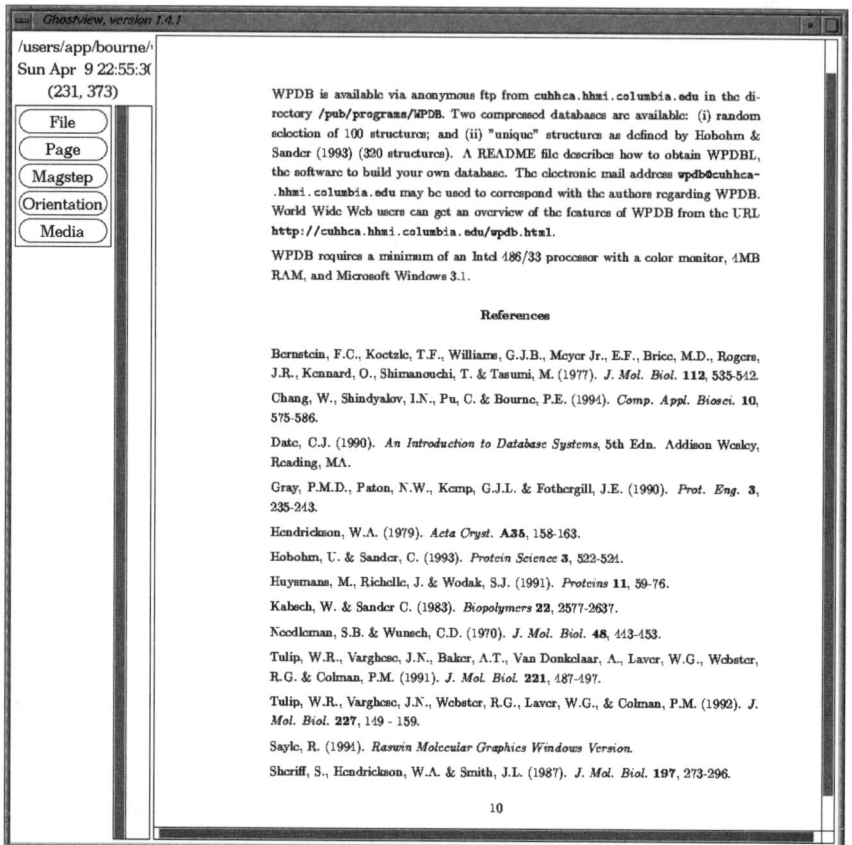

Fig. 6–3   Ghostview Screen

Figure 6–3 illustrates a typical Ghostview screen.

From Ghostview you can control the display of a PostScript file, for example, the specific page of the file to display, magnification of a portion of the image, and page orientation.

6.4.1.2 Installation Notes

If you are compiling from source you also will need the GhostScript software package, which is also freely available from the same site. Otherwise a binary can be used immediately upon being uncompressed.

6.4.2 xv

As introduced in Section 3.4.2 xv is a very useful graphics display and utility program written by John Bradley. It can be used to modify images and to convert them from one format to another.

6.4.2.1 Software Snapshot ☞

TABLE 6–10   xv Software Snapshot

Location	*ftp://ftp.cis.upenn.edu/pub/xv*
Binaries	None , but compiles on many platforms
Source	yes
Documentation	Extensive documentation is included
General Questions	*xv@devo.dccs.upenn.edu*
Licensing Issues	*xvbiz@devo.dccs.upenn.edu*
Bug Reports	*xvtech@devo.dccs.upenn.edu*
Features	Various graphics formats can be displayed, modified and filtered

6.4.2.2 Installation Notes

The README file has all the installation details you will need and they are not repeated here.

Figure 6–4 illustrates the xv control panel.

Here is a list of some of the tasks you can perform from this panel.

- "Grab" a window displayed on the screen.

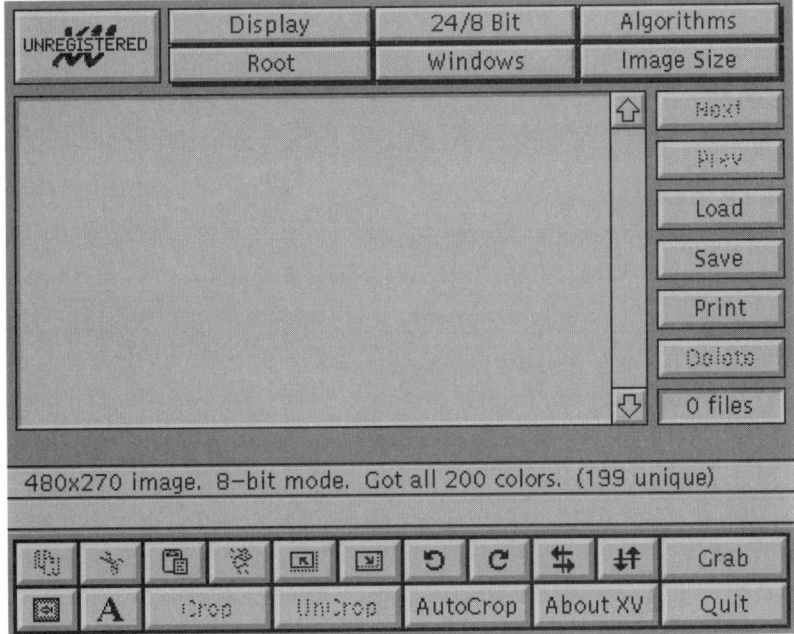

Fig. 6–4   xv Screen

- Save an image in a variety of formats e.g., GIF, PostScript, BMP, JPEG, TIFF, X11 Bitmap, Sun Rasterfile, IRIS RGB.
- Print an image after scaling, changing orientation, etc.
- Change the hue, contrast, shading, color.
- Convert between 8- and 24-bit color.
- Crop an image, i.e., remove surrounding non-image information.
- Change an image's size.
- Dither and smooth an image.
- Annotate an image.
- Cut and paste images.

6.5. SOUND PLAYERS

As I stated previously (Section 2.5.6), whether you can listen to sound on your UNIX client has more to do with supporting hardware than software. If you have hardware support, you will likely have a player already available. If you are not sure, here is a URL to visit and find out:

http://www-dsed.llnl.gov/documents/tests/au.html

This page has a test sound. If you do not hear it refer to

http://www.cuhk.hk/rthk/helper.html#xwindow

for a list of options.

6.6. VIDEO VIEWER

A popular video viewer mpeg_play, was developed at the University of California, Berkeley.

6.6.1.1 Software Snapshot. ☞

TABLE 6–11   mpeg_play Software Snapshot

Location (Web)	*http://bmrc.berkeley.edu/projects/mpeg/mpeg_play.html*
Binaries	Irix 4 and 5, SunOS, HP/UX, Ultrix, DEC UNIX, Solaris, Linux
Source	Yes
Documentation	Included
Bugs	*mpeg-bugs@plateau.cs.berkeley.edu*
Features	Tried and tested, includes demo files

6.6.1.2 Installation Notes

All of the information that you need is included with the distribution and not repeated here.

There are a variety of options that you can use when invoking mpeg_play. These can be viewed with the command **mpeg_play -help.** Most relate to coloring and dithering of the video. The most important option is **-loop,** which will repeat the clip until you terminate the player.

You should now have a fully functional Internet client from which you can begin to download the software you need to build your information server. In other words, we are now ready to start in earnest. Read on.

7

Server Installation

Ingredients:
- *Anonymous ftp*
- *A Listserver*
- *A Web server*
- *Using traditional Web browsers*

We have now come to recipes for the main course. You may serve a simple yet satisfying dish (anonymous ftp), an efficient diet-conscious meal (Listserver), or a variety of chef's specials (Web servers). The course should have the appropriate side dishes and condiments (search capability).

To this point, everything we have implemented has been to support a client activity. We are now at the point of server side implementation. Again I discuss implementation starting with the simplest methodology (ftp) and progress via Listserver implementation to the most complex activity: providing a Web server. Chapter Three discussed the rationale for which of these server types to install, and the most common software options for each type of server. This information is not repeated here. In this chapter I show you how to install and configure some of the common software options, namely, anonymous ftp, available as part of your standard UNIX operating system, the Washington University enhanced ftp server, *wu-ftp*, the Majordomo Listserver, and the NCSA httpd and wn Web servers. If you are supporting a Web server you may wish to provide an index of searchable information to help the user locate the item of interest. Harvest provides a complete package for searching, and I discuss the installation and configuration of Harvest. So let's get started with ftp.

7.1. ANONYMOUS FTP

Once you have decided to support anonymous ftp, as controlled by the *ftpd* daemon, there is one remaining decision—whether to run the basic ftp server, or an enhanced ftp server.

A discussion about making these decisions was given in Section 3.2.1. I install both here, the basic server first.

7.1.1 Basic Server Configuration

Setting up anonymous ftp is a straightforward lesson in UNIX system administration, and I treat it as a recipe. If you are responsible for administering your UNIX-based information server, and one or more of these steps does not make sense, refer to the sources of information on UNIX Administration given in Appendix B.

1. Decide where to put the ftp archive based on the discussion in Chapter 5. Create the root directory for the ftp archive—I use */var/spool/ftp* in this example.

2. Add the login name ftp to your UNIX system password file (*/etc/passwd* on most systems), if it is not present already. The entry should appear similar to:

   ftp::93:1:FTP Anonymous Account:/var/spool/ftp:/dev/null*

   Note: (i) the second field (fields are separated by colons), the password field, contains an asterisk (*), i.e., there is no specific password—under no circumstances should this be left blank; (ii) there is no shell specified (the last field), */dev/null* is a placeholder that prevents shell commands from being executed by user ftp; (iii) ftp should be a unique group not shared by other users or system level accounts (third field, group id 93 in this example)—*these are important points if a secure ftp environment is to be maintained.*

3. Create directories *~ftp/bin, ~ftp/etc,* and *~ftp/pub.*

4. Copy the */bin/ls* program to *~ftp/bin.* The *ls* program and any other executables you place here should have the correct level of protection (see below), since the ftp program has access to whatever executables you place here.

5. Copy the */etc/passwd* and */etc/group* files to *~ftp/etc and* edit them drastically so that they look exactly like the following:

```
% cat ~ftp/etc/passwd
root:*:0:1:Operator:/:/dev/null
daemon:*:1:1::/:
ftp:*:93:1:FTP Anonymous Account:/var/spool/ftp: \
    /dev/null

% cat ~ftp/etc/group
wheel:*:0:
nogroup:*:65534:
other:*:20:
ftp:*:93:
```

The file *~ftp/etc/passwd* is used by anonymous ftp to establish user and groups identifiers. We have created a group named "wheel" to be the owner of the ftp-related files an directories.

6. Set the file permissions as shown in Table 7–1.

7. Make sure the *ftpd* daemon is running with a command such as

    ps -el | grep ftpd

    or

    ps -aux | grep ftpd

    If the daemon is not running, check for the *ftpd* entry in the file *inetd.conf* (Section 2.2.2).

8. Load *~ftp/pub* and any subdirectories you create with the information to be served, making sure it is world readable.

At this point a client user should be able to access your ftp archive via anonymous ftp. Try it with the command

    ftp localhost

and log on with a login name of anonymous and a password that matches your e-mail address. If you are unable to log on, refer to Section 12.3. If accepting files into your ftp archive is important, test the uploading of a file to *~ftp/import*.

This simple recipe will require modification for some versions of the UNIX operating system. Often the man page for *ftpd* will include anonymous ftp configuration information. Problems you might encounter are:

- The need for *~ftp/dev/null*—the specification of a null device specifically for ftp, rather than using the system wide null device, */dev/null*.

TABLE 7–1   File Permissions for Anonymous ftp

File	Owner	Group	Permission
~ftp	ftp	wheel	555
~ftp/bin	root	wheel	555
~ftp/bin/ls	root	wheel	111
~ftp/etc	root	wheel	555
~ftp/etc/passwd	root	wheel	444
~ftp/etc//group	root	wheel	444
~ftp/import	ftp	wheel	777
~ftp/pub	ftp	wheel	777

- The need for *~ftp/lib* to support shared libraries used by *ls*, if the UNIX operating system uses shared libraries.

7.1.1.1 Security ☞

If you follow the above directions *exactly,* you should have a secure ftp environment. A good discussion on anonymous ftp security is maintained by the Computer Emergency Response Team (CERT) and is available at:

> *http://lucien.sims.berkeley.edu/CERT_anonymous_ftp*

If maintaining above-normal levels of security is important at your site, read the above.

7.1.1.2 Registering Your ftp Archive with Archie

You can register your ftp site so that it will be indexed by Archie (Section 2.5.1.1). There is a web form for doing this at

> *http://services.bunyip.com:8000/products/archie/-*
> *archie-ftp-reg.html.*

7.1.2 Enhanced ftp

If, based on the discussion in Section 3.2.1, you decide to install an enhanced *ftpd* daemon, a well documented, popular, free, and easy to install *ftpd* has been written by Bryan D. O'Connor, and is available from the University of Washington in St. Louis. It is referred to as *wu-ftpd.*

7.1.2.1 Software Snapshot ☞

TABLE 7–2   wu-ftp Software Snapshot

Location	*http://wuarchive.wustl.edu/packages/wuarchive-ftpd/*
Source	Yes—configuration files for AIX, HP/UX, Linux, DEC UNIX, Irix, SunOS, Ultrix and others.
Binaries	No
Help/Information	Subscribe to *wu-ftpd* at *listserv@wunet.wustl.edu* Book: Managing Internet Information Services (see *http://www.ora.com/www/item/miis.html*)
Bugs	*bryan@fegmania.wustl.edu*

7.1.2.2 Installation Notes ☞

Installation begins with downloading a compressed tar file (Section 6.3.1.2) The installation documentation is easy to follow and there are good man pages on how to configure *wu-ftpd* to meet your needs. There is little reason to repeat this information in detail here. Here are the major steps:

1. Set the correct pathnames in *pathnames.h* to find the configuration files included with the distribution.
2. Build the executable, which requires no changes to the *Makefile* for the more common operating systems.
3. Install the compiled software in the correct places.
4. Modify the file *ftpaccess* as needed (see below).
5. Edit */etc/inetd.conf* to point to the new *ftpd*.
6. Restart ftp with a command like (depending on the version of UNIX):

   kill -1 `ps t"?" | grep inetd`

   or

   /etc/killall -HUP inetd

7. If you wish to support on-the-fly tar builds or compression when uploading files, then load gnu tar and gnuzip (Section 3.3.3), making sure copies of these executables are located in *~ftp/bin*.
8. Copy the *ftpconversions, ftpusers,* and *ftpgroups* files to the locations specified in *pathnames.h*. There are examples of these files with the distribution.
9. Populate *~ftp/pub* with the files you wish to make accessible to users.
10. Run the *ckconfig* program that comes with the distribution to test whether *wu-ftpd* is installed correctly.

Step 4 above customizes the file *ftpaccess*. The *ftpd* daemon reads the file *ftpaccess* when that daemon is started. Additional details on how to configure this file can be found using the command **man 5 ftpaccess**, once the software has been installed. To get a good feel for the flexibility of *wu-ftpd,* consider what can be customized in a version of this file that I have annotated. Read it carefully.

```
# Annotated version of the file ftpaccess


# Terminate the ftp session after 2 login attempts
# have failed.
loginfails 2
```

```
# There are two classes of anonymous ftp user -
# local and remote. Which class the user belongs to
# governs the particular files they can access.
# A local user can be:
# (i) a real user (i.e., someone with an account);
# (ii) someone with a guest account;
# (iii) an anonymous user accessing the system from
#        the same Internet domain.
# The group local is defined in /etc/group.

# A user from another domain is of the class remote
# and may access files in the remote group.

class    local    real,guest,anonymous *.domain 0.0.0.0
class    remote   real,guest,anonymous *

# Limit local access to 20 simultaneous users at any
# time. An attempt to connect by the 21st user will
# echo the message found in the file
# /etc/msgs/msg.toomany.
# Remote users are limited to 100 any time on
# Saturday and Sunday and any week day
# between the hours of 6pm and 6am. At all other times
# they are limited to 60. The same message as for local
# users is displayed when that number is exceeded.

limit    local    20  Any        /etc/msgs/msg.toomany
limit    remote   100 SaSu|Any1800-0600 \
                                  /etc/msgs/msg.toomany
limit    remote   60  Any        /etc/msgs/msg.toomany

# When a user logs in show them the date and time when
# the file called README (in the ftp archive root
# directory) was last modified. Do the same when
# the user changes directory displaying the contents
# of the file called README in the current directory.
readme README*      login
readme README*      cwd=*

# Define a message to be displayed when the user
# logs in or changes directory.
message /welcome.msg            login
message .message                cwd=*
```

```
# Permit on-the-fly use of the UNIX compress and
# tar commands, by both local and remote classes
# of user.
compress           yes             local remote
tar                yes             local remote

# Allow the use of a private file for SITE GROUP and
# SITE GPASS providing a subset of users with enhanced
# access.
private         yes

# Define the level and enforcement of password checking
# done by the server for anonymous ftp. The form of
# the command is:
# passwd-check   <none|trivial|rfc822>  [<enforce|warn>]
# Here we only warn the user if the password is
# not rfc822 compliant - e-mail addressees are generally
# compliant.
passwd-check    rfc822  warn

# Log all commands issued by ftp users with real
# accounts.
log commands real

# Log file transfers, both inbound and outbound,
# for anonymous and real ftp users.
log transfers anonymous,real inbound,outbound

# File to display to the anonymous ftp user
# when a system shutdown sequence has been
# initiated.
shutdown /etc/shutmsg

# Permissions for each class of user.
# The defaults are yes for each operation for all
# classes of user.
delete      no   guest,anonymous    # delete permission
overwrite   no   guest,anonymous    # overwrite permission
rename      no   guest,anonymous    # rename permission
chmod       no   anonymous          # chmod permission
umask       no   anonymous          # umask permission

# Specify the upload directory.
# If upload is permitted set the owner, group and
# protection.
```

```
upload  /var/ftp   *            no
upload  /var/ftp   /incoming    yes root daemon   0600 dirs
upload  /var/ftp   /bin         no
upload  /var/ftp   /etc         no

# Directory aliases... [note, the ":" is not required]
# Thus cd inc with change directory to /incoming
# from anywhere in the directory tree,
alias   inc:     /incoming

# Define a search path when changing directories
# (as in the standard C shell).
cdpath  /incoming
cdpath  /pub
cdpath  /

# Define on a user-type basis a filter for regular
# expressions that can be used in filenames.
# If the file specified is invalid display the
# message in pathmsg
path-filter anonymous /etc/pathmsg ^[-A-Za-z0-9_\.]*$ ^\. ^-
path-filter guest     /etc/pathmsg ^[-A-Za-z0-9_\.]*$ ^\. ^-

# Specify which UNIX groups will be treated as
# "guests".
guestgroup ftponly

# e-mail address of ftp archive maintainer.
e-mail user@hostname
```

If you followed each of the installation steps above and configured *ftpaccess* in a manner similar to the example above, you should now have a functional, enhanced ftp server which allows you to control the features discussed in Section 3.2.1.

7.2. A LISTSERVER: MAJORDOMO

As stated in Section 3.2.2.2 we will install and configure the Majordomo Listserver. Majordomo was written by D. Brent Chapman, initially to service a variety of mailing lists on behalf of the USENIX Association. The story of its development and details of what it does, and does not do, are given in a paper by Brent Chapman included with the Majordomo distribution as a compressed Postscript file, *ftp://ftp.greatcircle.com/pub/majordomo/majordomo.paper.ps.Z.* I only need say here that if you intend to install a Listserver, Majordomo will likely meet your needs.

7.2.1 Software Snapshot ☞

TABLE 7–3   Majordomo Software Snapshot

Location	*ftp://ftp.greatcircle.com/pub/majordomo/*
Source	Yes—written in Perl (one program in C).
Binaries	No
Help/Information	Book: Managing Internet Information Services (see *http://www.ora.com/www/item/miis.html*). Chapters 24 and 25 are included with the ftp distribution.
	Subscribe to the list *majordomo-users* at *majordomo@greatcircle.com* for a general discussion.
	Subscribe to the list *majordomo-announce* at *majordomo@greatcircle.com* to receive information on new announcements.
Bugs	Subscribe to the list *majordomo-announce* at *majordomo@greatcircle.com* to report bugs and receive information.

7.2.2 Installation Notes ☞

Installation is particularly well documented since the chapters from the excellent book *Managing Internet Information Services,* published by O'Reilly and Associates (see above), are included with the ftp distribution. This supplements the installation documentation and paper from D. Brent Chapman.

There is little point in repeating this information here. Rather, I cover the basics of what you need to know before you attempt the installation. This is a useful supplement to the online information. If you are not the System Administrator for the UNIX server that is to run Majordomo, you will need to get help from the person who is, since parts of the installation require root access. For example, to set up the mail aliases for each mailing list requires root access.

The first concept to grasp is the notion of the three classes of people accessing a Listserver. They are

1. *User*—someone who subscribes to a list and receives all mail sent to that list and who also sends contributions to that list.
2. *List Administrator*—someone who administers a specific list, or lists, perhaps as a moderator (i.e., controls what passes from users who send messages to all who subscribe to the list).
3. *Listserver Administrator*—someone who has overall control of the Listserver and all the lists.

Classes 2 and 3 may be the same person, but this is not a requirement.

We discussed the user's view of a Listserver in Section 6.2. Note, however, that that discussion was for different Listserver software, a package called Listserv. I did this on purpose, not to make your life more difficult, but to indicate that the principles used by Listserv and Majordomo are the same, only the command syntax differs slightly. For example, to get help on available Majordomo commands it is necessary to send a mail message with the single word "help" to *majordomo@hostname* rather than to the *listserv@hostname* address used for Listserv.

The list administrator can have a simple or difficult job depending on the degree of control they choose to impose on a list. The *auto* list requires no input from the list administrator—all subscribe and unsubscribe messages are honored, regardless of who makes them. That is, anyone can subscribe and unsubscribe anyone else. This generally does not include enough security except for a small list among a group of trusted individuals. Even then, someone could stumble across the list and potentially wreak havoc. If you choose a more controlled list option, then you will receive four types of messages as list moderator:

1. Approve messages. Requests to approve subscriptions or unsubscriptions.
2. Notification messages. Messages detailing subscriptions and unsubscriptions.
3. Bounced messages. Messages that failed to be broadcast for some reason, for example, they were too big, had malformed headers, etc.
4. Messages that were broadcast successfully but could not be received by the remote client. This typically happens when the client is down for an extended period, or the login name to which the message has been sent has been removed from the remote machine.

These four types of messages can be received by the same or different e-mail addresses on the server. Majordomo includes *approve* and *bounce* scripts to handle the majority of these requests.

This takes us to the content and actual installation of the Majordomo distribution. Here are the major components:

- *majordomo:* the program which is started and used to interpret each mail message sent to *majordomo@hostname.*
- *resend:* the program that checks messages that arrive for a list, i.e., for *listname@hostname* and either passes the message to the list moderator or sends it to members of the list.
- *digest:* the program to build a digest (summary) of messages to the list which have accumulated over a particular time period.
- *wrapper:* the program that wraps around *majordomo* and runs it as a trusted user.
- *bounce:* the program to help the list owner handle subscribers whose mail is being returned. The *bounce_remind* script is used to notify subscribers about the problem.
- *approve:* the program to help the list owner approve subscriptions or moderate messages.

- *new-list:* the program to answer mail sent to a new list until it has been opened.
- *request-answer:* the program to automatically handle requests to a specific list that should have been handled by *majordomo@hostname*.
- *majordomo.cf:* the configuration file generated by the installation from a file *sample.cf* that defines the correct paths and contains information specific to each list.

As stated at the beginning of this Section, the actual installation is described fully in the README file and also in the file *Doc/majordomo.ora*, both of which come with the distribution. The latter is taken from the O'Reilly book named in the snapshot. None of that information is repeated here.

7.2.3 Using ☞

Your first task, once installation is complete, is to establish a list to which users can subscribe. Again, this whole procedure is described in a recipe-style fashion in the README and *Doc/majordomo.ora* files and not repeated here.

7.3. A WEB SERVER: NCSA

As outlined in Section 3.2.3 the NCSA Web Server, or NCSA httpd as it is frequently called, is a very popular Web server. If you just want to experiment with a server, and exceptional security is not a concern, start with NCSA httpd, it can be installed and serving Web pages in about 10 minutes. This will provide you with an excellent working environment in which to become proficient in serving Web pages, CGI scripts, and so on. Later you can move to another server if you need an enhanced set of features.

7.3.1 Software Snapshot ☞

TABLE 7–4 NCSA httpd Software Snapshot

Location	*http://hoohoo.ncsa.uiuc.edu/docs/*
Source	Yes (C language).
Binaries	AIX, HP/UX, Irix, Linux, DEC UNIX, SunOS, Solaris, Ultrix.
Help/Information	Tutorials and full documentation are available from the above location.
Bugs	*httpd@ncsa.uiuc.edu*

7.3.2 Installation Notes ☞

NCSA httpd has what NCSA refers to as a one-step downloader. The idea behind it is a very good one, and I would expect to see it adopted by more software distributors in the future.

The basic idea is that you fill out a Web form and submit that form to NCSA's server. The completed form defines the basic configuration parameters for your customized copy of the NCSA Web server software. The software distribution is then automatically built on NCSA's server and available for downloading as a compressed tar file. The custom-built software distribution will remain on NCSA's server for 15 minutes, after which time it is removed. The advantage of this approach is that you get a custom-built Web server with little effort. The disadvantage (minor in my opinion) is that if you need to change that configuration it is necessary to go back to the server and repeat the build process.

To build your Web server:

1. Fill in the Web form accessible from

   http://hoohoo.ncsa.uiuc.edu/docs/setup/Install.html

   providing the following information:
   - Hardware and software platform—available binaries are indicated in the software snapshot; source can also be chosen. If you do not know which binary you need, issue the UNIX command **uname -a** to determine the hardware on which you are running e.g.,

        % **uname -a**
        SunOS hercules 4.1.4 4 sun4m

   - Server type—choices are standalone and *inetd*. Standalone is recommended for all but moderately accessed servers. Under the control of *inetd* a copy of *httpd* is started for each server request. The overhead in doing this can be considerable. In standalone mode a single copy of *httpd* runs continuously and services all requests, thus reducing startup resource costs, but with a small on-going cost.
   - Binding Port—the port number to handle requests (see Section 2.3.1); the default is port 80.
   - The user id—the login name used by the server in serving requests. *This should NOT be root.* It is common to use a separate user called nobody. The files being served should be owned by nobody. Check the systems */etc/passd* or shadow password file for the user nobody. If it does not exist add it, or get your system administrator to do so.
   - The group id—the primary group used by the server in serving requests. *Again, this should NOT be a group of which root is a member.* It is common to establish a separate group called nobody, of which the user nobody is the sole member.
   - Server administrator's e-mail address—appears on a page served to the client, to be used when a problem is encountered.

- Server root directory (logical name *ServerRoot*)[1]—in which to place the root directory for the server. The directory */usr/local/etc/httpd* is commonly used.
- Document root directory (logical name *DocumentRoot*)[2]—in which to place documents you are going to serve (See Chapter Five).

2. Download, via the Web client, the compressed tar file that is built by submitting the above form.
3. Uncompress and untar the file in the directory you specified on the Web form for *ServerRoot*.
4. For standalone mode, start the server with the command

./httpd

If you want the server to be under the control of *inetd* you will need to add a line to *inetd.conf* as specified in the instructions that come with the server software (Section 2.3.2).

5. If you want the standalone server to start automatically, insert the above command in the UNIX local system startup file, *e.g., /etc/rc.local*.
6. Place an HTML document in the root document directory.
7. Use a Web browser to try and access the document, not as a local file, but as a URL. If this works, chances are your server is running correctly. For example, the file *index.html* in the *DocumentRoot* directory of the server *xtal1.sdsc.edu* will be served as *http://xtal1.sdsc.edu/* or *http://xtal1.sdsc.edu/index.html*. If the file does not serve refer to the file *ServerRoot/logs/error_log* (Section 12.1.3).

7.4. A WEB SERVER: WN

The wn server offers features not found in the more generic NCSA server, but if these features are used the server requires more effort to maintain. Install wn if you are serving complex pages or need an enhanced level of security.

Major features of the wn server, some of which are not available with the NCSA httpd server, are:

- *Searching*—a built-in search facility (as compared to using a separate search capability like Harvest, Section 7.5) will search titles, headers, and keywords, and generate a response by way of a Web form.

---

1. First used in Chapter Five to signify the logical root directory containing files used to run the Web server.

2. First used in Chapter Five to signify the logical root directory for all documents to be served by the Web server.

- *Parsed Text, Server Side Includes and Wrappers*—as we shall see in Chapter Nine, these are useful features for maintaining complex documents.
- *Filters*—rather than serve the page as written, the page is first processed by a filter. So, for example, rather than serve a compressed file, it could be decompressed on the fly for reading, yet downloaded as a compressed file for local use.
- *Ranges*—a range of lines in a document may be served rather than the whole document. For example, this is useful for serving entries in an address book.
- Security—a variety of options as described in Section 7.4.3.

7.4.1 Software Snapshot ☞

TABLE 7–5   wn Software Snapshot

Location	*http://hopf.math.nwu.edu/index.html*
	ftp://ftp.acns.nwu.edu/pub/wn/
Binaries	No
Source	Yes—see the configuration script in the following section for platforms on which wn is known to compile.
Bugs and Discussions	*http://hopf.math.nwu.edu/listserv.html*
Further Information	*http://hopf.math.nwu.edu/docs/manual.html*

7.4.2 Installation Notes ☞

1. Get the source, *ftp://ftp.acns.nwu.edu/pub/wn/wn.tar.gz*.
2. Use the *gunzip* program to uncompress the tar file *wn.tar.gz*.
3. Use the UNIX command **tar xvf wn.tar** to create the directory structure starting from an empty directory.
4. Follow instructions in the README file, which tell you to invoke the following Perl script called *configure*, to build a server. I have provided an annotated (denoted by a leading "#") version of this script below. If you have read the previous section on the NCSA httpd server, you will see the questions that need to be answered are very similar.

```
    # Refer to the Web page
    # http://hopf.math.nwu.edu/docs/setup.html
    # for a detailed discussion of this implementation.
    % ./configure


    This configuration script asks you several
questions. Default answers are printed in [square brackets]
so you can simply press return to enter that value.
```

(But don't use [square brackets] when you enter a
value.) You can quit at any time by pressing Ctrl-C
and nothing should be changed. An alternative to
running this script is to copy *Makefile.dist* and
config.h.dist to *Makefile* and *config.h* respectively and
edit them manually. You may rerun this script as many
times as you like, but it will only have an effect if
you rerun **"make"**.

    Currently supported operating systems are:
    AIX, AUX, BSDI, CONVEX_OS, DYNIX, FREE_BSD_2, HPUX,
IRIX, ISC, LINUX, NEXT, OSF1, PYRAMID, RISCOS, RTU, SCO,
SGI, SOLARIS2, SUN_OS4, SVR4, ULTRIX, UNIXWARE

    Under which operating system are you running?
          [SUN_OS4]: **osf1**

    # You should give some thought to this!! Refer to
    # Chapter Five if you need help.

    Enter the complete path to your data root.
          [**/usr/local/wn**]:

    When run as root the standalone server '**swn**' will
immediately change its user id giving itself only the
permissions of an unprivileged user, usually 'nobody'.
Most systems already have a user nobody and I recommend
you use it. If you choose another user it should not be
the owner of any of your data files. [HPUX users may
have to choose something other than 'nobody'].

    With which user's permissions should the server run?
        [nobody]:

    User nobody with user id 65534 and group id 65534
was found. These values will be used when the server is
run standalone (i.e. when using **swn**). For use with **inetd**
you must set the user in your *inetd.conf* file.

    Enter an e-mail address for the server maintainer.
            [webmaster@your.host]: **webmaster@sdsc.edu**

    # Refer to Section 2.3.1 if you are not sure what to
    # enter here.
    What port should be the default? [80]:

```
   What hostname should the server use? (Answer
"syscall" to get hostname from system.)[syscall]:

   Enter a complete path to your logfile.
        [/usr/local/wnlogs/wn.log]:

   Enter a complete path to your error log file.
        [same as logfile]:

# The majority of servers use "common log format"
# wn does not in fact use this format, however,
# there is a filter written by John Frank, the
# author of wn, to convert the wn log file to
# the standard format used by many programs.
# This is important if you desire to keep
# statistics on server use. This is discussed
# in Chapter Twelve.
Make sure that your logfiles exist and are writable
by user nobody or that you have specified a directory
for them in which nobody has write permission. Would you
like a verbose log file including entries for 'Referrer'
and 'User-agent'?
# These files are discussed in Sections
# 12.1.3.
        [No]:
# The following should NOT be permitted in secure
# environments

   Do you want to allow users to have home pages in
their home directories?
        [No]:

   In what directory should server binaries be
installed?
        [../bin]:
   In what directory should utility binaries be
installed?
        [../bin]:
   New versions of 'config.h' and 'Makefile' will be
written. Old versions will be saved as 'config.h.bak'and
'Makefile.bak'.
        Do this now? [Yes]:

   Configuration is now complete. You can now run
'make' or 'make install' to do the compilation. Further
```

```
configuration is possible by manually editing the files
config.h and Makefile.

    NOTE: IT IS NECESSARY TO RUN MAKE FOR THE CHANGES
MADE BY RUNNING THIS SCRIPT TO TAKE EFFECT.
```

5. Create a configuration file (*config.h*) and a *Makefile* specific to your site. Install the software as shown in the following annotated example:

```
    % make install
    Installing wn
    (cd wn; make CC="cc " CFLAGS="-I.. -I../wn" LIBS=""
BINDIR="../bin" install )
    cc -I.. -I../wn -c wn.c
    cc -I.. -I../wn -c prequest.c
    cc -I.. -I../wn -c init.c
    cc -I.. -I../wn -c chkcntrl.c
    cc -I.. -I../wn -c send.c
    cc -I.. -I../wn -c parse.c
    cc -I.. -I../wn -c util.c
    cc -I.. -I../wn -c misc.c
    cc -I.. -I../wn -c www.c
    cc -I.. -I../wn -c csearch.c
    cc -I.. -I../wn -c gsearch.c
    cc -I.. -I../wn -c isearch.c
    cc -I.. -I../wn -c regcomp.c
    cc -I.. -I../wn -c regfind.c
    cc -I.. -I../wn -c cgi.c
    cc -I.. -I../wn -c mod.c
    cc -I.. -I../wn -c tilde.c
    cc -I.. -I../wn -c rfc931.c
    cc -I.. -I../wn -c evalif.c
    cc -I.. -I../wn -c image.c
    cc -I.. -I../wn -c chkauth.c
    cc -I.. -I../wn -o wn wn.o prequest.o init.o
chkcntrl.o send.o parse.o util.o misc.o www.o csearch.o
gsearch.o isearch.o regcomp.o regfind.o cgi.o mod.o
tilde.o rfc931.o evalif.o image.o chkauth.o
    cc   -I.. -I../wn -c swn.c
    cc   -I.. -I../wn -c swninit.c
    cc   -I.. -I../wn -c standalone.c
```

```
    cc  -I.. -I../wn -o swn swn.o prequest.o swninit.o
chkcntrl.o send.o parse.o util.o misc.o www.o csearch.o
gsearch.o isearch.o regcomp.o regfind.o cgi.o mod.o
standalone.o tilde.o rfc931.o evalif.o image.o chkauth.o
    Installing wn and swn in ../bin
    touch inst-wn
    Installing wndex
    (cd wndex; make CC="cc " CFLAGS="-I.. -I../wn"
LIBS=""  BINDIR="../bin" install )
    cc  -I.. -I../wn -c wndex.c
    cc  -I.. -I../wn -c init.c
    cc  -I.. -I../wn -c content.c
    cc  -I.. -I../wn -o wndex wndex.o init.o content.o
    Installing wndex in ../bin
    touch inst-wndex
    Installing authwn
    (cd authwn; make CC="cc " CFLAGS="-I.. -I../wn"
LIBS=""  BINDIR="../bin" install )
    cc  -I.. -I../wn -c authwn.c
    cc  -I.. -I../wn -o authwn authwn.o
    Installing authwn in ../bin
    touch inst-authwn

    # Whether to run the server under inetd or
    # standalone is a major consideration. Refer to
    # Section 2.3.2 for a reminder of the role of inetd.
    # The reasons for using inetd or standalone are
    # the same as they were for the NCSA httpd server.
    # We have found a significant performance
    # improvement in running wn in standalone mode on
    # a heavily utilized server.

    Running the server under inetd

    This is an efficient way to run the server if the
load on it is relatively light (a few thousand hits per
day) and the host on which it runs is used for other
purposes. There are variations on how inetd works from
system to system so you may need to look at the man page
for inetd.conf(5). Here's how it works under many
systems, e.g. SunOS 4.1.3: Edit the file /etc/services
and create the line

        wn  80/tcp
```

(or replace 80 by the port you wish to use). Then edit the file */etc/inetd.conf* and insert the line

```
wn stream tcp nowait nobody /full/path/for/wn wn
```

After the last wn you can have optional arguments to turn on logging or use a different data directory. Some inetds limit the number of arguments you may use so I prefer to use a small script in place of wn here. My *inetd.conf* line looks like:

```
wn stream tcp nowait nobody /full/path/for/wnwrap \
wnwrap
```

and wnwrap contains only the two lines

```
#!/bin/sh
exec /full/path/for/wn -t 202 -L /my/log/file\
     /my/WN/root/dir
```

It is important to run wn as "nobody" (the fifth field in the *inetd.conf* line above) or some other user with no special access privileges. If you are using an inetd without the capability to set UID on startup (e.g., Ultrix), you should define the group ID and user ID in *config.h* so that the program is not running as root (look for the #defines USERID and GROUPID and set the values appropriately). *It should never be necessary to run wn under inetd as root and to do so would be a serious mistake for maintaining security.*

Every attempt has been made to make wn as secure as possible, even if it is run as root, however, no program accessible to remote users on the Internet can be assumed perfectly secure. (See the security guide)
```
# The security guide can be found at:
# http://hopf.math.nwu.edu/docs/security.html
```

After editing the *inetd.conf* and services files you should find the process id number of the **inetd** process and do the command **"kill -HUP process_id#"**. This must be done as root. You find the **process_id#** using the UNIX command **ps.** If you have never done this before, get someone who has to help you.

6. Test your setup. This information is given as part of the **make install** command.

```
    After compiling and setting up the software you can
test it on a sample directory provided with the
distribution. To do this first make a symbolic link in
your root data directory to the "docs" directory in the
source distribution. The command
    "ln -s /your/src/dir/docs docs"
    executed in the root directory should do this. If
your system does not support symbolic links you can copy
this directory and its subdirectories to your data
directory temporarily.


    % mkdir /usr/wn/data
    % mkdir /usr/wn/wnlogs
    % touch /usr/wn/wnlogs/wn.log
    % chown nobody /usr/wn/wnlogs/wn.log
```

Congratulations! You should now have a fully functional wn server, since with a Web browser, you should be able to see a test Web page as shown in Figure 7–1.

This page is being served by the wn server, indicating that the server is running.

7.4.3 Using—Security Implications

The reason the above Web page appears at all is because it has been indexed by the wn server, which is a fancy way of saying, "yes I specifically want this page accessible to Web users." By default, most Web servers make accessible every file in the *DocumentRoot* directory and all subdirectories. It is worth noting in passing that this has led to some embarrassing situations, since pages intended for a restricted audience have been indexed by *robots* and made accessible to the whole Internet community through the common search pages.

What gets indexed and made accessible through the wn server is controlled by a file called *index* that must exist in every directory containing files to be made available. You must create and manage this file. How to do this is described fully by the URL *http://hopf.math.nwu.edu/docs/index_desc.html* and only a synopsis, by way of an annotated example, is given here. Annotations begin with "#", a valid way of introducing a comment in the wn index file. Read this carefully.

```
% cat index
# Directory record - contains information pertinent
# to the whole directory:
```

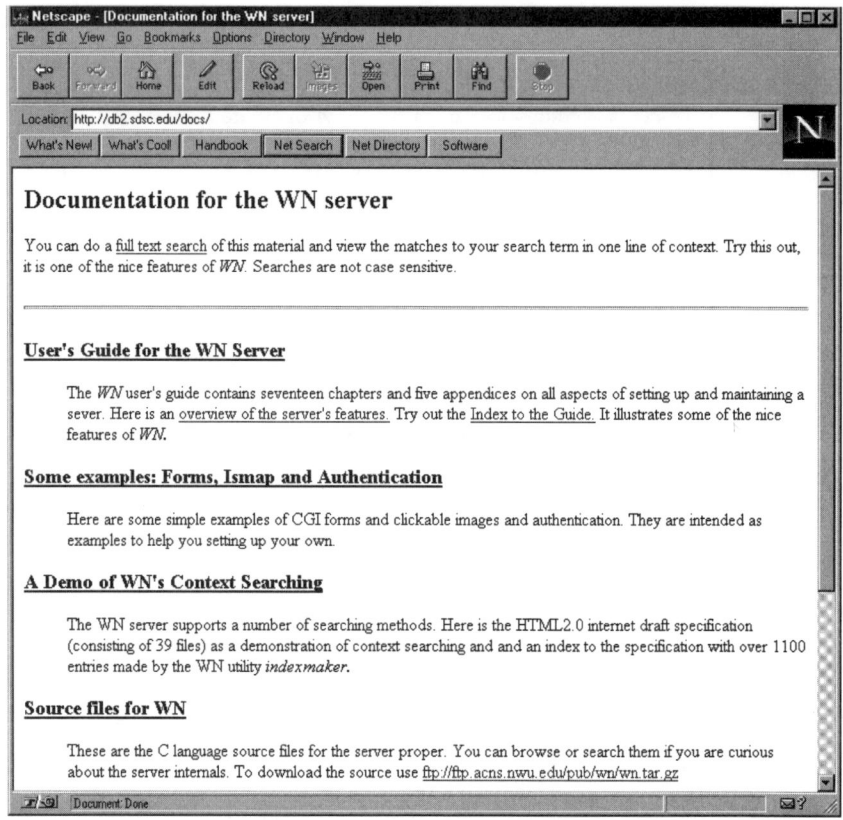

Fig. 7–1   The wn Server Test Home Page

```
# Owner is the maintainer of the directory;
# Accessfile is a file that lists what IP addresses
# have access to the directory.
# Searchwrapper is a specific kind of wrapper. As
# the name suggests, a searchwrapper wraps around
# the results of a search. A searchwrapper should
# be compared to a server side include, which we
# shall encounter in Section 9.3. A server side
# include is HTML which is served with every
# document for which an include is specified.
# Searchwrappers are only included with search
# requests.
```

```
# Subdirs are the list of subdirectories to be
# included in the index, any other subdirectories
# are inaccessible.

Owner=mailto:john@math.nwu.edu.edu
Accessfile = access
Searchwrapper=swrapper.html
Subdirs=examples,images,authentication

# File records - describe each file in the
# directory which is to be served.
# Content-type optionally specifies the MIME type
# of the file and is necessary if wn cannot
# deduce the type from the file extension.
# The Title record is optionally what is displayed
# in the Web browser to represent the file if the
# browser is given the directory as the URL.
# The search capability of wn operates from the
# title using titles as a set of keywords to be
# searched. In this way it is much more
# restrictive than Harvest, which optionally
# searches the whole HTML file.

File=CHANGES

File=index.html

File=howindex.html

File=manual.html
...
File=Gnu_License
Title=GNU Public License
Content-type=text/plain
...
# Includes are the server side include files to be
# included, in the order listed, when the file is
# server. Section 9.3 discusses server side
# includes in detail.
# A variety of additional Attributes may be applied
# to the file to be served (see http://-
# hopf.math.nwu.edu/docs/appendixB.html#attributes
# for a complete description. In this example
# nosearch indicates that this file should not be
# included in a title search.
```

```
File=complete.html
Includes=manual.html,overview.html,setup.html,\
index_desc.html,security.html,\
search.html
Title=Complete Documentation (suitable for printing)
Attribute=nosearch
...
```

Creating the file *index* is not the end of the story. Once created, that file must be explicitly cached since wn reads the cache file not the index file. The program *wndex* provided in the *bin* directory of the wn distribution will accomplish this task. The *wndex* program reads the file index and produces a file *index.cache*. It is the file *index.cache* that wn reviews when deciding whether or not to serve a file. Each time you decide to serve a new file you must add it to the index and then rerun *wndex* and reload the Web page in your browser to see the change. This does not apply to files which are already being served, but you then edit. The edited version of the file will automatically appear after a Web browser reload.

Files to be served by wn should be owned by the person who created them, not the user "nobody" (or whomever you assigned during the installation) who runs the wn server. These files should be world-readable, but writable only by the maintainer of the directory. The owner of the directory should be the one who creates the *index.cache* file. If these rules are not followed the file will not serve.

7.5. A SEARCH TOOL: HARVEST

Harvest is an integrated set of tools to gather, extract, organize, search, cache, and replicate relevant information. It is an ideal freeware tool for providing an *efficient* text search capability for all, or a subset, of the information on your server and, if desired, other servers. It can digest all of the most frequently used information types outlined in Section 3.3. Harvest was designed and built by the Internet Research Task Force Research Group on Resource Discovery (IRTF-RD) with Michael Schwartz of the University of Colorado as Principal Investigator. *You will be hard pressed to find better designed, better functioning, and better documented software in the public domain.* Much thought has been put into making the Harvest system meet a spectrum of needs, ranging from the simple to the complex. Thus, while it is very easy to provide an information index for your Web site, you can, with more effort and understanding, create a search engine for a complex array of information types at various sites. It is beyond the scope of this book to do the latter— it can all be found in the excellent users manual

http://harvest.cs.colorado.edu/harvest/user-manual/

It is within the scope of this book, however, to have you understand Harvest basics and be able to build a simple index.

Harvest extracts structured (attribute-value pair) information from many different information formats and builds indexes that allow these attributes to be referenced during queries (e.g., searching for all documents with a certain keyword or regular expression in the title field). So, for example, the title of an HTML document (as defined in Section 8.2.2 by its <TITLE>text_string</TITLE> HTML tags,) is an example of an attribute and the "text_string" the value. Harvest consists of a number of interrelated components shown in Figure 7–2.

Figure 7–2 represents a simplified view, since only one gatherer and one broker are drawn. However, Harvest can function as a client-server application. Information can be gathered (using the gatherer component) from multiple information servers and brokered (using the broker component) by multiple information servers. If there are large quantities of information being searched by many users it is advantageous to have multiple brokers, since the resource load for searching is distributed and, hence, shared.

The default index/search subsystem (Figure 7–2), that is, the part of the Harvest system used to index and subsequently search the index, is called Glimpse:

http://glimpse.cs.arizona.edu:1994/

This is adequate for most information servers. The Harvest user manual describes how to use the alternative search subsystems, WAIS, FreeWAIS, and Nebula, all of which are supported by Harvest, but not described here.

A Harvest server (the term for a specific collection of searchable information) is easily established. First, I give you the basic principles behind establishing a Harvest server. Subsequently, I will use a subset of these principles to make a queryable index of information typically found in a site's ftp and Web document areas. Once the queryable index is established, it can be updated automatically, with a frequency that you define based upon how quickly the information being indexed is changing.

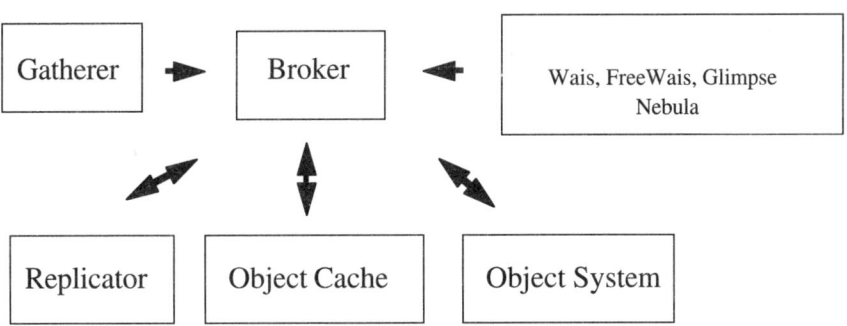

Fig. 7–2 Overview of the Harvest System

The basic principles behind a Harvest server are as follows:

- The *Gatherer* subsystem collects information for indexing (such as keywords, author names, and titles) from the resources available at *Provider* sites (such as ftp and Web servers). These are maintained as a set of *objects* in a local cache (Figure 7–2). What is to be gathered is specified by a set of URLs in a gatherer configuration file. We shall see what one of those files looks like below. The rules used to define what is gathered from each type of file may be modified to suit your needs. The details of controlling what is gathered is given in the User's manual. The extent of what can be modified is given in this book.

- The *Broker* subsystem retrieves indexing information from one or more Gatherers, suppresses duplicate information, indexes the collected information, and provides a WWW query interface to it. This is termed a *collection*, and the interface to such a collection is shown subsequently in Figure 7–4.

- The Replicator subsystem efficiently replicates Brokers around the Internet. We do not use the replicator in this book, but concentrate on just a single site as a broker.

- The Harvest Server Registry (HSR) is a distinguished Broker that holds information about each Harvest Gatherer, Broker, Cache, and Replicator on the Internet and can itself be searched.

7.5.1 Software Snapshot ☞

TABLE 7–6   Harvest Software Snapshot

Location	*http://harvest.cs.colorado.edu/*
Source	Yes—requires Perl, gcc, bison, and flex.
Binaries	Supported: SunOS, Solaris, DEC UNIX
	Unsupported: HP/UX, FreeBSD, Linux, AIX, Irix.
Help/Information	*http://harvest.cs.colorado.edu/harvest/doc.html*
	news:comp.infosystems.harvest

7.5.2 Installation Notes ☞

Installation of Harvest is straightforward and detailed instructions can be found at *ftp://ftp.cs.colorado.edu/pub/distribs/harvest/INSTRUCTIONS.html*. Here are the steps:

1. Download and unpack the distribution.
2. Configure your Web server to work with Harvest. There is a discussion for each of the major Web servers in the instructions. For the NCSA httpd server

this involves one minor addition to a configuration file and restarting the
server—both steps are documented and not repeated here.

3. Install the WWW interface to the broker. This involves minor path changes to
two files in the Harvest distribution; both changes are well-documented.

4. Execute the script RunHarvest, a dialog for setting up a complete gatherer and
broker. An example, which defines a Harvest server for part of a Web page
hierarchy, is given below. I have annotated the dialog with lines beginning
with "#***" (to distinguish them from "#" which are comments distributed as
part of the script) where additional clarification seemed necessary. The dialog
is followed with an explanation of how you can immediately begin searching
the hierarchy.

```
% ./RunHarvest


##################################################################
 Welcome to Harvest!
##################################################################


This program will create, configure, and run a Harvest Broker and
Gatherer. It will allow you to index one or more WWW, FTP, or
Gopher servers, using a set of defaults for content extraction
and indexing.
    We offer 3 standard configurations:

        1. Index your entire WWW site.
        2. Index an entire WWW site (or sites).
        3. Index selected parts of WWW, FTP, or Gopher sites.

NOTE: When this program asks you a question, you can accept the
      default answer shown within the square brackets [ ]'s by
      pressing ENTER, or you can enter your own answer.


Do you want to continue? [yes]:

You will be asked a few questions about what you want Harvest to
do, and about a few basic details of your WWW, FTP, or Gopher
server(s). You'll need several megabytes of disk space to run
these Harvest servers; the amount of disk space needed depends on
the size of the servers that you're indexing. If you are
uncertain about these questions, then stop now and contact your
server administrator.
```

This program is broken down into 4 question and answer sessions.
Based on your answers, it will create and configure Harvest
servers. It will also set up your system to run the Harvest
servers regularly.
A comprehensive user's manual is available for Harvest via WWW
at:
                 http://harvest.cs.colorado.edu/harvest/doc.html

Do you want to continue? [yes]:

STEP 1: Describe your local WWW server.

    The Harvest Broker requires that you have access to a WWW
server (e.g., NCSA httpd). If you don't currently run a WWW
server, then you will need to install and configure one before
you can run Harvest.

On which host does your WWW server run? [xtal1.sdsc.edu]:
On which port does your WWW server run? [80]:
*** See Section 2.3.2 for information on ports.

STEP 2: Select a standard configuration.

    We offer 3 standard configurations:

        1. Index your entire WWW site.
        2. Index an entire WWW site (or sites).
        3. Index selected parts of WWW, FTP, or Gopher sites.

Please select a configuration [1]:3

STEP 3: Configure your new Harvest servers.

    To configure your Harvest Broker and Gatherer, answer the
following:

Enter a short description of this Harvest server [none]:
Data Representation
Enter a one-word description of this Harvest server [none]:
DataRep
*** As you see below this name is used as part of the directory
*** structure.

```
Where do you want to install the Gatherer?:
        [/usr/harvest/Harvest-1.4.pl2/gatherers/DataRep]:
*** Each Gatherer and Broker should be run on a separate port.
*** This is a simple error that I have made!
On which port should the Gatherer run? [8500]:
Where do you want to install the Broker?:
        [/usr/harvest/Harvest-1.4.pl2/brokers/DataRep]:
On which port should the Broker run? [8501]:
Enter a password for the Broker administrative commands []:
<not shown>
Enter the list of URLs for the collections that you'd like to
index. The URLs that you enter below will be classified as
'RootNodes' and will be enumerated (e.g. by recursive FTP
directory listings for FTP URLs). Terminate this list by entering
a period ('.') on a line by itself.
Enter URL:    http://www.sdsc.edu/CompSci/pb/Group.html
Enter URL:    .
*** The concept of a root node is important and should be
*** understood before a selection is made. See the discussion in
*** the text.
*** Every URL subsequently referenced by Group.html will be
*** indexed down to a depth you define or until the total number
*** of URLs you define is reached. (see the
*** configuration file described subsequently).
-----------------------------------------------------------------
STEP 4: Registration information about your Harvest servers.
-----------------------------------------------------------------


   We ask that you register your new Harvest servers with our
global registry. Please answer the following short questions.
Later, after the installation is complete, we will ask you if
you'd like to register your Harvest servers or not using the
information that you provide below.

Enter your correct e-mail address: [sys853@xtal1.sdsc.edu]:
bourne@sdsc.edu


-----------------------------------------------------------------
STEP 5: Create and run the Harvest servers.
-----------------------------------------------------------------


   Now, this program will create Harvest servers based on your
input. Then, it will run the Harvest servers.

Creating the Gatherer...
Successfully created the Gatherer!
```

```
Would you like to edit the Gatherer's workload specification?:
        [no]:
Creating the Broker...
Successfully created the Broker!
Running the Gatherer.
WARNING:  For large sites, this may take several hours...
Done running the Gatherer!
Running the Broker.
WARNING:  For large sites, this may take several hours...
Done running the Broker!
Done.

    Your Harvest Servers are now running. To access them, refer
to:

    http://xtal1.sdsc.edu:80/Harvest/brokers/DataRep/summary.html

Would you like to register your Harvest servers now? [yes]:
Registered your Gatherer with the Harvest Server Registry.
Registered your Broker with the Harvest Server
Registry. Would you (bourne@sdsc.edu) like to join the
harvest-users@cs.colorado.edu mailing list (for software updates
and other discussions, etc.)?:
  [yes]:
```

The URL

> *http://xtal1.sdsc.edu:80/Harvest/brokers/-*
> *DataRep/summary.html*

defined in the installation above is your entry point for administering this particular Harvest server. You can set up as many Harvest servers as you need, each with its own administrative Web page. Figure 7–3 illustrates the options available through this URL.

In the following section I examine each option in more detail.

7.5.3 Using

I describe using the Harvest Server by working through each of the available options presented in Figure 7–3.

Query—This option presents the query interface to the information (i.e., the Harvest server) and is what the user making a search of your server sees by default.

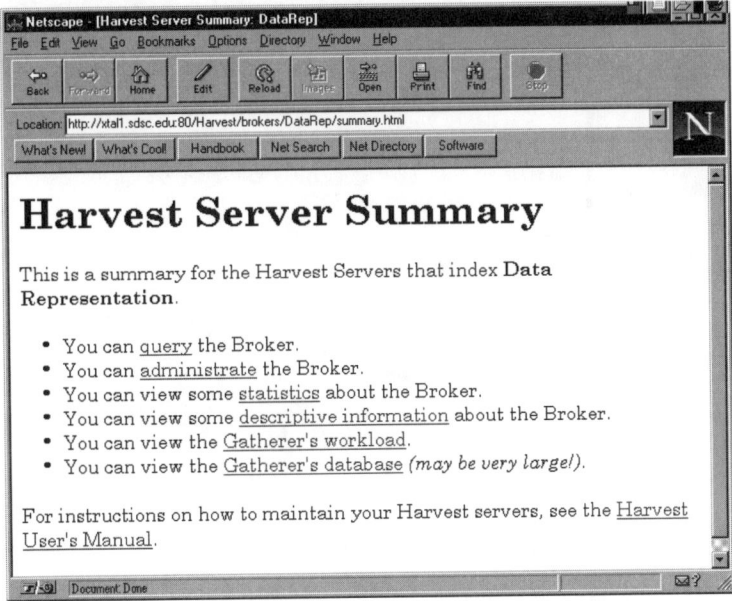

Fig. 7–3   Options Available through the Harvest Server

Hence, from your server's appropriate Web page, which introduces the accessible information, you would include a hyperlink to the query page like the one shown in Figure 7–4, indicating this is where to go to perform a search of these pages. You could customize this page, but that generated automatically by the Harvest system will likely meet the needs of the users accessing the information. A query can be made of any character string that the user chooses to enter. The features of the character string can be modified according to:

- Case sensitivity.
- Keywords match on word boundaries. That is, whether the query is a word surrounded by white space, or a substring of a word.
- Number of spelling errors allowed.

The appearance of the results of a search for a particular text string can be modified. Recall from the beginning of this section that an object is something that is searched during the gather operation, typically a Web page or ftp file. The modifications are to:

- Display the whole matched line containing the text string.
- Display object descriptions (if available).

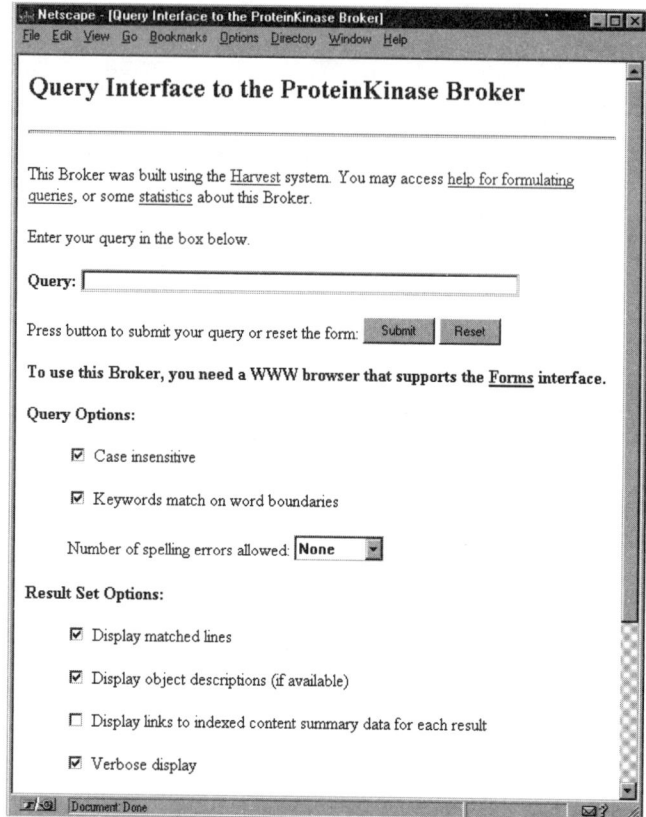

Fig. 7–4   The Harvest Query Interface

- Display links to indexed content summary data for each result.
- Display a verbose description.
- Control the maximum number of objects displayed.
- Control the maximum number of matched lines per object.
- Control the maximum number of results (i.e., objects+lines combined).

These options are discussed fully in the Harvest User's Guide.

Administrative

This option provides a Web forms based interface (Figure 7–5) to perform administrative functions on a specific broker.

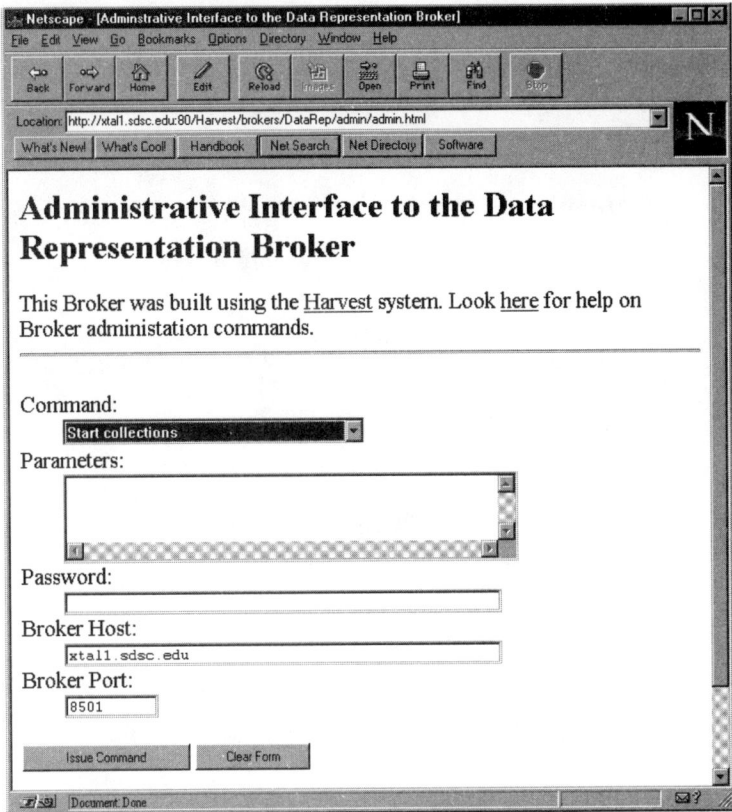

Fig. 7–5   The Harvest Administrative Interface

Here is a subset of the administrative tasks that can be performed through this interface. They are well documented in the user manual, and are given here to simply indicate
the range of administrative tasks.

- add objects to the broker
- remove expired objects from the registry
- delete objects based on a query
- maintain log files
- start and stop the Harvest server
- manage collections

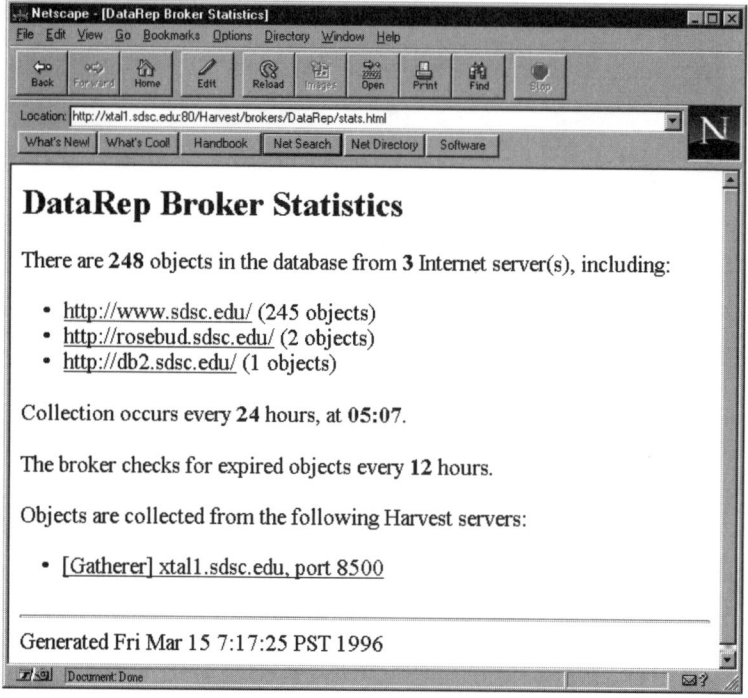

Fig. 7–6   The Harvest Statistics Interface

Statistics
The statistics (Figure 7–6) indicate where each object in the database came from, how many objects there are, how often new objects are gathered and how often expired objects are removed from the broker.

Description
A description of the broker, including information on:

- name
- last update
- maintainer
- description
- index type
- replication details

Gatherer's Workload
Displays the gatherer's configuration file, which is built and optionally edited when you create a Harvest server, or edited later if you wish to change what is gathered. Here it is

important to understand how you control the gathering process and enough of the syntax
to run a simple gatherer. Full details are left to the User's Guide.

```
#
#   DataRep.cf - configuration file for the
#   Data Representation Gatherer
#
#   Created by bourne@sdsc.edu on
#   Fri Mar 15 06:48:08 PST 1996
#
Gatherer-Name:   Data Representation
Gatherer-Port:   8500
Top-Directory:
 /usr/harvest/Harvest-1.4.pl2/gatherers/DataRep


<RootNodes>

# Enter URLs for RootNodes here
http://www.sdsc.edu/CompSci/pb/Group.html


</RootNodes>

<LeafNodes>
# Enter URLs for LeafNodes here
</LeafNodes>
```

What information is to be gathered and subsequently searched is defined by the *root
nodes* and the *leaf nodes*. Both are defined by URLs. A leaf node (at the end of the information tree) is a single piece of information contained in the URL (the object), that is, the
single file or part of a file defined by the URL. A root node cascades according to the type
of file it represents. For HTML files, any URLs found in the root URL are also gathered;
any URLs found in these first level URLs are also gathered, and so on. For root nodes
pointing to ftp archives, a recursive directory listing is done to include the whole archive.
For newsgroups it will follow the newsgroup.

It is not hard to image this gathering process getting out of hand very quickly
because of the complexity of local and remote hyperlinks to be found on the average information server. The trick is to customize the gathering process to gather just the right
amount of information.

7.5.4 Customizing

The full syntax for customizing the gathering process is given in the user's manual. Here
I tell you what can be customized and present a working example of a customization file
sufficient for simple gathering. The following may be customized:

- Total number of URLs to be gathered (default 250).
- Total number of hosts to search as defined by IP addresses (default is only the host defined by the root node).
- The types of nodes to gather, valid types are file, ftp, Gopher, HTTP, News, Telnet, or WAIS (default is HTTP only).
- Delay—the amount of time to wait between contacting servers. The intent is to balance network load as much as possible on a heavily used server (default is one second).
- Depth—how many depths of URL to follow. A depth of 1 implies that the root node and any URLs specified in that URL are gathered, but no further. *This can be a critical value since the amount of information being gathered may be huge even with a relatively small depth value.* There is no default value.

Further customization is possible by filtering either the URLs or the hosts that get searched. When filtering is being used the defaults apply *after* filtering. For example, the default number of URLs to be gathered is not that lesser number out of the default 250 which match the filter; but the first 250 that match the filter. Filtering is done using Posix regular expression syntax, which differs slightly from the better known C shell regular expression syntax. A URL filter applies only to the bold face part of the URL e.g., *http:/www.sdsc.edu/**moose.html**,* whereas the host filter applies only to the bolded part of the URL e.g., http://**www.sdsc.edu:80**/moose.html. Here are some examples of valid filters:

```
#URL Filters
# Deny access to any URL containing "gatherers" in
# the file name; allow all others.
Deny  /gatherers/
Allow  .


# IMPORTANT - the following filter prevents a
# movement back up an ftp archive. Recall that if
# you look at an ftp directory through a Web browser
# there is a link to the parent directory (..). This
# filter prevents a movement up to that directory
# and to even higher levels. If you think about how
# the following works you will realize that filters
# are applied sequentially.
Allow ^/my/ftp/achive
Deny .


#Host Filters
# Allow only hosts in the 128.59 domain (i.e., a B
# class Internet address)
```

```
Allow ^128\.59\..*
Deny  .
# Allow only a specific host
Allow rosebud.sdsc.edu
Deny  .
```

At this point you should have a fully functional information server for serving files via ftp, providing a service as a Listserver, and be ready to serve Web pages. You also have the means to index and provide a search service for this information. Congratulations! Let us now move on to what you need to do to prepare the information to be served.

8

Web Documents

Ingredients:

- *Existing online information*
- *New information written for a new medium*
- *A plan for how this information should appear*
- *The tools to make this plan a reality*

This is your main course—the pièce de résistance. Everything else was just a prelude to this moment. This is where you take existing information, any new information, and knead it and cook it just long enough to serve an Internet meal entrée that will be both lasting and satisfying.

While this book covers three modes of serving information—ftp, list serving, and Web serving, it is only the latter that requires significant attention to editing. Sure, you should put a README file in an ftp archive to assist people who access the archive in understanding its contents, but that is about the extent of the editing needed for ftp. Listservers require no editing at all. Your Listserver is simply a conduit for accepting mail and redistributing it to a list of recipients. As a list moderator, you could be creative in editing broadcasts to the list, but this serves little purpose. On the other hand, the editing of Web documents is crucial. Editing has a strong influence on how information content is perceived, navigated and absorbed by the audience. Presentation affects impact whether it is for a school project by ten-year-olds or a Fortune 500 company advertising their products. This chapter is devoted to the basics of Web page authoring, editing, and publishing.

8.1. AUTHORING VERSUS EDITING VERSUS PUBLISHING

I begin by drawing your attention to the notion of authoring versus editing information to be placed on your Internet information server, and to the concept that traditional publishing on paper is slowly being replaced. Initially, most of your efforts will be editing and publishing—converting existing information into a form suitable for Web access and making it available on the Internet.

Information technology has made editors out of all of us. Before the arrival of the PC, and hence of widespread word processing, authoring and editing were more distinct—you wrote something on paper, and if you were lucky enough, a secretary or office assistant performed the editorial role by controlling the look and feel of the document. Word processors have turned all of us into editors as well as authors. Today, much information is published directly from computer-generated, camera-ready materials, with no intermediate editing step. If the material is peer-reviewed, it is returned to the author to make the final corrections. In these cases there is no distinction between editor and author, and often, little distinguishing the publisher.

In authoring for the Internet (the Web in particular) this trend continues at an accelerated pace. The writing, editing, and publishing steps are indistinct, and what you write may be immediately made available to a potentially huge audience. I would suggest that lack of peer review for your creative efforts makes it essential that you do a good job, right from the start.

Editors will not disappear, but there will be a new type of editor who controls content and form in this new medium. If you work at a large organization that is using the Web extensively, you may well have an Internet editor already, even though he or she goes by some other name.

Good books have good content and are well organized. Good information servers are exactly the same. It is the implication of "organization" that has changed. Books are a sequential medium with a well-established form, and usually a single theme—the plot of a fiction novel, the explanation of words in a dictionary, the steps in setting up an information server, and so on. Hypertext is less structured and can present multiple themes. That is, the same Web page can be used to make many different points. Global hypertext has taken us away from the sequential organization with which we are familiar and has plunged us into the world of random access. I will give you some examples of what I think represent good organization in this new world disorder, and we will use these as templates for learning HyperText Markup Language (HTML), often referred to as the "language of the Web." I have based these selected templates on Web pages I have visited (in a virtual way of course) and found useful. That is, pages that have enabled me to achieve what I set out to do when I started looking for information on a specific topic.

Developments of the electronic authoring-editing-publishing continuum using hypertext and beyond are just beginning. A book is a very static medium. If you exclude pop-up books for kids, about all you can do to interact with a book is turn the pages. Web publishing brings the full world of interactive multimedia to bear. Authoring specifically for the Web is a different experience from traditional writing. Good writing skills are still critical, but are now accompanied by skills at using different media to get across the message.

I am getting ahead of myself here. What I am attempting to do is excite you to the possibilities of a new global medium with many new opportunities, but first we must cover the basics.

8.2. HYPERTEXT—THE BASICS ☞

Hypertext is not a new concept. Ted Nelson first coined the phrase back in 1965. It is beyond the scope of this cookbook to delve into the history of hypertext. If you are interested, refer to the references in Table 8–1.

One of the first commercial uses of hypertext was in the HyperCard products, initially for the Macintosh computer and then for PCs running DOS, and finally Windows. Some wonderful applications (hypercard stacks) have been built using these products. However, it is the global HyperCard stack, i.e., the Web, that has really popularized the use of hypertext.

The World Wide Web would not have proliferated if it were not easy to edit and publish for this new medium. Web authoring is not restricted to the computer savvy—anyone who wants to spend a few minutes can *mark up* text, thereby creating a *Web page* or perhaps a *home page*.

As we shall see subsequently, by "mark up" I mean insert additional text which has nothing to do with the information content, but when read by a Web browser causes a particular appearance or behavior. For example, displays a region of text in boldface, provides a link to another home page, or displays an image.

By home page, I mean the top of the information hierarchy on a particular theme. This is a physical idea in a virtual world, since the moment you link your page to the Web, there is no top, and for that matter no bottom. What's there is a complex pattern of cross links, hence the name, "Web." To help you orient yourself in this virtual maze, it helps to think of specific points that are referred to as "home pages." For example, a particular organization has a home page, which is the top level entry point for getting information on that organization. Likewise, an individual in the organization may have a home page which is the top level page for getting information on that individual. The individual's page exists somewhere in the company's hierarchy, where it is no longer the home page with respect to the organization. Hence, what constitutes a home page is dependent on how we are viewing the information, from the perspective of someone interested in the company or someone interested in the individual.

TABLE 8–1 Background Information on Hypertext

Location	Description
http://www.w3.org/hypertext/-History.html	Bullet list of hypertext developments.
http://www.isg.sfu.ca/~duchier/-misc/vbush/	"As We May Think," an aticle by Vannevar Bush, in which the hypertext concept was first suggested.
http://www.picosof.com/850	Home page of Xanadu, the company resulting from Ted Nelson's ideas.

8.2.1 Text Markup

Text markup, like hypertext, is not a new idea. It has been used in text processing for many years. You take your basic text, include (embed) a set of flags which describe how to format that text, pass that file to a program and have that program either display or print the formatted text based on the embedded tags. Markup for text processing was popularized by such markup formats as Digital Standard Runoff (DSR), nroff, troff, TeX, and LaTex. While these have enjoyed varying degrees of popularity over the years, none have become a standard, partly because they were overtaken by simpler to use (but not necessarily as powerful) word processing programs available on the PC and Macintosh.

Yet another of these markup languages is Standard Generalized Markup Language (SGML), which was, until recently, used mainly by the publishing industry. SGML is a well-developed language for describing the most complex documents. HTML is a subset of SGML, and, as such, does not have all the formatting features required for more complex documents. However, with each new release of HTML, more features described in SGML are included. The programs that process HTML and display the formatted text and graphics are the client Web browsers discussed in Chapter Six.

Using HTML, you can produce simple Web documents in a few minutes if you understand and remember a few markup tags. If you invest more time, you can produce more sophisticated Web documents using more advanced capabilities of HTML. HTML editors (Section 8.3) hide the details of HTML, however, given the sophistication of these editors at this time, it is useful to have some knowledge of HTML, since some manual "tweaking" of the page will be required to get exactly the effect you desire.

Web browsers assume many formatting features that are not explicitly specified in HTML. Further, these browsers are forgiving of poor HTML syntax—if the Web browser does not recognize the syntax it simply ignores it.

As I mentioned, HTML is evolving. HTML history is beyond the scope of this book. If you are interested in this topic refer to the following:

> *http://www.w3.org/hypertext/WWW/MarkUp/*

Everything in the printed version of this book should be compatible with at least HTML v3.0. The Web server

> *http://www.sdsc.edu/pb/Cookbook/UNIX*

will keep you updated on new HTML developments.

8.2.2 HTML—The Basics ☞

Much excellent material has already been written about HTML and is available on the Internet and in published books. I have provided you with pointers to what I have found most useful. I have subdivided these pointers into three types. (See Table 8-2)

(a) General information and detailed indexes of HTML-related information.

(b) Specifics of writing HTML.

(c) Pointers to publishers and book lists either devoted to, or containing large sections on HTML.

TABLE 8–2   Sources of Information on HTML

(a) General Information

Location	Description
http://www.yahoo.com/-Computers_and_Internet/-Software/Data_Formats/HTML/	Extensive index of HTML-related information.
http://akebono.stanford.edu/yahoo/-Computers/World_Wide_Web/-HTML/	Alternative site to the above.
http://www.gov.nb.ca/hotlist/-htmldocs.htm	Well-organized site with various levels of information content.
http://www.w3.org/hypertext/-WWW/MarkUp/MarkUp.html	The place that maintains information on the HTML standard, including past history and current developments.

(b) Writing HTML

Location	Description
http://snowwhite.it.brighton.ac.uk/-~mas/mas/courses/html/html.html	A nicely laid out guide to writing HTML.
http://www.ncsa.uiuc.edu/General/-Internet/WWW/HTMLPrimer.html	The *de facto* standard primer on HTML.
http://www.nashville.net/~carl/-htmlguide/index.html	Great page on the lesser known features of HTML.

(c) Books on HTML

Location	Description
http://www.mcp.com/-403822712823191/general-/workshop/books.html	HTML-related books from Macmillan.
http://www.diskovery.com/-Diskovery/EPG/Indices/Books/-ByPublisher/	List of publishers of HTML-related books.
http://www.davison.net/books/-www.top.html	A comprehensive list from a distributor.

What I do in this book is give you my own concise lesson in getting started with HTML. We begin with a discussion of the more crucial tags that make up the markup language.

8.2.2.1 HTML Tags ☞

An HTML tag tells the Web browser or other software reading the Web document to "Hey wake up and format me." This is not strictly true. Initially it is the MIME type as manifest by the *.html* or *.htm* file extension that says, ignore white space, line breaks, etc., and just obey the tags. HTML tags are distinguished from regular text by being contained in angle brackets as follows: <this_is_a_tag>. A tag nearly always has a terminator which is introduced by a slash: </this_is_a_tag>. Terminators are not always obligatory, but they are considered good coding practice. Consider a specific example of using an HTML tag:

```
<B> This text will appear in boldface </B> This will
appear in the standard font.
```

The <B> and </B> turn boldface on and off using a boldface version of the font currently selected. Some tags, such as the tag that forces an end of line
 (break) does not have a terminator—there is nothing to delimit in this instance. Appendix B summarizes a large variety of tags and serves as your reference guide. *On the server you will find a current list of tags for the currently accepted version of HTML.* Once you have mastered the principles behind HTML the reference guide should be all you need, since it serves to jog your memory as to what tags are available. How to use them will have become obvious. Here are a few of the principles behind using HTML tags.

- Certain tags have additional variables associated with them; these variables are referred to as attributes and modify the behavior of the tag. Attributes are tabulated in Appendix B along with their associated tags, and are covered in some detail in this and subsequent chapters.
- The characters comprising a tag are not case sensitive, that is, lowercase, uppercase, and a mixture, are all valid.
- Not all tags are understood by all browsers. If a browser does not understand a tag it will ignore it rather than misinterpret it.

8.2.2.2 HTML Anchors

An anchor is an example of a tag and represents the brilliance and simplicity of global hypertext. An anchor is used to reference other points in the same document, other documents on your server, or a document (or point in a document) any place in the world that the author (or editor) of that document wants you to access. Here is the syntax for a simple anchor.

```
<a href = "http://www.sdsc.edu/"> SDSC</a>'s home
page
```

What appears in the Web document is:

<u>SDSC</u>'s home page

Clicking on SDSC will take you to the URL *http://www.sdsc.edu/*, SDSC's home page. The <a ...> introduces the anchor and </a> terminates it. The "href = URL" (hypertext reference) is an attribute of the anchor tag and specifies the link to any piece of information on the Web.

When you are building HTML documents to serve from your own server, it pays to visit the site you intend your document to point to, cut the URL from the Web browser's URL locator text box, and paste it directly into your document. This serves two purposes: first, you know the URL is still active, and second, you are less likely to make typing errors when entering the URL. The context in which you reference the URL is completely up to you as author and editor. This is the heart of how the Web operates as an enabling technology. Once a document is served up on the Web, others can use it in any way they see fit. For example, one person could reference SDSC's home page as one in a list of National Computing Centers and another as part of a list of architecturally magnificent buildings in the La Jolla area of California (although that is unlikely if you have seen our building).

Variations on this simple anchor permit you to visit not only other documents referenced by URLs, but points in the current document and in other local documents. Here is an example.

```
<a href = "#introduction">Introduction</a>

....

<name = "introduction">Introduction
```

This is referred to as a relative anchor because the type (e.g., *http* and server, e.g., *www.sdsc.edu*) are not given, that is, it is an anchor relative to the current document. The "#" (hash mark) indicates a pointer to the named part of the document follows. Since there is no preceding URL, it is taken to mean the current document. Thus, in the current document there is a corresponding name tag, called "introduction." Using relative anchors is useful in large documents. You will see this a lot on the Web and examples are given in this book. For example, a hyperlink called Introduction would appear at the head of a document as part of a table of contents. Clicking on it would take you to the part of the document containing the name anchor.

Finally, then, you could have the following anchor.

```
<a href =
"http://www.sdsc.edu/index.html#introduction">
SDSC</a>'s home page introduction
```

This takes you to a particular point in SDSC's home page denoted by the named anchor "introduction."

8.2.2.3 Including Images ☞

Another great feature of the Web is the presence of images. From the reader's perspective, this makes material more visually pleasing and, hopefully, more informative. Images can also be used to navigate the reader to the information they are seeking (see Section 9.4 on clickable maps). From the author/editor perspective it is trivial to include images as long as they are in a format that can be read by browsers. This implies GIF or JPEG formats unless a *helper application* is present. Section 3.5 covers conversion between various graphics formats. Here we concentrate on how to display a graphic image as part of a Web page, assuming it is already in the correct format. The following examples illustrate the simplest form of image inclusion:

```
<IMG SRC="./mygraphic.gif">
<IMG SRC="http://www.sdsc.edu/Projects/Cookbook/Cover.gif">
```

The first example is relative and includes an image contained in a file called *mygraphic.gif* which resides in the same directory as the Web page which references that image. The second example is fully qualified and includes an image located somewhere on the Web in a document—the <IMG ...> tag (image) introduces an image and the SRC (source) attribute of that tag indicates where to find the image. It is not good nettiquette to include hypertext links from other people's images for selection in your Web documents, for two reasons. First, such an action places a demand on their server that you have no right to make, not to mention placing high bandwidth demands on the network and causing a delay in serving the page. Second (and a problem not restricted to images), you do not have the right to use someone else's material without permission. If you want to use someone else's image you should contact the owner of the image and request permission to download that image and serve it locally (see below).

The above example says nothing about the characteristics of the image presented, for example, size or the relative position of the image on the page, both of which can be specified. By default, the image will be left justified and presented at the size it is stored in the GIF file or shrunk just enough to fit the browser window. An image displayed using the IMG tag is referred to as an *inline image* since it can appear within a line of text.

There are some wonderful sources of images on the Web that you are invited to download and use in your own pages—a further example of enabling technology. Table 8–7 provides sources of images that you can use in your own Web pages.

You can, of course, grab many of the images that you see in Web documents. As stated above, you should give suitable acknowledgment and respect any copyright associated with the page. Assuming it is permissible to grab an image seen in a Web page, proceed as follows when using a Web browser that does not support downloads.

1. Use the "View Source" option (a feature available with all Web browsers) to view the HTML source of the page containing the image in which you are interested. Determine the SRC attribute for that image.
2. From the URL of the Web page and the SRC attribute determine the URL of the image only (see below for an example).
3. Load that URL to display the image only. If it is file- protected on the remote server this will not be possible.
4. Download the image using the "Save As…" option of your Web browser.

For example, the source of the Web page *http://www.sdsc.edu/pb/Cookbook/UNIX.html* includes the HTML statement <IMG SRC = "./images/cover.gif">. Let us assume this is the image you are interested in downloading. In your Web browser you load the URL

http://www.sdsc.edu/pb/Cookbook/UNIX/images/cover.gif

and just the image should appear. This image can now be downloaded to local disk as a GIF file with the "Save As..." option of the Web browser.

When including images in your own documents, the IMG tag can be supplemented with a number of additional attributes. The ALT (alternative to the image) attribute should always be used, for it is this attribute that provides an alternative display for text only browsers (e.g., lynx) and for all browsers when image display is turned off—a likely situation when display is via a slow network connection. Here is an example of using the ALT attribute.

```
<IMG ALT= "Cookbook Cover"
SRC="http://www.sdsc.edu/Projects/Cookbook/Cover.gif">
```

In text-only Web browsers, the words "Cookbook Cover" will appear instead of the image. This preserves the reader's ability to comprehend the page when an image cannot be displayed.

The last display features of an inline image that we need to consider in this introduction are: (i) the alignment of text and the image, and (ii) changing the characteristics
(e.g., size and border) of the image. Both of these features are seen in Figure 8–1.
Here is the HTML used to create this Web page.

```
<HTML>
<HEAD>
<TITLE>Associating Inlined Images with Text</TITLE>
</HEAD>
<BODY>

<P><IMG SRC="email3.gif" HSPACE=5 VSPACE=5 BORDER=0
HEIGHT=50 WIDTH=50 ALIGN=TOP>
ALIGN=TOP - A single text line will appear at the top
of the image and will then wrap from left to right under
the image.

<P><IMG SRC="email3.gif" HSPACE=5 VSPACE=5 BORDER=0
HEIGHT=50 WIDTH=50 ALIGN=CENTER>
```

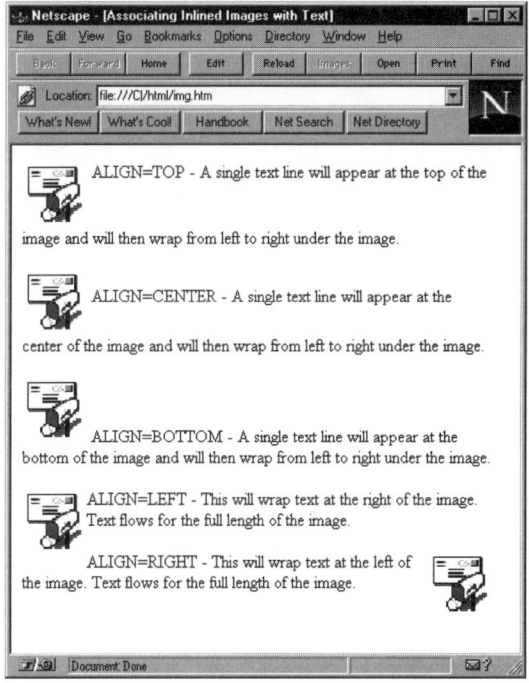

Fig. 8–1   Image Alignment in HTML

```
ALIGN=CENTER - A single text line will appear at the
center of the image and will then wrap from left to
right under the image.

<P><IMG SRC="email3.gif" HSPACE=5 VSPACE=5 BORDER=0
HEIGHT=50 WIDTH=50 ALIGN=BOTTOM>
ALIGN=BOTTOM - A single text line will appear at the
bottom of the image and will then wrap from left to
right under the image.

<P><IMG SRC="email3.gif" HSPACE=5 VSPACE=5 BORDER=0
HEIGHT=50 WIDTH=50 ALIGN=LEFT>
ALIGN=LEFT - This will wrap text at the left of the
image which will then continue to flow from left to
right under the image.

<P><IMG SRC="email3.gif" HSPACE=5 VSPACE=5 BORDER=0
HEIGHT=50 WIDTH=50 ALIGN=RIGHT>
ALIGN=RIGHT - This will wrap text at the right of the
image which will then continue to flow from left to
right under the image.

</BODY>
</HTML>
```

Note the following attributes of the <IMG ...> tag.

- The attribute ALIGN is used to align text with the image as described on the page.
- The attributes HSPACE and VSPACE define horizontal and vertical space (in mm) to be left outside the image.
- The attribute BORDER defines a border (in mm) of white space to be placed around the image. A value of 0 indicates no border.
- The attributes HEIGHT and WIDTH specify the height and width of the image in mm. In enlarging or shrinking the image these values should be set to the same relative value so as to maintain the aspect ratio of the image.

The above example introduces some HTML tags we had not encountered previously. The tag <P> (paragraph) forces a paragraph break, and along with the tags <HTML>, <HEAD>, and <BODY>, introduces the concept of basic page layout.

8.2.2.4 Basic Page Layout

Page layout using HTML is straightforward. If you get it wrong, or do not format the page at all, something sensible will usually result when viewed with a Web browser. Without any HTML tags, provided the file has an *.html* or *.htm* file extension, the contents of that file may[1] appear in the browser. Any white space, blank lines, indents, paragraph breaks, etc., will be ignored and the text will be autowrapped. That is, carriage returns at the end of lines are ignored and lines will be wrapped to fit the width of the browser. You can see this effect just by adjusting the width of your Web browser window. You can override this default effect with a couple of basic HTML tags. We already met <BR> to force a line break and <P> to start a new paragraph. There is also <PRE> ... </PRE> (preformatted), which will present the text exactly as it appears on the page, BUT will interpret hyperlinks. The tags <XMP> ... </XMP> have the same effect, except that hyperlinks are ignored. With just a few basic commands the text will take on a whole new appearance. Here is a simple example.

```
<HTML>
<HEAD>
<TITLE>This text appears in the bookmark.</TITLE>
</HEAD>
<BODY>
<H1>This is the first level heading for the
page</H1>
This is the body of the document.
...
</BODY>
</HTML>
```

The whole document is delimited by <HTML> ... </HTML> tags. The <HEAD> ... </HEAD> tags delimit the header part of the document, which is not displayed and is used to annotate the document for your own use, and for anyone displaying the HTML source code of your document. The <TITLE> ... </TITLE> tags define what appears in the title bar of most Web browsers and what appears in the list of URLs that you have visited. Similarly, it is the title that is added to your Web browser's hotlist of frequently accessed URLs. Thus, the title string is an important way for people to recognize your page, and you should think carefully about its content. The text string should be a short and concise description of what is on the page. The <BODY> ... </BODY> tags delimit the body of the document. This simple example includes

---

1. This is dependent on the Web server. For example, it will appear using NCSA's httpd, but will not appear with wn.

<H1> ... </H1>, which is a first level header. Up to six levels of header are permissible in HTML. Text at each level is emphasized according to its header level and header levels can be nested. The following example of using header levels in a table of contents illustrates these features.

```
<H1>Chapter 1</H1>
        <H2>Section 1.0 Introduction </H2>
                <H3>Phase I</H3>
                <H3>Phase II</H3>
        <H2>Section 2.0 The Guts</H2>
<H1>Chapter 2</H1>
```

You can take this type of hierarchy one step further with the use of lists. This is not, strictly speaking, a page layout feature, but it takes us to the point where we can format a nice looking page. Lists are groups of items where each item is identified by a bullet (unordered list—<UL> ... </UL>) or number (ordered list—<OL> ... </OL>). Some browsers also support roman numerals and letters to identify lists. We will revisit this detail when we discuss the more advanced features of HTML in Chapter Nine. Here is an example of using unordered and ordered lists.

```
<UL>
<LI> First list item
<LI> Second list item
  <UL>
  <LI> Part 1 of second item
  <LI> Part 2 of second item
  </UL>
<LI> Third list item
</UL>

Here is an ordered list:<BR>

<OL>
<LI>Numbered item 1
<LI>Numbered item 2
  <OL>
  <LI> Part 1 of second item
  <LI> Part 2 of second item
  </OL>
<LI>Numbered item 3
</OL>
```

As you see, unordered and ordered lists can be nested.

8.2.3 Learning through View Source and Downloading

There is only one way to really learn how to write Web pages—do it. Fortunately, doing it is easy, and is made even easier by the enabling capabilities of Web browsers. When you run an executable program, unless you have the source there is no way of seeing what makes the program tick. With Web pages you frequently have access to the source through the "View Source" option available in all Web browsers. Any time you see a nifty Web page, you can view the source HTML and see exactly how it was done. What is even better, you can download that source and use it as a template for your own information. If you do this, be sure to not violate any copyrights and give credit where credit is deserved.

8.2.4 Putting It all Together—Your Home Page

With this simple understanding of anchors, inline images, and page layout you are ready to build your first page. As an example, we will take my personal home page, which could be used as a template for your own home page. Here is an annotated outline from which we will build the final page. Note I have used the comment tag, <! comment string > to annotate the page. The comment may extend over multiple lines.

```
<HTML>
<HEAD>

<!-- This page is used as a sample page in the book,
A Cookbook for Serving the Internet published by
Prentice Hall -->

<TITLE>
Phil Bourne's Personal Page
</TITLE>
</HEAD>
<BODY>
<!-- The ALT attribute displays the text specified
in a text only browser, or when images are turned
off.-->
<H1><IMG ALIGN="MIDDLE" ALT="[Phils Face]"
    SRC="./images/photo.gif">Phil Bourne</H1>

<HR>         <!--"HR" is a horizontal rule-->
<H2>Synopsis</H2>

Hi, I am a computational biologist at the
<A HREF="http://www.sdsc.edu/">San Diego
```

```
Supercomputer Center</A>. My professional interests
revolve out of making the most of biological data.
This implies data representation, databases, query
languages and the Web as a research tool. When not
thinking about this I am playing squash, walking,
driving fast or writing on computing trends.

<H2>For More Information</H2>

<UL>
<LI><A HREF="#contact_info">Contact Information</A>
<LI><A HREF="#res_projects">Research Projects</A>
<LI><A HREF="#other_projects">Other Projects</A>
<LI><A HREF="#papers">Recent Publications</A>
<!-- Second level nesting of lists -- >
<UL>
<LI><A HREF="#journal_papers">Scientific Journal
    Papers (1994-)</A>
<LI><A HREF="#comp_papers">Magazine Articles
    (1994-)</A>
</UL>
<LI><A HREF="#grants">Current Grants</A>
<LI><A HREF="#committees">Current Committees </A>
<LI><A HREF="#collabs">Current Collaborators</A>
<LI><A HREF="#education">Education</A>
<LI><A HREF="#profession">Work History</A>
</UL>
<!-- First level 3 header -- >
<A NAME="contact_info"><H3>Contact
Information</H3></A>
Philip E. Bourne <BR>
San Diego Supercomputer Center <BR>
PO Box 85608 <BR>
San Diego CA 92186-9784 <BR>
<P>
Voice:   (619) 534-8301 <BR>
Fax:     (619) 534-5117 <BR>
<!-- See the NOTE below -- >
<A HREF =
"MAILTO:bourne@sdsc.edu">bourne@sdsc.edu</A> <BR>
<HR>
<A NAME="res_projects"><H3>Research
Projects</H3></A>
...
<HR>
```

```
<A NAME="other_projects"><H3>Other Projects</H3></A>
I am currently involved in one none research related
project:
<H4><A HREF =
"http://www.sdsc.edu/Projects/pb/Cookbook/Cookbook.html">
A Cookbook for Serving the Internet</A></H4>
...
<HR>
<A NAME="papers"><H3>Recent Publications</H3></A>
...
<HR>
<A NAME="journal_papers"><H4>Scientific Journal Papers
(1994-)</H4></A>
...
<HR>
<A NAME="comp_papers"><H4>Magazine Articles (1994)
</H4></A>
...
<HR>
<A NAME="grants"><H3>Current Grants</H3></A>
...
<HR>
<A NAME="committees"><H3>Current Committees</H3> </A>
...
<HR>
<A NAME="collabs"><H3>Current Collaborators</H3></A>
...
<HR>
<A NAME="education"><H3>Education</H3></A>
...
<HR>
<A NAME="profession"><H3>Professional Background
</H3></A>
<HR>
</BODY>
</HTML>
```

When interpreted by a Netscape browser, the result is shown in Figure 8–2.

Figure 8–2 is a simple, yet effective, layout for your home page. It could be more sophisticated, but yet is functional in the current form. For example, a closing address (e.g., a copyright notice) could be formatted using the <ADDRESS> ... </ADDRESS> HTML tag. Refinements like this come later. A major attraction of HTML is basic information with only a slight learning curve.

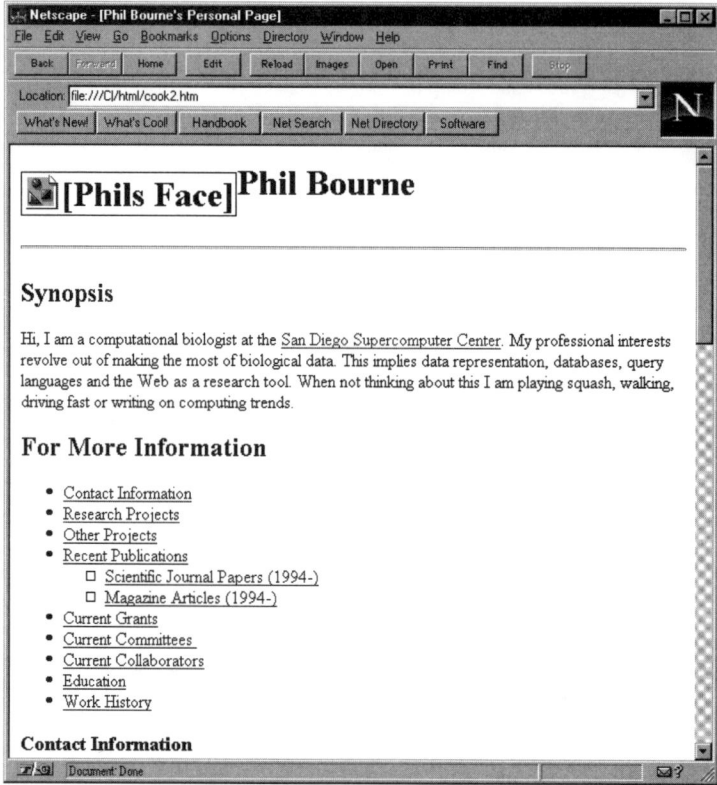

Fig. 8–2   An Example of an Individual's Home Page

Associating a face with this personal profile seems like a good idea. It is best, however, to include what is referred to as a thumbnail image—a small image of low quality that is quickly downloaded. The thumbnail image can then be made a hyperlink to a larger image. Should the readers of the Web page be interested in the image, they can click on it and wait while the larger image is downloaded. An example of the HTML used in a thumbnail sketch is shown below.

```
<A HREF="./images/big_face.gif"><IMG ALIGN="MIDDLE"
ALT="[Phils Face]" SRC="./images/photo.gif"></A>
Phil Bourne</H1>
```

Thus, clicking on *photo.gif* (the thumbnail sketch) will display the GIF file *big_face.gif* (the more detailed image).

The synopsis at the top of the above Web page (Figure 8–2) provides enough information for the reader to decide whether it is worth reading further, or to move on. The remainder of the information is organized like a table of contents, where each item in the list is a hyperlink to another named part of the document. In this way the reader can easily move to the section of interest. Since my whole profile is in one document organized sequentially, the reader can also simply scroll through it, reading it as if it were a printed resume. The reader can also print the whole profile.

This is an important point. Web browsers do not currently follow links when printing, but simply print the complete HTML file. *In organizing your pages you need to think of the logical blocks of text that will likely be printed. Each block should be a single Web page represented by a single file.*

8.2.5 More HTML Basics

8.2.5.1 Modified Anchors

There is a feature in Figure 8–2 that we have not discussed, and that is the following anchor:

```
<A HREF="MAILTO:bourne@sdsc.edu">bourne@sdsc.edu</A>
```

This is a neat feature supported by the majority (but not all) Web browsers. Clicking on the text associated with the hyperlink, in this instance my electronic mail address, *bourne@sdsc.edu*, will bring up a window that permits the user to enter a mail message which is then sent to the "MAILTO:" address. Thus, the reader of the page can send mail directly from the browser without the necessity of invoking a separate mail program and transcribing the email address by retyping or cutting and pasting.

8.2.5.2 Character Formatting ☞

One area we have yet to cover in our introduction to writing HTML documents is formatting special characters. This is straightforward and is illustrated with a few simple examples.

Consider a bibliographic reference as it might appear in my Web page profile.

```
<A <ul>
<LI> A. Smith and P.E.Bourne <I>The Journal</I>,
<B>The volume number</B>, 1995, The alpha subunit at
2.2 &Aring;
...
</UL>
```

Note first, as we have already seen, single or groups of characters may be surrounded by tags to force specific formatting of the characters between the tags. In the above example, <B> ... </B> forces boldface and <I> ... </I> forces italics. A number of other character formatting features of this type are possible and are tabulated in Appendix B under Text Layout. The best way to learn them is to just start using them with Appendix B as a guide. We will be meeting more of these character formatting options as we progress to writing more complex Web pages.

Note second, the character formatting denoted by Å which will appear in most browsers as Å (Ångstrom). This is an example of a special character. Think of the character as special, either because it is not to be found on the standard keyboard, or if it is found on the keyboard, it has a special HTML function. The < (less than) and > (greater than) characters are examples of the latter since they are found on the keyboard, yet are used to delimit a tag. Characters that have a role in specifying HTML syntax are referred to as metacharacters. (HTML metacharacters are analogous to shell metacharacters, which have a special meaning to the UNIX shell).

What if you wish to use a metacharacter literally, that is, display an HTML metacharacter in your Web page? You use the same kind of special notation we used for Ångstrom—precede the entity description of the character by an ampersand (&) and follow it by a semicolon. (;). In our example above, "Aring" is referred to as an entity and is interpreted in a special way by the Web browser. Similarly, less than (<) is represented as < and greater than (>) as >.

There is an alternative form of special character representation referred to as "character decimal reference." This representation uses a decimal code to represent the special character, which is preceded by an ampersand (&) and a hashmark (#) and followed by a semicolon (;). So less than (<) appears as < and greater than (>) as >

The extent to which these special characters are supported is browser dependent.

For a complete list of special characters using the character decimal reference notation refer to sources in Table 8–3.

With a basic understanding of character representation we are now ready to move on to a more complex example which introduces a few new tags and one form of interrelationship between your Web pages.

TABLE 8–3   Special Character Listings

Source - Internet	Description
http://www.bbsinc.com/-iso8859.html	The current character set and its interpretation derived from a number of sources.
http://www.w3.org/pub/WWW/-MarkUp/htmlspec/html-spec_9.html#SEC9.7	Alternative source of the above.

8.2.6 Structuring Web Documents

By now you should sense that writing and serving Web pages is straightforward. As I stated earlier, that is part of the appeal. Where skill is required is in conveying the information.

A key feature of conveying information is advance planning of how you organize the information. To plan, you need to understand your intended audience. How are they going to want to view this information? How will they likely discover the components that they are interested in? Once you have contemplated the answers to these questions, you need to relate those answers to the following practical questions.

- What are the logical chunks of information I should be serving?
- How should those chunks be referenced, as separate HTML files or by named anchors within one or a smaller group of HTML files?
- What hyperlinks (i.e., relationships) should I establish between those chunks of information? In other words, what are the various views that people seeking the information are going to want, and therefore, what pathways should I set up for them to follow?

There is a whole discipline emerging, complete with its own jargon, that deals with the notion of authoring and editing hypermedia. Here we will keep it simple. Let us explore the practical considerations with respect to the three major questions above. First, by analyzing the example we already have, and then by applying those principles to a more complex example.

The layout of information used for my personal home page is represented by Figure 8–3.

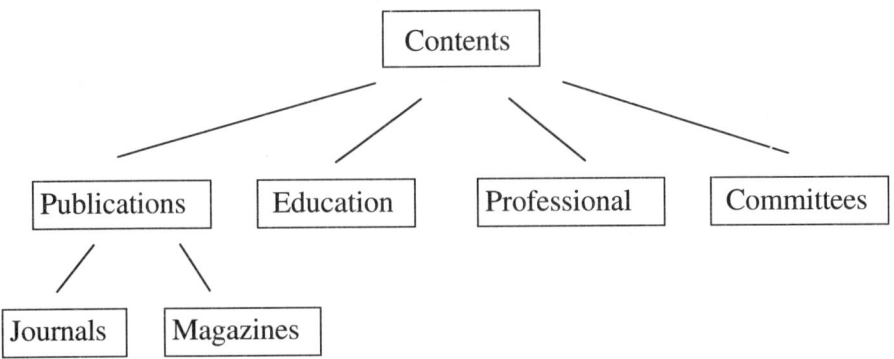

Fig. 8–3   A Simple Information Layout

This is about as simple as it gets. My professional life is broken down into a few discrete categories—education, professional, publications and committees, each represented by a square box (the logical chunks of information). If the scope of what someone is interested in is my resume, then this structure works well by keeping the contents in a single file, structured the way most written resumes are structured. You can scroll through the whole document as if you were reading the resume. Also, by printing the page, you print the *whole* resume, which is what most people would want to do (point 2 above).

The relationships (represented by the lines) between chunks of information are equally straightforward: a single root (contents) from which I can navigate down one level, and then, in the case of publications, down to a second level. There are no cross-pointers to other chunks of information at this level. All navigation is by going back to the contents. This structure is adequate, and facilitates navigation when the information content is of this complexity. I have included reference points in the form of name anchors for each chunk of information (e.g., <A NAME = "papers"><h3>Recent Publications</h3>). These reference points are not used by this document, but they could be referenced by other documents, as we shall see subsequently (point 3 above).

8.2.7 A Group's Home Page

Let me take this notion of organization between chunks of information to the next logical step with a more complex body of information. In this instance we have information that covers a group of related areas and requires a set of relationships at the second level. This idea of levels has no absolute meaning, it simply provides a point of reference. One person's notion of the first level may be someone else's notion of the tenth. Assigning levels is simply a way of referencing the hierarchy from one viewpoint. Someone interested in a summary of our research group would view this information as the first level and any software we have developed as the second level (Figure 8–4).

The important idea here is that we can now navigate directly between items at the second level. This implies more links. *Having more links implies that it is more difficult to maintain and to navigate these Web pages.* More links may confuse the reader, such that they navigate around in circles becoming increasingly frustrated, and in the end see only a subset of the information in which they are interested. *It is important to think through a complex information scheme before you implement it.*

What I have done to support the layout given in Figure 8–4 is to create a template that will appear at the top of each chunk of information (represented by the boxes) and which provides the appropriate navigation facilities. This template is shown below.

```
<HTML>
<HEAD>
<!-- A template for Web page navigation
```

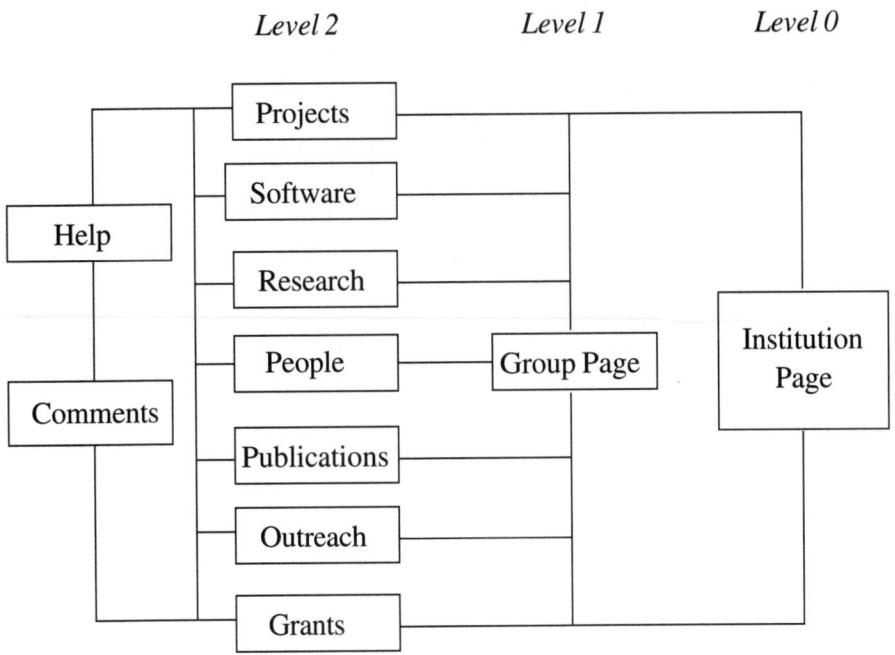

Fig. 8–4   A More Complex Information Layout

```
     This is the Top Level Page -->
<TITLE>Title Goes Here </TITLE>
</HEAD>
<!-- This introduces a background image. -->


<BODY BACKGROUND="./images/bg.gif">
<CENTER>
<H1>Top Level</H1>

<!-- Use a horizontal blue line as separator -->
<IMG ALIGN="MIDDLE" SRC="images/hrblue.gif">
<P>
<!-- Here is the navigation which appears at the top of
each page. On the databases page the URL for the
database page would be replaced with a URL pointing back
to the top level, and so on for the other pages. -->
```

```
<A HREF="./Databases.html"> Databases</A> |
<A HREF="./Software.html"> Software</A> |
<A HREF="./Research.html"> Research</A> |
<A HREF="./People.html">   People</A>   |
<A HREF="./Pubs.html"> Publications</A> |
<A HREF="./Grants.html">   Grants</A>   |
<A HREF="./Comments.html"> Comments</A> |
<A HREF="./Help.html">     Help</A> <BR>
<A HREF="./Search.html">   Text Search</A> |
<A HREF="http://www.sdsc.edu/"> SDSC Home Page</A>
<BR>
<IMG ALIGN="MIDDLE" SRC="./images/hrblue.gif">
</CENTER>


<H2>Synopsis</H2>

A summary of the page contents goes here.

<H2>Content</H2>

The content of the page goes here.

</BODY>
</HTML>
```

The corresponding page is shown in Figure 8–5.

What we have created is a compact, yet easily navigable, set of pages in which it is easy to move between a variety of topics or back to the top level. When creating, for example, the database page, you could change the URL pointing to the database page in the above example to a URL pointing back to the top level. You would not want to call it top level, since it is only the top level from a single perspective. A term like "Group Page" would be more appropriate.

```
<!-- On the databases page the following: -->
<A HREF="./Databases.html"> Databases</A> |
<!-- would be replaced by: -->
<A HREF="./Group.html">Group Page</A> |
```

So far, so good. However, there is a maintenance issue in what we have done here. Suppose I decide to add a new topic, for example, "Education," to indicate classes and other student related activities that are performed by our group. I now have to go back and

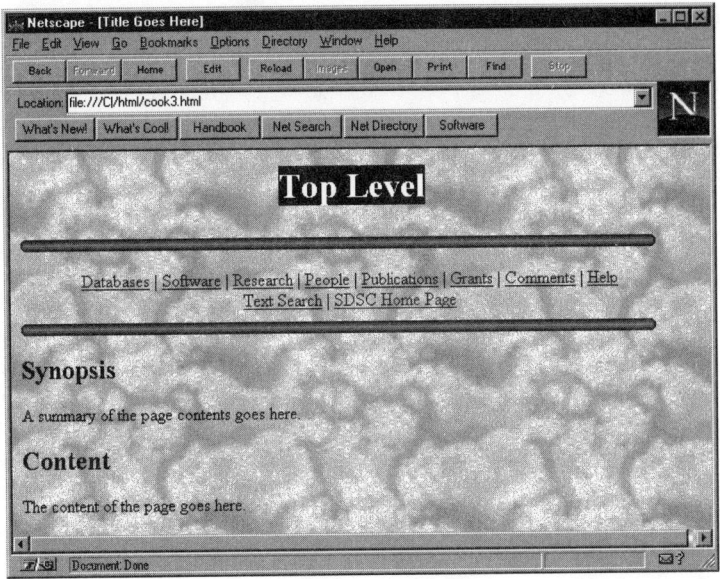

Fig. 8–5   A Web Page for a More Complex Information Layout

add that option to every page that has this menu! Not a big deal for the small number of pages here, but what if I have a complex structure with hundreds of pages? I can avoid this maintenance headache with what is termed a *server side include*. In practical terms, this means I define the menu once as a separate page, and include that menu page in each page at the time it is served to a Web client. Let me make that quite clear—the inclusion is not done at the time I create the page, but when the page is served to a Web client. When I want to add a new item to the menu, I need only add it once to the include page, and it will appear on every page that includes that menu. Server side includes are discussed in more detail in Section 9.3. It should be apparent here, however, that server side includes are useful for including the same volatile information, that is, information that changes frequently, in a variety of pages.

The group Web page introduced a couple of new features that have nothing to do with content, but everything to do with presentation. They lead us to our next topic on authoring and editing Web pages, that of creating a specific look and feel.

8.2.8 The Look and Feel (Style) of Web Pages

The terms "look" and "feel," as applied to Web pages, are often clumped together and referred to as style, and described in a variety of *style guides*. For our purposes, I consider *look* to imply how a Web page is presented and *feel* as the organization of the page and its relationship to the organization of other pages. The personal and group home pages described above have a lot to do with feel and little to do with look. As you will have ascertained from reading other parts of this book, I regard feel to be more important than look, which is why I discuss them separately. Here, look affects how easy it is to read a page, and feel how easy it is to navigate and, hence, find the correct piece of information. I start with a couple of useful items related to look that were introduced on the page above.

8.2.8.1 Look: Controlling the Background

The background of a Web page can be filled with a particular color or image. The trick is to avoid colors or images that make the text harder to read, although, as we shall see in the next section, the text color may also be altered. Be aware that what appears as a suitable background on one display type may be unreadable on another display type! For example, I have seen a page look fine on a color X terminal, but unreadable on an active matrix display using the 256-color palette found on many laptop computers.

Try out your Web pages on as many display types and as many Web browsers as possible to make sure they are readable before releasing them to the world (see Section 8.2.10 on debugging HTML).

To fill the background with a particular image use the BACKGROUND attribute to the <BODY> tag to define the image file to use. From the previous example:

```
<BODY BACKGROUND="./images/bg.gif">
...
</BODY>
```

will fill the background with the image contained in the GIF file *bg.gif*. If the background image is smaller than the Web browser display window, the image will automatically tile to fill the available background. This is yet another image for the client to download and should be kept simple (i.e., a small GIF file). The *xv* program (Section 3.8) is a good tool for setting the contrast and intensity of an image so that it does not overwhelm the text.

It is appropriate here to introduce the idea of a transparent background. By modifying the background of an image to match that of the browser background, the image appears to float on the Web page and provides a pleasing look. Good instructions on creating images with transparent backgrounds can be found from the sources in Table 8–4.

An alternative to using a specific background file is provided by the BGCOLOR attribute of the <BODY> tag. BGCOLOR sets the background color on a display device. It has the form

```
<BODY BGCOLOR="#rrggbb">
...
</BODY>
```

where rrggbb are the hexadecimal values for the red, green, and blue primary colors, respectively. If you do not know, or cannot remember your hexadecimal numbering, and/or you cannot remember what the effect of mixing primary colors is, Table 8–5 provides a quick look up, to at least give you the extremes of color you might wish to use for a background.

Table 8–6 indicates some good sites for obtaining background images.

TABLE 8–4   Information on Transparent Background Images

Location	Description
http://members.aol.com/htmlguru/-transparent_images.html	Step by step guide, including sources of image editing tools.
http://www.magi.com/~kk/tbi2.html	Another step by step guide, but using Lview Pro on the PC.
http://www.icce.rug.nl/misc/-examples.html	Examples of opaque versus transparent backgrounds.

TABLE 8–5   Hexidecimal RGB Color Specifications

Hex Value	Color
#000000	White
#FFFFFF	Black
#FF0000	Red
#00FF00	Green
#FFFF00	Yellow
#FF00FF	Magenta
#00FFFF	Cyan
#00000FF	Blue

TABLE 8–6   Sources of Background Images

Location	Description
http://-the-tech.mit.edu/KPT/bgs.html	Thumbnail sketches of a variety of backgrounds and how to make transparent backgrounds.
http://cameo.softwarelabs.com/-gini/index.htm	A large collection of images, including a large number of backgrounds.

8.2.8.2 Look: Controlling the Foreground ☞

Once you have colored the background it may also be desirable to color the text itself to provide the correct contrast. This is also done with attributes to the <BODY> tag. I say attributes (plural) because you may want not only to set the color of the basic text, but also the color of the text representing the various classes of hyperlinks. The attributes are given in Table 8–7.

Here is a simple example taken from the Netscape documentation that creates an interesting contrast.

```
<HTML>
<HEAD>
<TITLE>Color Control Example</TITLE>
</HEAD>

<BODY BGCOLOR="#000000" TEXT="#F0F0F0"
      LINK="#FFFF00" VLINK="#22AA22"
      ALINK="#0077FF">

This is an example document. Text is light-gray on
black, and <A HREF="nowhere.html">anchors</A> are
yellow at first, flashing blue-green when activated,
and pale green if already visited.
</BODY>
</HTML>
```

The URL

http://www2.netscape.com/assist/net_sites/bg/

provides additional information on the use of foreground and background images.

TABLE 8–7   Text-based Attributes of the HTML <BODY> Tag

<BODY> Attribute	Description
TEXT	Basic text
VLINK	Visited link
ALINK	Active link
LINK	All other links

8.2.8.3 Look: Using Clip Art ☞

In a previous example we saw the use of the following

```
<IMG ALIGN="MIDDLE" SRC="./images/hrblue.gif">
```

which, like the horizontal rule (<HR>), defines a separator, but in this instance is a thick line presented on an off-white background. The thick line is contained in a file in GIF format. Such clip art images are used very frequently in Web pages. Table 8–8 provides sources of clip art images as well as catalogs of other useful images.

8.2.8.4 Feel: Some Guidelines ☞

Here is a list of guidelines that I and others have found useful in writing Web pages. If you forget all the items on this list just remember the following. The best way to write good pages is: (i) take note of the features of Web pages you have visited and like; (ii) solicit and listen to feedback from readers on the pages you have written; and (iii) strive for *maximum information transfer in minimum time.*

Navigation

- Make the <TITLE> ... </TITLE> as concise, i.e., short and informative, as possible, since this is what a user maintains in their hotlist. When they visit their hotlist sometime hence they should recall from the title what the entry for your page contained.

TABLE 8–8   Sources of Clip Art and Other Images

Location	Description
http://cameo.softwarelabs.com/-gini/index.htm	Over 1500 buttons, bars, and other common icons.
http://cameo.softwarelabs.com/-hotlist/hotlist.htm	Pointers to a very large collection of images.
http://wuarchive.wustl.edu/-multimedia/images/gif/	A comprehensive album of images with a searchable catalog.
http://home.netscape.com/-assist/net_sites/starter/-samples/index.html	Images from Netscape.
http://www.stars.com/Vlib/-Providers/Images_and_Icons.html	A variety of images and icons.

- Avoid the phrase "click here." Browsing does not necessitate a mouse and so the term may be meaningless. More importantly, the phrase is redundant, bears no useful information, and only draws attention away from the description of where you might go, since you have to read back to and figure out why to "click here."

- Make the URL reference as informative and as locational as possible. I believe people like a sense of knowing where they are on the Web. I always have the location preference turned on if the browser supports it, since I like to see where in the world I am. It also raises one's tolerance level for waiting for pages to download when they are coming from far-off places (or places known to have slow network links). Here is an example of what I mean:

Excellence in scientific computing is part of the mandate of the <A HREF="http://www.sdsc.edu/">San Diego Supercomputer Center</A> which is located in <A HREF="http://www.lajolla.com/">La Jolla</A> California.

- Use links judiciously by first considering the various views that you want a visitor to have of the information. Avoid linking in such a way that navigation becomes circular and leaves large chunks of information unseen. This is especially irritating when waiting for pages to download using slow connections.

- Make the home page (i.e., the top of the document tree) self-explanatory, yet concise, and have links to all the obvious places.

- Use conventional publishing techniques as a guide—an index, table of contents, list of figures, etc., remain very effective navigation tools for hypertext.

- In long pages, use named links to navigate backward and forward to appropriate points in the page. For example, named links supplement scrolling by immediately taking you backward or forward to appropriate sections in the document.

- Break your documents into appropriate chunks, and have a reference anchor for each chunk. Granularity is also a consideration when printing (see below).

- Provide links to related sources of information, but be judicious.

- Cater to text-only access:
     use the ALT attribute with images
     avoid navigation only by images

- Cater to slow data links between client and server.

- Specify the size in kilobytes of files and images to be downloaded.

- Have a small version of the image (a thumbnail), which itself is a reference to a larger image, as was described earlier.

- Avoid Web pages that are longer than 10-15 screens of text.

<u>Page Layout</u>

- Experiment with the appearance of your pages by using a Web browser to view them using various page lengths and widths. The autowrap feature of HTML is satisfactory for most features, but for titles and other special blocks of text, a forced break tag (<BR>) should often be used.
- Draw the readers attention with:
  - putting important information up front—do not waffle at the beginning
  - the use of bullets
  - the use of appropriate separators
  - the use of eye-catching icons (with text substitutes of course)
- Avoid using headers <H1> through <H7> for anything other than headings, notably to display text of different sizes. This destroys the logical structure of the document if that document uses headers for their intended purpose. This will come back to haunt you in large documents where the header levels are useful markers and likely to be used later, for example in developing a tool that automatically generates a table of contents on a fast growing document. Use <EM> ... </EM> and <STRONG> ... </STRONG> to emphasize text and keep an eye out for what emerges as standard HTML to emphasize text.
- Do not use esoteric icons, but instead, those icons readers will recognize.

<u>Printing</u>

- Since printing only prints the current Web page, make each page a self-contained body of information.

<u>Images</u>

- Use MIME types that you consider generic, and then inform the "reader" of what is required to view the image.
- Limit colors—the use of extensive color maps increase the size of the file dramatically and make downloading to the client Web browser slow.
- Use thumbnail sketches of images as discussed previously.

Table 8–9 contains some useful sources of style guides.

8.2.9 HTML Templates ☞

As stated, you can learn good techniques of Web page writing from pages you stumble across while surfing the net. A more directed approach is to look at templates that others

TABLE 8–9   Sources of HTML Source Guides

Location	Description
http://www.w3.org/hypertext/-WWW/Provider/Style/-Overview.html	The style guide from CERN.
http://www.cl.cam.ac.uk/users/-gdr11/style-guide.html	Useful extensions to the CERN Guide.
http://info.med.yale.edu/caim/-StyleManual_Top.HTML	Another useful style guide that considers performance issues.

have prepared for different types of pages and use those as a starting point. Table 8–10 provides some places to go for templates.

8.2.10 Debugging HTML

In contrast to a high-level compiled programming language like C or C++, debugging HTML is easy. Unlike a core dump that cannot be interpreted without the use of a debugging tool, you can generally see what the problem is with the HTML just by viewing the page with a Web browser. The page does not have to be served by your http server to be viewed. Provided you have read access to the file, it can be loaded with the "open file" (or similar name) option available with all Web browsers. *Remember to reload the file (and perhaps empty the disk and memory caches) after making changes, otherwise you will not see the changes. It is the cached (i.e., unchanged) file that will be viewed again.* Let me make this point quite clear. Browsers use various caching schemes, but the basic idea is the same. Once a page is downloaded to the client, it remains there for a period of time, since the likelihood that file will be revisited is high. It is faster to retrieve the page from the client than go back to the server to get it. A problem arises when the page has been changed (by you or someone else).Without a reload (a function available on all browsers), those edits will not be seen since you are viewing the previously unedited, cached version.

TABLE 8–10   Sources of Web Page Templates

Location	Description
http://home.netscape.com/assist/-net_sites/starter/samples/templates/-index.html	Netscape's contribution—15 or so useful starting points.
http://www.inform.umd.edu:8080/-EdRes/-Faculty_Resources_and_Support/-template	Templates for course material.

TABLE 8–11   Lists of HTML Editors

Location	Description
http://www.w3.org/hypertext/WWW/-Tools/Overview.html	Extensive list from the WWW Consortium.
http://www.yahoo.com/Computers/-World_Wide_Web/HTML_Editors	Yahoo List.
http://sdg.ncsa.uiuc.edu/~mag/-work/HTMLEditors/unixlist.html	UNIX-specific list.

Browsers all have a view source option, and on more recent browsers you can view the page and the source simultaneously.

Some HTML editors (see below) also have a debugging capability. That is, when you load an existing page into the editor some problems in the HTML syntax may be highlighted.

8.3. HTML EDITORS ☞

There are far too many HTML editors to document here. Moreover, their number and the capabilities of each are changing rapidly, as is the official HTML standard and the *de facto* HTML standard imposed by some Web browsers. A question to ask yourself at any time is, does the HTML editor support the advanced features that I wish to use? Currently, this implies tables, forms, and frames (see Chapters Nine and Ten). Table 8–11 provides sources of lists that tabulate available HTML editors.

8.4. PUBLISHING YOUR WEB PAGES ☞

Writing pages should be done in your personal directory. You then view the results by opening the file (rather than the URL) from the Web browser. Once you are satisfied with the pages and ready to publish, you can move the files to somewhere in the server document hierarchy. If you have used appropriate relative file references in your URLs, then all pages should be found and served after they are moved. (If you are using a Web server like wn, they will need to be indexed first). Keeping Web documents out of the server hierarchy until you are ready prevents readers stumbling across them or having them indexed by Web *robots* (if you are using a server for which files need not be explicitly served to be read by clients) .

If your goal is to make your pages widely known, you need to do more than simply make them accessible on your server. The Web robots used by the various search engines

TABLE 8–12   Further Reading on Getting Your Web Pages Known

Location	Description
http://www.webcom.com/html/-publicize.html	A comprehensive discussion of the various options for getting your pages known.
http://www.cl.cam.ac.uk/users/-gdr11/old-publish.html	As above.

will eventually find and index your pages, but you may wish to expedite this process in various ways.

Here are some specific suggestions, including specific Web pages to visit for more information (See Table 8–12).

- Notify Webmasters of heavily utilized sites relevant to your material and request a link be made.
- Notify relevant newsgroups of your pages.
- Submit your URLs to maintainers of individual search engines, but be aware that the number and popularity of these search engines is constantly changing.
- Use a free service. This entails your filling in a Web form that is then translated into the many formats required to register with each of multiple sites, search engines, bulletin boards, comprehensive lists e.g., the Virtual Tourist, NCSA's What's New, Yahoo, and WWW Virtual Subject Library.
- Use a commercial service, which operates like a free service, but for a fee and with guaranteed coverage.

You should by now have grasped the basics of writing HTML. We'll now move on to the more advanced features of HTML namely, tables, clickable maps, frames, and forms (Chapter Nine). Forms, which enable data submission to the server, open up a new world of client server interaction, which we'll explore in Chapters Ten and Eleven.

9

Advanced Web Documents

Ingredients:
- *Tables*
- *Frames*
- *Server Side Includes*
- *Server and Client Based Clickable Maps*

We have learned how to prepare a simple main course; now for the culinary delights. The difference between a good meal and a great meal is the subtle use of spices and sauces and, of course, presentation.

If you spend more than a couple of minutes surfing the Web, you will come across what I term advanced Web documents. Sometimes these documents are highly informative and easily navigable. Other times they serve no useful purpose and take longer to download to the client browser than would a simple document with the same information content. *Use the features found in advanced Web documents judiciously in your own Web pages.*

I begin with the simplest advanced feature for use in Web documents, namely tables. Tables can be used not only for data that are tabular in nature, but also to format text and graphics in a way not possible otherwise. An example would be to present a page in multiple columns, as found in a newspaper or magazine format. A more advanced and newer feature for page formatting is frames. Frames are used to divide your Web page (a frame set) into arbitrary, separately addressable frames. That is, a different URL is used to address each frame. A different type of advanced feature is a clickable map, which acts as a visual form of navigation aid.

Maintenance of Web documents is an important consideration. Server side includes provide a mechanism for including the same volatile (i.e., fast changing) information on a number of Web pages. Finally, not all the information you may wish to provide can be handled by a Web browser, in which case a helper or plug-in application is required. A helper application is called from the Web browser, but executes as a separate application. A plug-in application executes within the browser window.

9.1. TABLES

If you are presenting numeric data or information that, in printed form, would best be presented in a table, then it is also best presented in a Web page as a table. Tables can also be used to address current shortcomings in HTML for justifying text, that is, controlling its exact location on a page. Having text in multiple columns is an example.

At the time this is being written, not all Web browsers recognize the HTML tags associated with tables. *The literal translation of a table by a browser that does not support tables is often unreadable.*

Tables are easy to construct, once you understand the following.

- A table consists of a number of rows (horizontal divisions).
- A table consists of a number of columns (vertical divisions).
- A table consists of a number of cells, where each cell is, by default, one vertical and horizontal division.
- Cell size scales automatically, based on content.
- It is easy to make a cell span more than one horizontal and/or vertical division.
- There are normal (data) cells and cells that contain header information.
- A table optionally can have a border. The border can have a number of specific characteristics.
- The alignment of information in a cell (could be text or image(s)) may be explicitly defined. By default, header cells have their information centered, and normal cells have their information left justified.

9.1.1 A Simple Example

Here is a simple table that introduces the basic HTML tags used in table construction.

```
<TABLE BORDER>
  <CAPTION>A Very Simple Table</CAPTION>
  <TR><TH>Header for Column 1</TH>
      <TH>Header for Column 2</TH>
  </TR>
  <TR><TD>Cell(1,1)</TD><TD>Cell(1,2)</TD></TR>
  <TR><TD>Cell(2,1)</TD><TD>Cell(2,2)</TD></TR>
</TABLE>
```

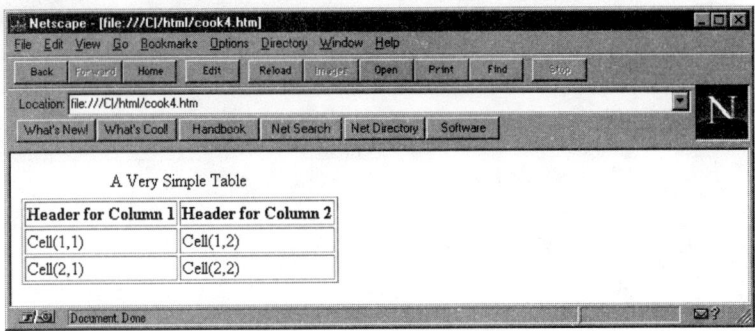

Fig. 9–1   A Very Simple Table

This table is shown in Figure 9–1.
Note:

- A table is delimited by the <TABLE> . . . </TABLE> HTML tags with an optional BORDER attribute. The width of the border may be specified.
- The HTML tags <CAPTION> . . . </CAPTION> define a caption for the table, which appears centered above the table.
- The HTML tags <TR> . . . </TR> (table row) define a table row.
- The HTML tags <TD> . . . </TD> (table data) define a cell in a row.
- The HTML tags <TH> . . . </TH> (table header) define the heading for a column.

9.1.2 A More Complex Example

Here is an example of a table where cells span rows and columns.

```
<TABLE BORDER>
  <CAPTION>A Table with Cell Spanning</CAPTION>
  <TR><TH ROWSPAN=2><TH COLSPAN=2>Average
      <TH ROWSPAN=2>other<BR>category<TH>Misc
  <TR><TH>height<TH>weight
  <TR><TH ALIGN=LEFT>males<TD>1.9<TD>0.003
  <TR><TH ALIGN=LEFT ROWSPAN=2>females<TD>1.7
      <TD>0.002
</TABLE>
```

The table is shown in Figure 9–2.

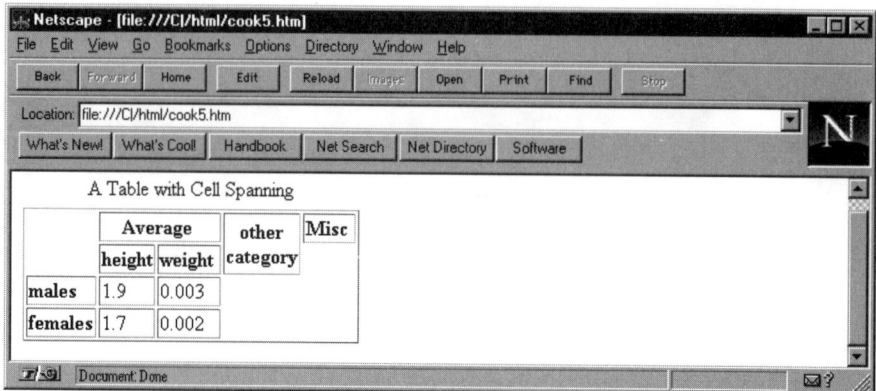

Fig. 9–2   A Table with Cells that Span Rows and Columns

Note:

- ROWSPAN and COLSPAN are attributes of <TH> or <TD> that cause the cell to cover multiple rows and columns, respectively.
- The trailing </TH> or </TD> is subsumed by a new <TH> or <TD>, respectively, or by </TABLE> and can be omitted.
- The ALIGN=LEFT/CENTER/RIGHT attribute of <TH> or <TD> will align text or images in a cell.
- The
 HTML tag is used to force a break in a text line, this, in turn, affects the default size of each cell. The NOWRAP attribute (not shown) can be use with <TD> and <TH> tags to exert some control over the size of cells.

9.1.3 Further Information ☞

Table 9–1 indicates good sources for a more extensive discussion of tables.

TABLE 9–1   Sources of Information on HTML Tables

Location	Description
http://webreference.com/-html3andns/table.html#border	The HTML 3.0 specification for tables.
http://www.w3.org/hypertext/-WWW/MarkUp/html3/tables.html	A full description of how to write tables in HTML.
http://www.utirc.utoronto.ca/-HTMLdocs/NewHTML/tables-5.html	Another good source including a discussion of tables within tables.

Here are some of the additional features that you will find in the above Web pages.

- The CELLPADDING and CELLSPACING attributes can be used with <TH> and <TD> to define the white space around a cell with a border, and the width of the border between cells, respectively.
- The WIDTH attribute can be use to define the absolute width of tables.
- The THEAD, TBODY, and TFOOT tags can be used to group rows for border rendering etc.
- The COLS = n attribute can be used to set the absolute number of columns in a table to n.

The HTML standard for describing tables is in a state of flux. There are many good working examples found in the tutorials below which introduce the current capabilities. Study them and use them as templates for your own tables. Note that HTML is upwardly compatible. That is, while there may be new features, features used today will continue to function.

9.1.4 Online Tutorials ☞

TABLE 9-2   Online Tutorials for Writing HTML Tables

Location	Description
http://www.newbies-netguide.com/web_pa~1/table2.html	Approximately 20 useful examples of tables.
http://raptor.rit.edu/Nick/tlesson2.htm	A few simple examples, including an orphan cell.
http://www.ozemail.com.au/-~dkgsoft/html3/tables.html	Includes nested tables.
http://math-www.uni-paderborn.de/HTML/Dictionaries/HTML-Dictionary/netscape/tables.html	Another good example of nested tables.
http://home.netscape.com/assist/-net_sites/table_sample.html	A sampler from Netscape Inc.

A summary of the more common table-based HTML tags and their attributes is given in Appendix B.

9.2. FRAMES

Including frames in HTML documents divides the browser window into one or more independently accessible regions of arbitrary layout. Each region is referred to as a frame and is referenced by way of a unique URL. Hyperlinks in framed documents can then not only update and control the contents of their own frames, but also the contents of other frames and windows as well. This capability adds a new dimension to hypertext browsing, since there can be a number of interoperable Web pages in the same browser. For example, a table of contents can be displayed in one frame while a specific section of the document is displayed in another frame. Selecting a specific section of the document from the table of contents will update the frame containing the document section to display the new section. Alternatively, a database query of some kind could be present in one frame and the results of that query present in another frame, since it is often useful to see the query and the result at the same time.

At the time of writing frames are not part of the HTML standard, but have been introduced by Netscape Communications Inc. and are supported by Netscape's browsers. So compelling is this development, and so large is Netscape's share of the browser market, that few people care that it is not part of the standard and HTML authors are using frames enthusiastically.

Possible disadvantages of frames are: (i) the inability to "view source" without some effort; (ii) the inability to print a browser window, but only the contents of the active frame, i.e., the frame that has the input focus based on a mouse click, and (iii) the failure of text-based Web browsers to recognize frames.

Frames introduce the concept of *layout* documents and *content* documents. A layout document, as the name suggests, defines the layout of the frames and the content document the content of each frame. The content document is the kind of HTML document we have been considering thus far. A layout document includes an explicit or implicit reference to a content document for each of its frames. Browsers that do not support frames will not recognize layout documents, and if read will, by default (see the use of <FRAME> ... </NOFRAME> below), present a blank screen, whereas content documents will appear as they always have.

Here is a very simple layout document.

```
<HTML>
<HEAD>
<TITLE>A very Simple Layout Document</TITLE>
</HEAD>
<FRAMESET COLS=*,*>
     <FRAME SRC=fig1.htm NAME=left>
     <FRAME SRC=part2.htm NAME=right>
</FRAMESET>
</HTML>
```

with the result shown in Figure 9–3.

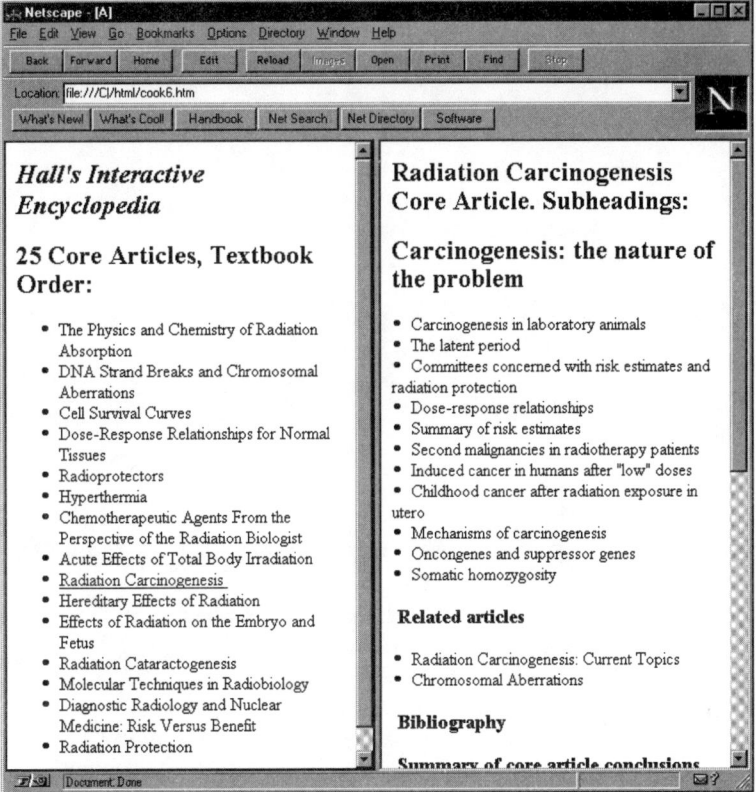

Fig. 9–3 A Simple Frame Environment

Note:

- There is no text displayed in the layout document, but rather hyperlinks to two content files (*fig1.htm* and *part2.htm*).
- The content files are displayed in two columns and each has a name reference ("left" and "right" in this example). The names become important when we wish to create interrelationships between frames. For example, clicking on a link in one frame updating the other frame.
- The frames are introduced with the <FRAMESET> ... </FRAMESET> tags, which replace the <BODY> ... </BODY> tags of content documents.
- The COLS=*,* attribute of the <FRAMESET> tag will be explained subsequently.

It is possible to nest frames either directly or indirectly. Here is an example of direct nesting.

```
<HTML>
<HEAD>
<TITLE>An Example of Direct Nesting</TITLE>
</HEAD>
<FRAMESET COLS=*,*>
     <FRAME SRC=fig1.htm NAME=left>
         <FRAMESET ROWS=*,*>
         <FRAME SRC=part2.htm NAME=right_top>
         <FRAME SRC=part3.htm NAME=right_bottom>
         </FRAMESET>
</FRAMESET>
</HTML>
```

with the result in Figure 9–4.

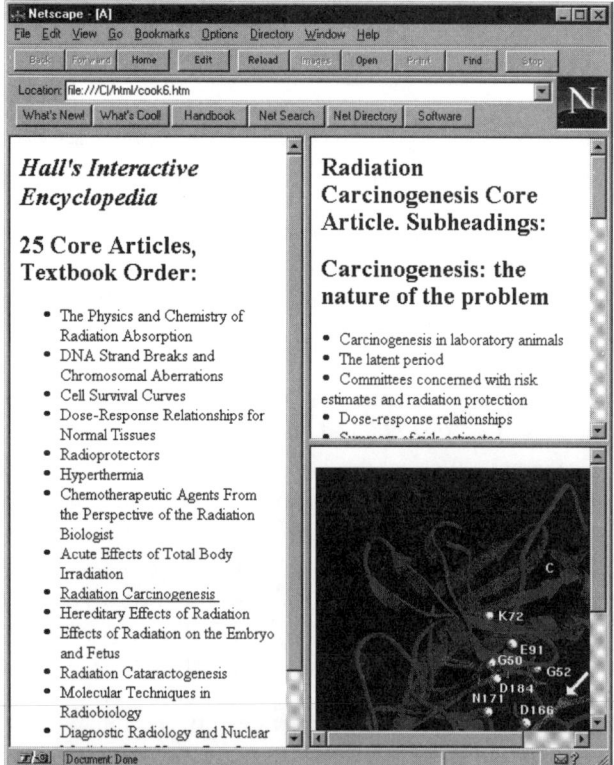

Fig. 9–4   Direct Nested Frames

A possible disadvantage of this approach is that since the addressing is done at the frame level, you lose the ability to jointly address both the frames in the right column. For example, by clicking on an item in the left-hand frame, you may wish to update both right-hand frames. Indirect addressing solves this problem by making the SRC of a frame actually a layout rather than a content file.

```
<HTML>
<HEAD>
<TITLE>An Example of Indirect Nesting</TITLE>
</HEAD>
<FRAMESET COLS=*,*>
      <FRAME SRC=fig1.htm NAME=left>
          <FRAMESET ROWS=*,*>
          <FRAME SRC=part2-3.htm NAME=right>
          </FRAMESET>
</FRAMESET>
</HTML>
```

where the file *part2-3.htm* looks like

```
<HTML>
<HEAD>
<TITLE>A Layout as Part of Indirect
Nesting</TITLE>
</HEAD>
      <FRAMESET ROWS=*,*>
      <FRAME SRC=part2.htm NAME=right_top>
      <FRAME src=part3.htm NAME=right_bottom>
      </FRAMESET>
</HTML>
```

To simplify the discussion, let us go back to our original two-frame Web page and explore the interrelationships that you can create between frames. In Figure 9–3 we have a table of contents in the left frame and the article selected in the right frame. When we selected "Radiation Carcinogenesis" from the table of contents, how did the browser know to update only the right frame and display the article?

Without frames, clicking on a hyperlink in, for example, a table of contents, will refresh the whole Web browser window with the new URL. Now we are faced with updating only part of the browser window defined by the NAME attribute of the <FRAME> tag. To address this, NAME requires an extension to the HTML hyperlink syntax of the form

```
<A HREF=documentURL TARGET=targetname>Hyperlink
Text</A>
```

We have introduced the concept of a hyperlink target, which in our example will appear as

```
<A HREF="./part2.htm" TARGET=right>Radiation
Carcinogenesis</A>
```

This is an example of an explicit target. The URL references "right" an explicit frame name that we have defined. It is also possible to use implicit (i.e., predefined) frame names having a specific relationship to the frame containing the hyperlink. Here are some examples of implicit frame names, which begin with a leading underscore (_).

- *_self*—Directs the browser to update the frame in which the link is located. This is the default target if no target is specified.
- *_parent*—Directs the browser to update the parent frame if the frame containing the hyperlink is a child frame, otherwise has the same effect as *_self*. Parent and child are defined by the nesting relationship between frames.
- *_top*—Directs the browser to update the entire window, regardless of the current frame layout.
- *_blank*—Creates a completely new browser window.

The last example is noteworthy, since it does not reference a frame in the existing window, but creates a new instance of the complete browser (referred to as a new window) and displays the contents of the hyperlink. For example,

```
<HTML>
<HEAD>
<TITLE>An Example of Generating a New Window</TITLE>
</HEAD>
<A HREF = "./part2.htm" TARGET = _blank>part 2 </A>
</HTML>
```

displays the contents of *part2.htm* in a new copy of the browser. Cloning new browsers in this way should be used judiciously. It is not always obvious to the user that this has happened, since browser windows may lie one on top of the other, and each new browser window expends a significant amount of client resources, notably memory.

9.2.1 Examples ☞

The best way to learn how frames are utilized is to view the source of the layout files and their associated content files for examples that use frames well. Some good examples can be found in Table 9–3.

TABLE 9–3   Examples of Using HTML Frames

Location	Description
http://home.mcom.com/comprod/-products/navigator/version_2.0/-frames/eye/index.html	A tutorial on vision.
http://www.spunwebs.com/sites2c/-fotoalbum.html	The Ava Gardner Photograph Collection.
http://www.netscape.com/comprod/-products/navigator/version_2.0/-frames/frame_users.html	A large list of sites that use frames supplied by Netscape Inc.

A question you should be asking yourself at this point is, *how do I control the size and characteristics of a frame?* To begin to answer this question you need to understand the COLS and ROWS attributes of the <FRAMESET> … </FRAMESET> tags. In our examples so far we have used:

<FRAMESET COLS = *,*> and <FRAMESET ROWS = *,*>

The "*,*" value autosizes the frames in a useful way. The window will be divided equally into two frames (Figure 9–3) with identical size and characteristics. If we use COLS= *,* it will be two equal columns and if we use ROWS = *,* it will be two equal rows. In Figure 9–4 we nested the frames so that the right hand column was, by default, further subdivided into two frames of equal size.

To specify the dimensions of each frame you can specify them in pixels (absolute measure) or percentages (relative measure). Whether you use percentages or pixels (or both) depends on what you wish to take place when the reader resizes the Web browser window. Percentages are useful when you wish to expand or contract frames equally, relative to each other; pixels are useful when you wish to specify the absolute size of frames. An absolute or relative value is given as "horizontal, vertical". Consider an example similar to that used for the tutorial on vision, for which the URL was given above. That example has a frame layout similar to the following.

```
<HTML>
<HEAD>
<TITLE>A Common and Useful Type of Frame
     Layout</TITLE>
</HEAD>
<FRAMESET ROWS="70,*">
     <FRAME SRC = "./header.htm" MARGINHEIGHT=0
     MARGINWIDTH=0
     NAME = "header" SCROLLING = "no" NORESIZE>
```

```
      <FRAMESET COLS="373,*">
      <FRAME SRC = "./image.htm" MARGINHEIGHT=0
       MARGINWIDTH=0 NAME = "image"
       SCROLLING = "no" NORESIZE>

      <FRAME SRC = "./info.htm" NAME =
       "information" >
      </FRAMESET>
</FRAMESET>

<NOFRAME>
This page requires Netscape 2.0 or later
</NOFRAME>
</HTML>
```

It produces the Web page shown in Figure 9–5.
Note the following:

- The window is divided into 2 rows, with the second row divided into two
  columns (defined by the FRAMESET nesting).
- At the top we have a header frame, which is the width of the browser window
  and is 70 pixels long (rows). There is no margin (white space) reserved around
  this frame (defined by MARGINHEIGHT and MARGINWIDTH). The frame

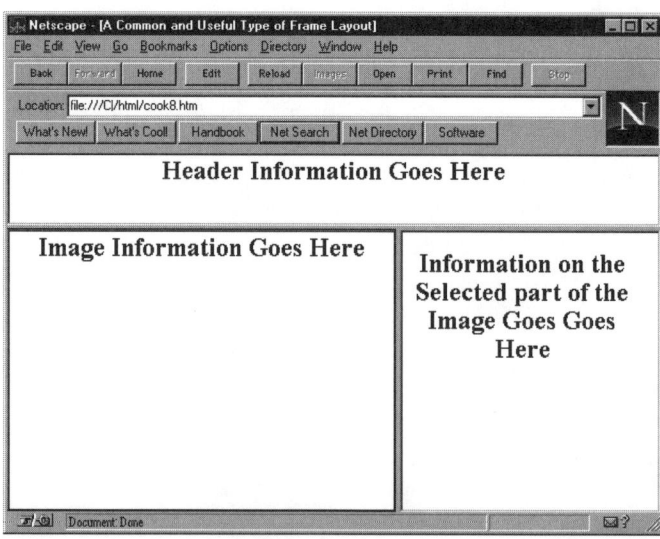

Fig. 9–5   Frame Sizing

will not have scroll bars (SCROLLING = "no") and cannot be resized (NORE-SIZE). If the window is resized below 70 pixels in height, the contents will simply be truncated and a scroll bar will not appear. This is an ideal frame environment for a banner (header message) for a particular Web page that is not going to change, irrespective of the contents of the other frames.

- Under this header frame are two columns for the image frame and the information frame. The image frame is fixed at a width of 373 pixels (COLS="373,*"), whereas the information frame will take up the remains of the browser window width.

- Pixel and percentages could be mixed (not shown), for example, COLS="373,*,40%" would represent 3 columns where the first is 373 pixels wide, the last is 40% of the overall window width and the middle column takes up the remainder (if there is any). The question then arises as to what happens when 373 pixels is greater than 60% of the window width. The answer is, try it and find out! A good habit to adopt for all Web pages prior to making them available on the Internet.

- The <NOFRAME> ... </NOFRAME> tags delimit what will happen if a Web browser that does not support frames is used to display the HTML, assuming it can at least recognize the <NOFRAME> ... </NOFRAME> tags. In the example above, a simple message is displayed to tell the user they need a frames capable browser to view the page.

9.2.2 Online Tutorials ☞

If you need further information on using frames, some good sources are given in Table 9–4.

TABLE 9–4   Online Tutorials for Using HTML Frames

Location	Description
http://sharky.nomius.com/frames/menu.htm	Step by step introduction, including Frequently Asked Questions (FAQs).
http://www.spunwebs.com/sites2c/-frmtutor.html	Another step by step introduction.

9.3. SERVER SIDE INCLUDES ☞

An example of where you might use a server side include was given in Section 8.2.7 where we defined a menu bar as a navigation tool. Simply stated, the *main use* of server side includes is any situation where you have the same information that you wish displayed on multiple Web pages. Server side includes are particularly useful when that same information is going to change frequently. Thus, server side includes save you the labor of editing each page to make the same changes. You keep that information in a separate file, make the change to that one file and have the multiple pages *include* (read) that file when they are served by the Web server. If you are familiar with the use of #include statements in one or more programming languages, the idea is the same. So, in our example (Section 8.2.7), by keeping the menu bar in a separate file we can update it, adding or deleting options and immediately see those change on all the Web pages that include the menu bar.

There are negative aspects to using server side includes, notably, performance and security. Performance is an issue since you are not just sending some HTML to a client but building that HTML on the fly, or, as we shall see, actually executing commands on the server. Security is an issue since the client has access to these server commands.

While the principle is the same, what you need to do to invoke server side includes differs from one Web server to another. The description given here is for NCSA's httpd Web server.

An important point to note is what happens when you "view source" in a Web browser that has read a Web page with a server side include. *What you see is the page after the include. There is no indication that the contents came from a separate file that was included with a server side include.*

Notice that I said earlier that the "main use" of server side includes is for including the same information on multiple Web pages. There are other uses. All involve the server performing some action and including the results of that action in the Web page sent to the client. We begin our discussion by examining how to include a file.

To allow server side includes in NCSA's httpd:

1. Edit the file *ServerRoot/conf/srm.conf* and uncomment the line:

   #AddType text/x-server-parsed-html .shtml

   This line indicates that all files with the *.shtml* file extension are server side includes. *This is the recognized file extension for server side includes, and I suggest you use it.* If you have forgotten, or did not read Chapter Seven on installing a server, *ServerRoot* is the top level directory containing the server software.

2. Edit the file *ServerRoot/conf/access.conf* and specify any directory trees (the specific directory and any subdirectories) that are authorized to use server side include files. By default, the *DocumentRoot* and the *ServerRoot* directories are already specified. For each directory tree specified there are two possible levels of access: Read or Read and Execute. *For security reasons it is unwise to have a large number of directories capable of including files since, as we shall see, these directories can also contain programs that can potentially be executed through a Web browser.*

Here is what to look for and change in the file *access.conf.* I have annotated this file to better explain the options.

```
# A section of the ServerRoot/conf/access.conf file.
# See http://www.oac.uci.edu/X/W6/httpd-
# howto/access.conf.a.html for further details.
# Here is the default location of executables allowed
# by the server
<Directory /usr/ncsa/cgi-bin>
Options Indexes FollowSymLinks Includes
</Directory>

# Here is the DocumentRoot for this server

<Directory /usr/htdocs>

# This may also be "None", "All", or any combination of
# "Indexes", "Includes", or "FollowSymLinks"
Options Indexes FollowSymLinks IncludesNoExec
</Directory>
```

In the above example, changes to the file *ServerRoot/conf/access.conf* are shown in bold. The *cgi-bin* directory (Chapter Ten) and any subdirectories can use include files, either reading them or executing them. The document root and any subdirectories can read them but not execute them (*IncludesNoExec*). These are the recommended settings.

3. Create the HTML file with the server side include. Here is a simple example.

```
<HTML>
<HEAD>
<TITLE>An example of a Server Side Include</TITLE>
</HEAD>
<BODY>
<!-- Include a menu bar -->
<!--#INCLUDE FILE = "./includes/menubar.shtml" -->
</BODY>
</HTML>
```

The <!--#INCLUDE ...> tag introduces the HTML syntax to invoke a server side include. Attributes may be FILE (as shown), which includes a file specification relative to the original document, or VIRTUAL, which specifies a file relative to the document root.

9.3.1 Other Types of Server Side Includes

The <!--#INCLUDE ...> HTML tag I introduced above is only one of a number of commands that can be used to invoke server side actions. Table 9–5 has the complete list of commands for the NCSA httpd server.

The following are examples of how you might use each of these server side commands.

```
<HTML>
<HEAD>
<TITLE>An example of a Server Side Include</TITLE>
</HEAD>
<BODY>
...
<!-- Include the date modified -->
<I>Last Modified by Phil Bourne on
<!--#ECHO VAR="LAST_MODIFIED"--></I>
</BODY>
</HTML>
```

In this example the modification date of the file is determined from the file header itself. You do not have to be bothered with remembering to change this date each time you modify an HTML document. Including the date of modification is a powerful way of informing the reader of how current, or alternatively how seminal, is the information on the Web page. The LAST_MODIFIED variable is just one of several variables that can be used with the ECHO command. Table 9-6 lists all the variables that can be used with the ECHO command. ECHO and its associated variables is supported by most Web servers.

TABLE 9–5 Server Side Commands for the NCSA httpd Web Server

Command	Description
ECHO	Insert the value of one or more variables.
INCLUDE	Insert the text of a document.
FSIZE	Insert the size of the specified file.
FLASTMOD	Insert the last modification date of the specified file.
EXEC	Insert the output of a cgi-script or shell command.
CONFIG	Control features of server side include processing.

TABLE 9–6   Variables Associated with the ECHO Command

Variable	Description
DOCUMENT_NAME	The current filename.
DOCUMENT_URI	The virtual path to the file.
QUERY_STRING_UNESCAPED	The unescaped version of any search query the client sent, with all shell-special characters escaped with \.
DATE_LOCAL	The current date and time in the local time zone.
DATE_GMT	Current Greenwich Mean Time.
LAST_MODIFIED	The date the current file was last modified.

Here is an example using the commands FLASTMOD and FSIZE.

```
<HTML>
<HEAD>
<TITLE>An example of a Server Side Include</TITLE>
</HEAD>
<BODY>
...
<!-- Use of FSIZE and FLASTMOD -->
The file you are about to download is
<!--#FSIZE FILE="myfile.html" --> byes in length
and was last modified on
<!--#FLASTMOD FILE="myfile.html" -->
</BODY>
</HTML>
```

The commands FLASTMOD (an alternative to ECHO VAR="LAST_MODIFIED") and FSIZE are useful to readers of the Web page, since they automatically indicate the size and age of a file that the reader may be about to download. Important information if the reader has a slow Internet connection, or is looking to update a version of a file they already have.

Here is an example that causes the execution of a specific command on the server. *This should be used with caution for security reasons.* It would not be wise, for example, to execute code provided by a client user, unless you were positive that this code would not have any undesirable effects.

```
<HTML>
<HEAD>
<TITLE>An example of a Server Side Include</TITLE>
```

```
</HEAD>
<BODY>
...
<!-- Use of EXEC to return the results of the w
     command -->
The current load on this server is:
<!--#EXEC CMD="/usr/bin/w" -->
</BODY>
</HTML>
```

The EXEC command can have either a CMD (command) or CGI (cgi-script) attribute. In invoking a cgi-script the results of that invocation are returned, and, as we shall see in Chapter Ten, this is usually in the form of HTML, which gets displayed by the Web browser. The results of a command are returned as they would appear when invoked from the UNIX command line.

Finally, the CONFIG command effects the behavior of some of the above commands. CONFIG can have one of several attributes (Table 9–7).

ERRMSG will be sent to the user if one of the server side include commands fails. Examples include failure to find an include file, failure of a script executed with the EXEC command, and file protections that prevent files from being served. Example,

<!--#CONFIG ERRMSG="There was a server side include error">

SIZEFMT controls how a file size defined by FSIZE and ECHO will be displayed: "bytes" provides the size in bytes; "abbrev" displays the size rounded to the nearest megabyte or kilobyte, depending on the size of the file.

TIMEFMT controls how a date and time are displayed for the FLASTMOD and ECHO commands. TIMEFMT uses the syntax of the *strftime()* UNIX system call, which is:

"%d.%m.%y %H:%M:%S"	4.10.96 17:21:00
"%a. %b. %d, %Y %I:%M %p"	Wed. Apr. 10, 1996 5:21 PM
"%m/%d/%y %I:%M %p"	4/10/96 5:21 PM

TABLE 9–7   Variables Associated with the CONFIG Command

Parameter	Description
ERRMSG	Display an error message, which you define, and which is displayed if the server side event produces an error.
SIZEFMT	Control the format of the file size specification.
TIMEFMT	Control the format of the time format specification.

See the UNIX man page for **strftime** for further details. Here is an example of how to use these formatting options.

```
<HTML>
<HEAD>
<TITLE>An example of a Server Side Include
with a #CONFIG directive</TITLE>
</HEAD>
<BODY>
...
<!-- Use of FSIZE and FLASTMOD with CONFIG➔
The file you are about to download is
<!--#CONFIG SIZEFMT="abbrev">
<!--#CONFIG TIMEFMT="%m/%d/%y %I:%M %p">
<!--#FSIZE FILE="myfile.html" --> in size and
was last modified on
<!--#FLASTMOD FILE="myfile.html" -->
</BODY>
</HTML>
```

9.3.2 Online Tutorials ☞

Table 9–8 has pointers to online tutorials for learning about server side includes.

TABLE 9–8   Online Tutorials for Using Server Side Includes

Location	Description
http://hoohoo.ncsa.uiuc.edu/docs/-tutorials/includes.html	Tutorial for NCSA httpd.
http://media.ucsc.edu/docs/parse.html	Tutorial for wn.
http://www.w3.org/hypertext/WWW/-Daemon/User/CGI/Overview.html	Tutorial for the CERN server.
http://www.theworld.com/ssi/ssiplus.htm	Basics of server side includes and a comparison to using the Common Gateway Interface (CGI).

9.4. CLICKABLE MAPS

A clickable map is a visual navigation tool that can be used to great effect. Before you go crazy with clickable maps, however, remember they are based on images that take time to download, and they are of no use to someone who is using a text-only browser. If you

TABLE 9–9   Good Examples of Using Clickable Maps

Location	Description
http://pubweb.parc.xerox.com/map	Xerox Parc map viewer.
http://www.sgi.com/	Silicon Graphics Inc. home page.
http://home.mcom.com/comprod/-products/navigator/version_2.0/-frames/eye/index.html	The previously reviewed (in the context of frames) page on the human eye.
http://www.duke.edu/~mccann/clickexa.htm	Traffic reports for San Diego.
http://www.duke.edu/~mccann/clickexa.htm	A pointer to a collection of clickable maps.

want some good examples of what can be achieved with clickable maps, refer to the pointers given in Table 9–9.

Tools for helping you make clickable maps are described at the end of this section. Whether you are using a tool or making the clickable map manually, it pays to understand the basic principles. Here is the basic recipe for making a clickable map.

1. Select an image in the form of a GIF file that readers will click on.
2. Define the regions of the image that will map to the various URLs. Regions can be circles, rectangles, and a variety of other polygons.
3. Place this coordinate reference to URL mapping information in the *imagemap* file.
4. Register the *imagemap* file with the Web server. How you do this is server dependent.
5. Create the HTML documents defined in the *imagemap* file if they do not already exist. That is, make sure there are Web pages to go to when clicking on different parts of the map.
6. Create the HTML document that will contain the inline image of the clickable map.
7. Distinguish the inlined image in the HTML document by: (i) making it the anchor tag to the server's imagemap program; (ii) giving the anchor tag an additional ISMAP attribute.
8. Check each link in the map to make sure it works as expected.

Here is a specific example using NCSA's httpd Web server. It is a map of the United States; when I click on various regions, I get a list of job vacancies in that region. The job vacancy information is actually solicited through a Web form, and we will see how to do that in the next chapter. For now, worry about how to display information when a region of the map is selected.

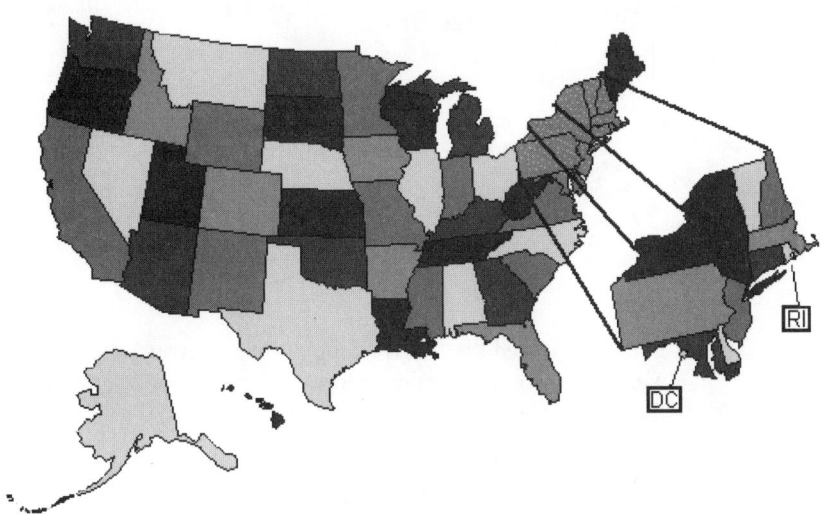

Fig. 9–6   An Example of a Clickable Map

1. The GIF file is shown in Figure 9–6 and can be found at

   http://www.sdsc.edu/CompSci/Xtal/images/states.gif

2. I use *xv* (Section 3.4.2) to divide the map into three rectangles for west, central and east (Figure 9–7). Holding the middle mouse button down in *xv* provides the positional information for the cursor in pixels, as specified below.

3. I then create the image map file which I call *us.map*. This file contains the following.

```
# Imagemap file for the US example:
default http://www.sdsc.edu/CompSci/Xtal/ACA/Jobs/error.html
rect http://www.sdsc.edu/CompSci/Xtal/ACA/Jobs/pacific.html 0,0 120,300
rect http://www.sdsc.edu/CompSci/Xtal/ACA/Jobs/central.html 120,0 275,300
rect http://www.sdsc.edu/CompSci/Xtal/ACA/Jobs/east.html 275,0 500,300
```

Note that in this file:

• Comments begin with a # and end with a line break.

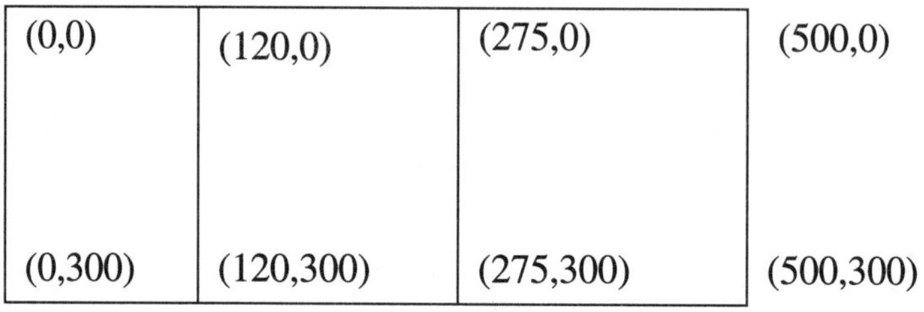

(0,0)	(120,0)	(275,0)	(500,0)
(0,300)	(120,300)	(275,300)	(500,300)

Fig. 9–7   Coordinates for a Clickable Map

- I have only used the rect (rectangle) shape. As such, I specify the coordinates in the top left corner followed by the bottom right. I could have specified other shapes as follows:

  circle URL {center} ,{point on circumference}

  polygon URL {point1}, … {pointn}

  For the circle I define the coordinates of the center and a point on the circumference. For a polygon with an arbitrary number of sides I define the coordinates of the apices. Thus, a triangle would be defined by three points.

- The default specification defines a URL if I click on a region of the GIF file not specifically defined.

4. I register the map file with the server by creating the file *ServerRoot/conf/imagemap.conf* and adding the following:

```
# Web Server image file (NCSA httpd format)
# Format:
# symbolic name: absolute map file name

acamap: /var/spool/gn/CompSci/Xtal/ACA/Jobs/us.map
```

5. I create the HTML document that contains the clickable map.

```
<HTML>
<HEAD>
<TITLE>Select Jobs by Geographic Area</TITLE>
</HEAD>
<BODY>
<P ALIGN=center>
<H1>Select Jobs by Geographic Area</H1>
```

```
<I>Click on the region of interest</I>

<P ALIGN=center>
<A HREF="http://www.sdsc.edu/cgi-bin/imagemap/acamap">
<IMG SRC="http://www.sdsc.edu/CompSci/Xtal/images/states.gif"
    ISMAP></A>
</BODY>
</HTML>
```

Note:

- The first hypertext reference (HREF) points to the location of the *imagemap* program, which is usually in the directory *ServerRoot/cgi-bin/imagemap*. The URL is completed by the symbolic name we gave to the map in the *imagemap.conf* file.

- The anchor text is the inlined image of the map with the ISMAP attribute added.

6. I create the files *pacific.html*, *central.html*, and *east.html* which get served when the reader clicks on the appropriate region of the map.

7. I test to see whether all this works!

9.4.1 Online Tutorials ☞

Additional information on setting up image maps can be found at the locations given in Table 9–10.

9.4.2 Clickable Map Editing Tools

Editors are available to help you in preparing clickable maps. A clickable map editor is often included as part of an HTML editor (Section 8.3). However, for UNIX systems the most popular and comprehensive map editing tool is *Mapedit*.

TABLE 9–10   Tutorials on Server Side Clickable Maps

Location	Description
http://hoohoo.ncsa.uiuc.edu/docs/-tutorials/imagemapping.html	Tutorial for NCSA's httpd server.
http://www.spyglass.com/techspec/-img_maps.html	A tutorial by Spygalss Inc.
http://media.ucsc.edu/docs/click.html	Tutorial for the wn server.
http://www.w3.org/pub/WWW/-Daemon/User/CGI/HTImageDoc.html	Tutorial for the Cern server.

9.4.2.1 Mapedit Software Snapshot ☞

TABLE 9–11 Mapedit Software Snapshot

Location	*http://www.boutell.com/mapedit/*
Binaries	Linux, Solaris, SunOS, DEC UNIX
Source	Yes
Bugs	*mapedit@boutell.com*

Mapedit is fully documented and requires no further explanation here.

9.4.3 Client Side Clickable Maps

Note that everything I have discussed to date on clickable maps refers to server side click-able maps—the map specification requires a map description file be resident on the serv-er. Newer browsers support what are termed client side image maps where the map description is downloaded as part of the Web page. Client side image maps have the fol-lowing advantages.

- They may be used with local files, i.e., there is no necessity for using the http protocol.
- There is no need to have a server transaction to resolve a map reference. That is, clicking on the map can be resolved on the client without reference back to the server, thereby improving performance.
- There is visual feedback. That is, when the user moves the cursor over a region of the map, there is an indication of the URL that they will visit should they click on that region. This does not happen with server side image maps since that information is on the server only.

Here is a simple example of selecting pages using a menu bar.

```
<MAP NAME="buttonbar">
<AREA SHAPE="RECT" COORDS="10,10,49,49"
HREF="about_us.html">
<AREA SHAPE="RECT" COORDS="60,10,99,49"
HREF="products.html">
<AREA SHAPE="RECT" COORDS="110,10,149,49"
HREF="index.html">
<AREA SHAPE="RECT" COORDS="0,0,159,59" NOHREF>
</MAP>
<IMG SRC="../images/tech/bar.gif" USEMAP="#buttonbar">
```

Note the following:

- The <MAP> ... </MAP> HTML tag delimits the specifications of the clickable map. The NAME attribute is used to identify the specific map.
- The <AREA ...> HTML tag defines the regions of the map in the same way they were defined for a server side clickable map.
- The USEMAP attribute of the <IMG ...> HTML tag associates a map with a specific image.

This will only work if the Web browser you are using supports client side clickable images. A foolproof method for having a map recognized is to specify it both as a client and server side map.

```
<A HREF="/cgi-bin/imagemap/pic2"> <IMG
SRC="../images/tech/pic2.gif"
USEMAP="maps.html#map2" ISMAP></A>
```

That is, it is okay to use the ISMAP and USEMAP attributes of the <IMG ...> HTML tag together. Table 9–12 has pointers to further information on client side clickable maps.

At this point you should be able to provide a comprehensive and useful set of Web pages that can be *browsed*. We can now move on to the next step beyond browsing of information, which is to allow the user to interact with your Web server. In the next chapter we begin to explore how the client user can solicit specific responses from your server by way of a Web form.

TABLE 9–12   Tutorials on Client Side Clickable Maps

Location	Description
http://www.iwaynet.net/~rtyler/- htmltutorial/imagemaps.html	A concise introduction on which the material given in this book is based.
http://www.dallas.net/~jwill/html/- appenda.html	A more detailed description, including itself as a good example.
http://www.hway.net/ihip/cside.html	Another concise description, including pointers to what browsers support client side clickable maps.

10

Web Input Processing

Ingredients:

- *A Web form through which the user can provide input*
- *The Common gateway Interface (CGI) for processing that input on the server*
- *Returning output to the client Web user*

Many people are satisfied after the main course and rarely eat desserts. For others, no meal is complete without a dessert. Here we learn how to make your basic dessert.

10.1. INTRODUCTION

Thus far, our discussion of serving information via the Web has been "passive"—simple requests for information that the client user reads and subsequently navigates by way of a hypertext link to more information on the same or other servers. There is another very powerful aspect of Web technology that you will likely need to support—specific user input from the client and an appropriate response to that input by the server. I like to think that, from a user's perspective, this makes your information server an "active" as opposed to a simple passive provider of information.

On an active server, the same information is not served to everyone. What gets served is in response to specific input from the user. For example, you may use the server to collect information from Web users and see a simple customized acknowledgment based upon their input. Alternatively, the Web user could provide input to a program that gets executed on the server and the results of that program would be returned to the Web client browser for display. Finally, you might upload information to the server and see that information immediately made available to a worldwide audience. These are the three examples of the role of an active server that I will show you in this chapter. There are many other possible ways in which the active server could be used, but the principles are the same.

The support of input processing, i.e., an active server, can be thought of as a four-step process.

1. Provide a Web page that collects user input—a *Web form.*
2. Pass that input through a *Common Gateway Interface (CGI)* for processing.
3. Process the input with a program (called a *CGI program or CGI script*) that produces some form of output.
4. Return the results to the user as HTML, or graphics, or plain text, that can be displayed by the client browser.

This chapter discusses these four steps. I will give you the basic principles, followed by some examples that you can adapt to your own needs. The sophistication of the interaction between client and server depends, for the most part, on step 3, that is, the capabilities of the program processing the input from the Web form.

The majority of existing programs for processing Web forms input are written in Perl, an interpreted language. The major reasons for the use of Perl are:

- Perl is an interpreted and not a compiled language, which facilitates portability and ease of use.
- Perl works well with the UNIX shell, for example, in recognizing environment variables (also true of some compiled languages, e.g., C).
- Perl is available *free* for a wide variety of platforms (see Section 3.8 for where to get Perl and for further sources of information).
- Perl is a very good language for string manipulation.

This last point is important, since it is a text string that gets passed to the CGI program from the Web form. Given the popularity and above-mentioned advantages of Perl, I chose to use Perl for the CGI program examples given in this book. If you are more familiar with other languages, they can be used equally well once you have written (or obtained from elsewhere) the appropriate code to parse the input stream from the Web form.

The last consideration, before we get into the nitty-gritty of Web forms and input processing, is the notion of state. You will see the phrase "the Web is stateless" used in any detailed discussion of the World Wide Web. A Web server receives a request from a client and processes that request by returning a stream of HTML, which is interpreted by the client browser. Under normal circumstances the server does not "remember" which of the many clients requested which piece of information. When the same client makes a second request, the server does not recognize that client as one that made the previous request. This works okay for requesting Web pages of information where each request is independent and gets treated in *exactly* the same way. Stating this another way, there is no need for the server to know anything about the previous request, since each request is treated independently.

On the other hand, consider the implications of this stateless behavior when, for example, you are querying a database through a Web server. You pass the query to the server and results are returned. No problem here, but what if you wish to use those results in a subsequent query? With independent steps, all the needed information must be passed *back* to the server for the second query, since the server retains no results from the first query. This is inefficient in terms of the network bandwidth required, the load on the server, and the management of the information that needs to be sent back and forth between server and client with each incremental request.

It is more desirable to have the server store the results of the query and pass to the client only the subset of information needed to make a decision about whether a second query is needed. If needed, the query is performed on the data already stored on the server. However, since the server is stateless and many queries from various clients may be being made at the same time, how do you associate a set of query results with a particular client for subsequent access?

There are various tricks for making this association. All use the same basic idea—provide each client with a unique identifier so that it may be identified repeatedly by the server. On the first query, the results are stored on the server with a certain identifier. That identifier is then passed back to the client. A subsequent query passes both the new query information and the identifier back to the server so the correct information already resident on the server can be recognized and used. There is a security issue here, however. There is little to stop another client from gaining access to this information on the server if that client acquires the token. Nevertheless, this methodology works well if the security of the information being sent to the server is not a major concern.

I will point you to an example that uses this methodology and we will explore other more secure options that involve making a direct TCP/IP connection between client and server in Chapter Eleven. Meanwhile, let us start with the basics.

10.2. WEB FORMS ☞

If you have ever written a graphical user interface in X and Motif for a UNIX platform, you will appreciate the simplicity of writing a Web form in HTML. You may also appreciate that this same interface will run unchanged on a PC or Macintosh computer. While simple to write, the HTML form is limited in what can be represented, in comparison to an interface generated with a graphical user interface language and extensive widget library. However, like other features of the HTML standard (for example, tables and frames) the syntax to describe forms is evolving, and better interfaces for passing information to server programs for processing will be produced. As we shall see in Chapter Eleven, Java provides more detailed, computer-independent graphical user interfaces, but requires more programming effort.

Here is your recipe for building a Web form.

1. A form is defined using the same basic HTML constructs that we saw in Chapters Eight and Nine.
2. A form is delineated by <FORM ...> ... </FORM> HTML tags and associated attributes.
3. There are several HTML tags and associated attributes that you can use within a form to collect input. Each of these input collection types associates the input with a variable name that will be used for processing on the Web server. These input types are
   - a text box, which allows a single line of text
   - a text area, which allows multi-line text input
   - buttons of two types

     radio buttons, for selecting one of a number of options

     checkbox buttons, for selecting one or more of a number of options
   - pop-up menus, from which a single option is selected
   - scrollable lists, from which one or more options are selected
4. The contents of a form can be cleared (reset) with a reset button.
5. A form can be submitted to the server for processing from either
   - a submit button
   - a text box
   - a clickable image

We will see examples of all these features. For the impatient, a summary of the syntax for creating a Web form is given in Appendix B.

Here is a simple form to get us started. This is the form from which I solicit comments from readers of the page that was shown in Section 8.2.7.

```
<HTML>
<!-- A simple form to solicit input from "readers" -->
<HEAD>
<TITLE>Reader's Comments Form</TITLE>
</HEAD>
<BODY BACKGROUND="./images/bg.gif">
<CENTER>
<H2>Reader's Comments Form</H2>

<FORM METHOD = POST
 ACTION="http://www.sdsc.edu/CGI/CompSci/pb/comments.cgi">
```

```
<!-- Solicit input in the form of a table -->
<!-- The table provides better control over text box placement-->
<TABLE CELLPADDING = 5>
<TR ALIGN = LEFT VALIGN = TOP>
 <TD><B> Name:</B></TD>
 <!-- Associate input in this field with the variable called "name" -->
 <TD><INPUT NAME = "name"></TD>
</TR>
<TR ALIGN = LEFT VALIGN = TOP>
 <!-- Associate input in this field with a variable called "email" ->
 <TD><B> E-mail Address:</B></TD>
 <TD><INPUT NAME = "email"></TD>
</TR>
<TR ALIGN = LEFT VALIGN = TOP>
 <TD><B> Phone Number:</B></TD>
 <TD><INPUT NAME = "phone"></TD>
</TR>
<TR ALIGN = LEFT VALIGN = TOP>
 <TD><B> Comments:</B></TD>
 <!-- Associate anything entered in this text box to a variable called
 "comments" -->
 <!-- Define a text area of 7 rows and 60 columns in which to enter
 comments -->
 <TD><TEXTAREA NAME = "comments" ROWS = 7
   COLS = 60></TEXTAREA></TD>
</TR>
</TABLE>

<!-- Define the buttons to either submit the form for processing
            or clear the form -->
<INPUT TYPE="SUBMIT" VALUE = "Submit Comments">
<INPUT TYPE="RESET" VALUE = "Reset Form">

</CENTER>
</BODY>
</HTML>
```

Figure 10–1 illustrates this page when viewed through a Netscape Web browser.

To make this example more interesting, I have embedded this form in a table to reinforce what we learned about tables in Section 9.1 and to illustrate the use of tables as a formatting feature as well as a data representation feature. The <TD> .. </TD> (table data) tags to define a cell in a table are used here, not to contain plain text, but to contain a text box from which, as we will see below, information will subsequently be passed

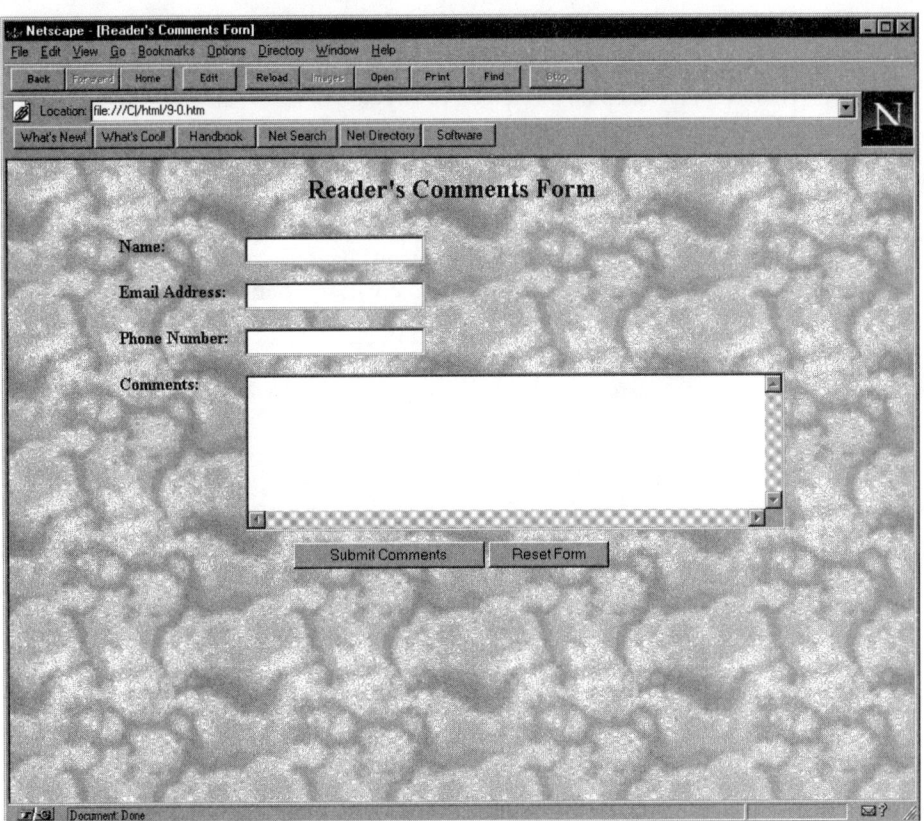

Fig. 10–1   A Simple Web Form—The Comments Page

to a processing program on the server. Embedding the various forms options in a table gives you greater flexibility over the exact placement of forms features. The result is to left justify and vertically align the names of the forms fields (Name, Email Address, Phone Number, Comments) as the first column and the text entry fields as the second column. For example

```
<TD><INPUT NAME = "name"></TD>
```

defines a cell in the table through the use of the <TD> ... </TD> (table data) HTML tags. Recall that the sizes of table cells scale automatically based on the information they contain, but that this may be overridden with specific tags. Automatic scaling is what happens here based on the INPUT tag with the NAME attribute. The INPUT tag defines a text box with a default size (since no SIZE attribute is specified) of 20 characters. Hence, the table cell is set to a width of 20 characters. If more than 20 characters are entered, the text will scroll from right to left as defined by the text box. The full text string is retained, but only 20 characters are seen on the screen at any one time. Whatever the user types in that text box is associated with a variable name called "name" and passed to the server for processing. There are three such text boxes in this form (Figure 8–1), all of which align nicely thanks to the use of the HTML <TABLE> tag.

I also define a table cell that is actually a text area of 7 rows, with each row having 60 columns. This is to contain the comments made by the reader. Comments are passed to the server having been associated with the variable name "comments."

```
<TD><TEXTAREA NAME = "comments" ROWS = 7
COLS = 60></TEXTAREA></TD>
```

The user of the form is not limited to making a comment of 7 lines with a maximum of 60 characters per line. The 420 characters are simply the part of an arbitrarily long comment that will be seen on the form at any one time. Vertical and horizontal scroll bars will automatically be added if the user enters text beyond 7 lines or 60 characters per line, respectively.

At the bottom of the form is the option to either submit the form for processing, or clear it and start again.

```
<INPUT TYPE="SUBMIT" VALUE = "Submit Comments">
<INPUT TYPE="RESET" VALUE = "Reset Form">
```

The TYPE attributes to the <INPUT ... > HTML tag define the type of input and the VALUE attributes define what text appears in the button. Since we are all human and prone to screw up it makes sense to *always* include a TYPE="RESET" button since this resets the form with empty or (as we shall see) default values.

The remaining and most crucial question regarding Web forms is, "what happens when I submit the form?" This is where the one remaining unexplained line in our form comes in. I refer to

```
<FORM METHOD = POST
    ACTION="http://www.sdsc.edu/CGI/CompSci/pb/comments.cgi">
```

There are three components to this HTML <FORM ... > tag.

• <FORM ...> introduces the form and has an associated </FORM> to indicate the end of the form

TABLE 10–1   Tutorials for Writing Web Forms

Location	Description
http://robot0.ge.uiuc.edu/-~carlosp/cs317/cft.html	Interactive forms tutorial.
http://www.soton.ac.uk/devpages/-forms/pf_t1.html	Forms tutorial from Europe.
http://www.ncsa.uiuc.edu/SDG/-Software/Mosaic/Docs/-fill-out-forms/overview.html	Good tutorial from the folks at NCSA.
http://www.w3.org/hypertext/WWW/-MarkUp/html3/forms.html	Forms syntax supported in the HTML 3.0 specification.

- < ... METHOD = POST ... >, the FORM attribute that defines how the form will be processed by the server
- <... ACTION="http://www.sdsc.edu/CGI/CompSci/pb/comments.cgi"> the FORM attribute that defines a URL which is actually a program on the Web server that processes the form

The file extension *cgi* is the clue to the role of *comments.cgi* and stands for *common gateway interface*. I will show you how the CGI works and then we will come back to some examples on designing more complicated forms.

10.2.1 Online Tutorial ☞

Appendix B has a summary of HTML forms syntax; Table 10–1 contains pointers to online tutorials covering Web forms.

10.3. THE COMMON GATEWAY INTERFACE ☞

The Common Gateway Interface (CGI) is a feature of the Web server distinct from Web forms. Forms happen to be the most convenient way of getting information from the Web client to a CGI script or program using the http protocol. Chapter Eleven introduces other methods of client server exchange.

The CGI takes care of steps 2 through 4 from our introduction to Web input processing. That is, it executes the program indicated by the Web form, using as input arguments the values from the Web form passed with the URL from client to server. Typically, this will generate some output (text and graphics), which is passed back to the client browser for display.

How does the Web server know this is a script or program to be executed and not just a request for some HTML to be served? The file type *.cgi* provides the distinction—

files with this extension are referred to as *CGI scripts* or CGI programs. Whether execution of the CGI script on the server is permitted depends on how you configured the Web server (e.g., Section 7.4 and 7.5). The two usual scenarios are:

1. Any file with an extension of *.cgi* located below *DocumentRoot* in the directory hierarchy can be executed.
2. The file must be resident in the *DocumentRoot/cgi-bin* directory distributed with all Web servers.

Debugging of CGI scripts is done in one of two ways. Either you can run them standalone by passing the script the argument it would normally get from the Web form, or you can run the application through the client Web browser since, like standard output, standard error is passed back to the client through the CGI (this is dependent on the particular Web server and how that server is configured).

Here is a detailed sequence of events for what happens when a CGI script or program is invoked.

*   When you hit the "submit" button on a Web form, a text string containing all input to the form is passed to the URL specified in the form by the ACTION attribute of the FORM tag.
*   Specifically, the text string is attached to the URL to form a single string. The text string and URL are separated by a question mark (?).
*   The overall format of this text string depends on the METHOD attribute of the FORM tag. Currently, one of two METHOD attributes may be specified, POST or GET. The GET method operates like any request for a URL from the server, except that the URL has added variables that are used by the script. The POST method opens up a separate channel of communication.
*   GET passes a text string to the CGI, whereupon the server equates it with the UNIX environment variable *QUERY_STRING* and the *REQUEST_METHOD* environment variable is set to GET.
*   The *QUERY_STRING* defined by the GET method is of limited size (256 characters in most UNIX implementations) and is not suitable for large amounts of input. For example, our reader's comment form including name, email address, and comment, would easily exceed 256 characters.
*   The POST option solves the text string size limit since it processes the whole input stream as standard input and there is, therefore, no limitation on its size. In using the POST option the UNIX environment variable *REQUEST_METHOD* is set to POST and *QUERY_STRING* is set to null. Further, the UNIX environment variable CONTENT_LENGTH defines the length, in bytes, of the query string.
*   Regardless of whether the POST or GET method is used, the information will have a well-characterized format in which all the variables being passed to the

CGI script are attached to the URL. As a Web client user you will have most likely seen these strings in the "Location" field of your Web browser. The particulars of the typical formats that you may have seen are described below.

- When the text string gets to the server, what happens next is a function of your program, as we shall see below.

Here are typical formats for the text string passed to the CGI program or script. What gets passed depends on whether you are using the GET or POST methods, and whether you are using named parameters (i.e., name-value pairs), as we did in the one example of a form we have seen so far.

```
Keyword List (escaped)        HREF="/cgi-bin/script_name?John%20Smith"
GET method, unnamed
parameter

Keyword List (delimited)      HREF="/cgi-bin/script_name?John+Smith+Jr"
GET method,
unnamed parameter

Named Parameter List          HREF="/cgi-bin/script_name?first_name-
POST method, named            =John&last_name=Smith&title=-
parameter                     Assistant%20Professor"
```

Keyword List (escaped)—The text string is of the form: HREF="/cgi-bin/script_name?John%20Smith" The ? separates the script name (the program used to process the input stream) from the variable information. Thus, I am passing the words "John Smith" to *script_name* on the server for processing. Then *script_name* could, for example, trigger a database lookup for the name John Smith. Spaces, tabs, carriage returns, etc., are examples of special characters and if they are to be taken as literal text they must be represented correctly when passed to the CGI script or program. That is, they must be marked to indicate their special meaning. This marking is achieved using the percent (%) followed by the two-digit hexidecimal code for each character. For example, %20 represents a single space. A complete conversion table for hexadecimal, decimal and ASCII can be found at

http://www-nmlt.uchicago.edu/courses/intro_c/src/labs/lab2b.txt

Keyword List (delimited)—Variables are delimited by the "+" (plus) character and is the old style delimiter commonly seem in the "Location" text box of a Web browser when doing a word search.

Named Parameter List—The named parameter list *is used by all forms and is by far the most common way of getting information to the server.* We will be using this exclusively in subsequent examples. Again, the question mark (?) is used to separate the URL describing the CGI script to be executed from the arguments to be passed to that script. The rest are name=value pairs each separated by an ampersand (&). Again, special characters such as white space are marked.

Code already exists in a variety of programming languages for decoding the various text strings passed to the CGI, so there is no need to rewrite these. Examples you can use are given in Section 10.4.

10.3.1 CGI Online Tutorials ☞

Tutorials on CGI programming (Table 10–2) also indicate where to get various parsers. Parsers are often distributed with Web servers and can be found in the *cgi-bin* directory.

10.3.2 Sources of Perl Information ☞

As stated, Perl is the most common programming language used in processing input from Web forms. Table 10–3 has pointers to online sources of information on Perl.

TABLE 10–2   Tutorials on CGI Programming

Location	Description
http://hoohoo.ncsa.uiuc.edu/cgi/forms.html	Decoding forms tutorial.
http://www.comp.it.bton.ac.uk/~mas/mas/-courses/html/html3.html	Good CGI tutorial.
http://www.best.com/~hedlund/cgifaq/faq.html	Frequently asked questions about CGI programming.
http://www.yahoo.com/Computers/-World_Wide_Web/-CGI___Common_Gateway_Interface/	Yahoo listing associated with CGI.
http://www.merlin.nrw-online.de/schulung/html/overview.html	Tutorial on CGI programming.
http://www.best.com/~vincek/hp/hp.html	Tutorial, including interfaces to data bases.
http://www.awpa.aust.com/awpa_html/cgi/	Good introduction to CGI programming and pointers to other places.

TABLE 10–3   Information on Perl

Location	Description
http://www.charm.net/~web/Vlib/-Providers/Perl.html	Collection of useful links to Perl resources, including libraries.
http://www.perl.com/perl/	Definitive source of Perl information.
http://www.perl.com/perl/info/software.html	Source of Perl software.
http://www.seas.upenn.edu/-~mengwong/perlhtml.html	Index of Perl archives.
http://www.cs.cmu.edu/htbin/perlman	Perl manual on line.

10.4. HANDLING WEB FORMS INFORMATION BY EXAMPLE

It is beyond the scope of this book to teach you Perl. However, by closely following the annotated examples below, you could modify these scripts for your own use.

10.4.1 Soliciting Feedback—A Comments Page

If we take an example posting of the form shown in Figure 10–1, what gets passed to the CGI script is

> *http://www.sdsc.edu/CompSci/pb/Comments.cgi?*
> *name=Phil&email=bourne@sdsc.edu&phone=xxx%20yyy*
> *-zzzz&comments=comments%20go%20here*

What follows is an annotated version of the Perl script, *comments.cgi*, used to parse and process this input stream. With respect to Perl programming, this is a very simple read-write exercise. We are simply writing, in a specific format, the comments we have solicited to a file for later use and sending an acknowledgment back to the user. Familiarity with any programming language should make it possible to follow this Perl script, even if you are not familiar with Perl syntax.

```
#!/usr/local/bin/perl
# The above must appear as the first line of the script if Perl is to
# be invoked,and must appear as written, except for the path to the
# Perl executable.

# Standard subroutine to parse the string sent from the Web client.
# This is freely available (see below) and will process strings sent
# by both the POST and the GET methods. Typically you would call this
# as a function from a separate library as we shall see in the next
# example.
#++++++++++++++++++++++++++++++++++++++++++++++++++++++++++++++++++++++
# Perl Routines to Manipulate CGI input
# S.E.Brenner@bioc.cam.ac.uk
# $Header: /cys/people/seb1005/http/cgi-bin/RCS/cgi-lib.pl,v 1.6
1994/07/13 15:00:50 seb1005 Exp $
#
# Copyright 1994 Steven E. Brenner
# Unpublished work.
# Permission granted to use and modify this library so long as the
# copyright above is maintained, modifications are documented, and
# credit is given for any use of the library.
#
```

```
# Thanks are due to many people for reporting bugs and suggestions
# especially Meng Weng Wong, Maki Watanabe, Bo Frese Rasmussen,
# Andrew Dalke, Mark-Jason Dominus.

# see http://www.seas.upenn.edu/~mengwong/forms/ or
#    http://www.bio.cam.ac.uk/web/         for more information

# The following is a minimal example for using ReadParse and is
# included as a comment.

# Example of minimalist http form and script
# (http://www.bio.cam.ac.uk/web/minimal.cgi):
# if  (&MethGet) {
#   print &PrintHeader,
#      '<form method=POST><input type="submit">Data: <input
# name="myfield">';
# }  else {
#   &ReadParse(*input);
#   print &PrintHeader, &PrintVariables(%input);
# }

# ReadParse
# Reads in GET or POST data, converts it to unescaped text, and puts
# one key=value in each member of the list "@in"
# Also creates key/value pairs in %in, using '\0' to separate multiple
# selections

# If a variable-glob parameter (e.g., *cgi_input) is passed to
# ReadParse,information is stored there, rather than in $in, @in,
# and %in.

sub ReadParse {
  local (*in) = @_ if @_;


 local ($i, $loc, $key, $val);

# Read in text
# The text is equated to the variable "in"
# For the GET method in comes from the environment variable
# QUERY_STRING
# For the POST method it is read from standatd input. Note that since
# new line characters are escaped there is no telling where this vari-
# able ends. The CONTENT_LENGTH environment variable specifies
# exactly how many bytes are to be read into in from STDIN.
```

```
 if ($ENV{'REQUEST_METHOD'} eq "GET") {
   $in = $ENV{'QUERY_STRING'};
 } elsif ($ENV{'REQUEST_METHOD'} eq "POST") {
   read(STDIN,$in,$ENV{'CONTENT_LENGTH'});
 }

 @in = split(/&/,$in);

 foreach $i (0 .. $#in) {
  # Convert plus's to spaces
  $in[$i] =~ s/\+/ /g;

  # Split into key and value.
  ($key, $val) = split(/=/,$in[$i],2); # splits on the first =.

  # Convert %XX from hex numbers to alphanumeric
  $key =~ s/%(..)/pack("c",hex($1))/eg;
  $val =~ s/%(..)/pack("c",hex($1))/eg;

# Associate key and value
# This gives us an associative array (a neat feature in Perl, C and
# some other languages, which has entries of the form, in this
# example, of:
# in(name) = phil
# in(email) = bourne@sdsc.edu

  $in{$key} .= "\0" if (defined($in{$key})); # \0 is the multiple
                                             # separator
  $in{$key} .= $val;

 }

 return 1;
}
#++++++++++++++++++++++++++++++++++++++++++++++++++++++++++++++++

# Now our specific application code which is simply going to write out
# the contents of the associative array in the desired format.

&ReadParse();

# Open the file comments.txt which resides in the same directory as
# the CGI script and which already contains comments and append to it.

open (COMMENTS, ">>comments.txt") || die "Cannot open comment.txt:
$!\n";
```

```
# Enter the date and time taken from the UNIX date command.

$date = `/bin/date +%D`;

print COMMENTS
"##########################################################\n\n";
print COMMENTS "$date\n";

if ($in{'name'} ne '') {
        print COMMENTS "Posted by: $in{'name'}\n";
}
if ($in{'email'} ne '') {
        print COMMENTS "Email: $in{'email'}\n";
}
if ($in{'phone'} ne '') {
        print COMMENTS "Phone number: $in{'phone'}\n";
}

$in{'comments'} =~ s/\//g;

print COMMENTS "\nComments:\n\n$in{'comments'}\n\n";

# That does it for the output file now we worry about what to pass
# back to the client Web browser that indicates that the comments have
# been registered. To do this we simply write to standard output. We
# first tell the browser that we are passing back HTML and it should
# be interpreted accordingly.

print "Content-type: text/html\n\n";
print "<TITLE>Posting Successful</TITLE>";
print "<BODY BACKGROUND=\"bg.gif\">";
print "<CENTER><P>";
print "<B>Your comments were succesfully logged.</B>";
print "<P><img ALIGN=middle SRC=\"images/hrblue.gif\"><p>";
print "<a href = \"./Databases.html\"> Databases</a> |";
print "<a href = \"./Software.html\"> Software</a> |";
print "<a href = \"./Research.html\"> Research</a> |";
print "<a href = \"./People.html\"> People</a> |";
print "<a href = \"./Pubs.html\"> Publications</a> |";
print "<a href = \"./Grants.html\"> Grants</a> |";
print "<a href = \"./Comments.html\"> Comments</a> |";
print "<a href = \"./Help.html\"> Help</a> <BR>";
print "<a href = \"./Search.html\"> Text Search</a> |";
print "<a href = \"http://www.sdsc.edu/\"> SDSC Home Page</a> <P>";
print "<img ALIGN=middle SRC=\"images/hrblue.gif\">";
print "</CENTER>";
```

The comment that appears in the file *comments.txt* resulting from the execution of this script is

```
##########################################################

05/24/96

Posted by: phil
Email: bourne@sdsc.edu
Phone number: (xxx) yyy-zzzz


Comments:

My Comments
```

and the page displayed in the Web browser of the person submitting the form is shown in Figure 10–2.

10.4.2 Executing a Server Program

This example sends input variables to a program that is executed on the server. Results are sent back to the client Web browser for review. The example introduces additional Web forms syntax, namely,

- passing a hidden variable to the CGI script
- using a scrolling list
- using radio buttons

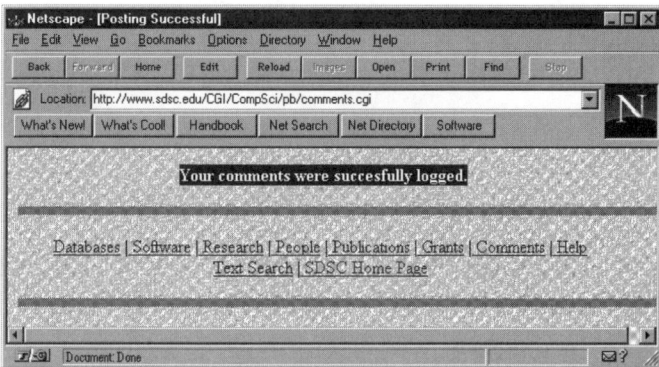

Fig. 10–2   A Simple Page Generated by a CGI Script

The example can be used as a template for running any program on the Web server using a Web form as a Graphical User Interface (GUI).

Here is the annotated Web form for soliciting input to the program.

```
<!-- Meaning short title to appear in Hot List etc. -->
<TITLE>
MOOSE - Fast Protein Structure Search by Conformational Likeness
</TITLE>
<!-- Set background color to white -->
<BODY BGCOLOR="#FFFFFF" >

<!-- CGI script to accept input from the form -->

<FORM METHOD="GET"
 ACTION="http://xtal1.sdsc.edu/misha/cgi-bin/misha1.cgi">

<P>
<CENTER>

<H2>Fast Protein Structure Search by Conformational Likeness</H2>

<B>Other Queries:</B>
  <A HREF="http://db2.sdsc.edu/moose">Moose</A> |
  <A HREF="misha.html">Alignment</A><P>
<HR>

<!-- Define a text box that can contain up to 8 characters and with an
     initial value of 4HHBA. The value entered will be assigned to the
     name value of entity_code1 -->

<B>Entity:</B>
<INPUT NAME = "entity_code1", VALUE="4HHBA", SIZE=8>
<HR></CENTER>

<!-- Define a radio button which is on by default (CHECKED). The value
     "julia" will be passed to the CGI and equated with the name
     "ent_or_frag" -->

<INPUT TYPE="radio" NAME="ent_or_frag" VALUE="julia" CHECKED>

<B> Entity Search </B><P>

<!-- Define a second radio button which is not on. Since the name
     value is the same selecting this button will deselect the previ-
     ous button -->
```

```
<INPUT TYPE="radio" NAME="ent_or_frag" VALUE="misha" >

<B> Fragment Search
<!-- Associate two additional text boxes with the radio button.
     Note that this is a loose association, that is, values entered
     here will not be used unless the button is selected (this is con-
     trolled by the CGI script not the form). -->

From </B>

 <INPUT NAME = "entity_frag1", VALUE="10", SIZE=4><B> To </B>
 <INPUT NAME = "entity_frag2", VALUE="30", SIZE=4>
<HR>
<!-- Define a scrollable list of options. Since this list lacks the
     MULTIPLE attribute the single option selected will be equated
     with the name variable "mode" . SIZE = 10 indicates that 10
     options on the list will be visible without scrolling. The OPTION
     designated as SELECTED is the default. -->
<CENTER>
<B>Select Mode:</B>
<SELECT NAME="mode" SIZE = 10>
<!-- Without the VALUE attribute "mode" is defined by the option value
     e.g.,LocalDist -->
<OPTION> LocalDist
<OPTION> LocalAngle
<OPTION> LocalTwist
<OPTION> LocalSurface
<OPTION> LocalPhiPsi
<OPTION SELECTED>LocalSecStr
<OPTION> SeqPAMatrix
<OPTION> FeatSurface
<OPTION> FeatShape
<OPTION> FeatFreq

<!-- Options omitted here -->

</SELECT>

<HR><P>
<B>Length Criterion:</B>
<!-- Define a pop-up list (distinguished from a scrolling list by the
     lack of a SIZE attribute). Again the SELECTED OPTION defines the
     default value. -->
<SELECT NAME="length">
<OPTION VALUE=10 SELECTED> 10%
<OPTION VALUE=50> 50%
<OPTION VALUE=200> 200%
```

```
<OPTION VALUE=300> 300%
<OPTION VALUE=1000> Any
</SELECT>

<B>Likeness Criterion:</B>
<!-- A text box as describe above. -->
<INPUT NAME="likeness", VALUE="0.25", size=6>
<P>
<I> Click <A HREF="julia_help.html"><B>here</B></A> for details.</I>
<HR><BR>

<!-- The input type hidden does not appear on the Web form but sends
     the value "search" to the CGI with a name value of "query_type".
     The VALUE attribute for the submit and reset buttons defines the
     text that appears in the buttons. -->
<iINPUT TYPE=hidden NAME="query_type" VALUE="search">
<INPUT TYPE=submit VALUE="EXECUTE QUERY">
<INPUT TYPE=reset VALUE="RESET FORM"><BR>

</CENTER>
</FORM> <!-- End of form -->
<HR>
</BODY>
```

Figure 10–3 illustrates the appearance of this form in a Netscape 2.01 browser.

Information entered on the Web form is processed by the following annotated script resident on the server.

```
#!/usr/local/bin/perl

# This script simply takes the input from the Web form (Figure 10-3)
# and  converts it to a command string that is executed on the server
# converts it to a command string that is executed on the server and
# the results are returned as HTML to the client Web browser.

# Define locations (server dependent) for temporary files.
$SCRATCH_PATH = "/scratch/s1/moose_output";
$SCRATCH_URL = "http://xtal1.sdsc.edu/scratch";

# Include a Perl library which contains a routine to parse the input
# string from the GET operation.
require "cgi-lib.pl";

# Routine from cgi-lib.pl to parse the input stream into array input.
&ReadParse(*input);
```

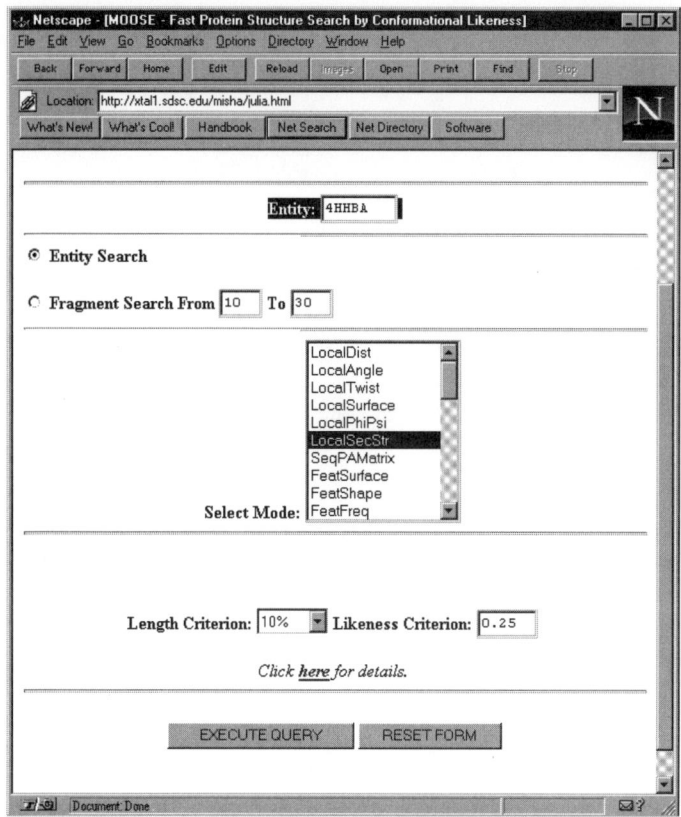

Fig. 10–3   A More Complex Form—Input to a Program

```
# Build a variable "command" from the input parameters. Note that the
# "query_type" is the hidden variable in the above form. In the above
# form the value of "query_type" is "search" hence this part of the
# script will get executed by submitting the above form. This offers a
# convenient way to have a single Perl script process multiple Web
# forms.

if($input{'query_type'} eq 'search')
# Build the command string from the input array.
{
  $ent1=$input{'entity_code1'};
  $mode=$input{'mode'};
  $length=$input{'length'};
```

```
    $likeness=$input{'likeness'};
    $ent_or_frag=$input{'ent_or_frag'};

    $command ="/misc/x1/moose/pon/"."$ent_or_frag"." "."$ent1"."
"."$mode".",".".$length".",".".$likeness";

# Modify the command string for the fragment case.
if($ent_or_frag eq 'misha')
    {
        $frag1=$input{'entity_frag1'};
        $frag2=$input{'entity_frag2'};
        $command .=",".".$frag1".",".".$frag2";
    }
# Define the output to be sent back to the Web client.
# First define the content type and header information.
    print "Content-type: text/html\n\n";
        print "<TITLE>Pure Output</TITLE>\n";
        print "<BODY BGCOLOR=\"#ffffff\">\n";
# Execute the command appending an HTML line break to each line.
    open (RES, "$command |");
    while (<RES>) {
        print; print "<BR>";
    }
        print "</BODY>\n";
}
```

The simple function of this Perl script is to recognize each named variable passed from the form and to construct a command string that is executed by the program */misc/x1/moose/pon/$ent_or_frag,* which we can see from the script, implies */misc/x1/moose/pon/misha* or */misc/x1/moose/pon/julia.* Output from the program is passed back to the client browser in a format determined by the program being executed, not the CGI script.

Returning to the Web form, notice the HIDDEN attribute to the <INPUT ... > HTML tag. This provides a mechanism for submitting variables to the CGI script from the form which are not provided by the user. I use it here to identify the Web form, since the same CGI script can process input from multiple Web forms.

The script uses the same Perl routine *ReadParse(*input)* from the library developed by Steven Brenner that was annotated in the first example. The difference is that here we use the Perl *require* statement to make it accessible to our application, rather than include it as part of the source code.

Table 10–4 has pointers to free libraries containing useful routines for Perl CGI programming.

TABLE 10–4   Perl Routines for Use in CGI Programming

Location	Description
http://www.oac.uci.edu/indiv/ehood/-perlWWW/dev/	Summaries and locations of the more popular Perl libraries.
http://www.ics.uci.edu/pub/websoft/libwww-perl/archive/	libwww-perl mailing list archives—a good source for current happenings with Perl and Web related libraries.
http://iamwww.unibe.ch/~scg/-Veranstaltungen/PSE96/cgi-perl.html	Large list of useful Perl/CGI related links.

10.4.3 An Automated Archive: The Positions Vacant Page

A major problem with any information server responsible for maintaining volatile information (i.e., information that changes frequently) is keeping that information current. In many cases the only hope of keeping information current is by off-loading the update tasks to client users. I call this type of resource, which is fully automated and updated by the user, a self-sustaining archive. The negative features of such an archive are (a) no opportunity to moderate the contents, and (b) difficulty in validating the data being placed in the archive. However, for certain forms of information for which accuracy and appropriateness are not critical, it works very well.

Another feature of this example is the notion of multiple views—making the same information accessible in different ways. In this example this implies two views: (i) by level of position (faculty, post doc., industrial, or other) and (ii) by location in the US (western, central, eastern).

The example can be found at

http://www.sdsc.edu/Xtal/ACA/Jobs/jobs.html

It works as follows.

1. Employers post details of vacant positions via a Web form.
2. Using information provided on the form, the position is posted to different Web pages based on U.S. location and level of position. (Accessing jobs via a map of the U.S. was shown in Section 9.4 during the discussion of clickable maps).
3. Information is also posted to an ftp archive, so that it is accessible to those readers without Web access (not included in this example).
4. Jobs are automatically removed from the list after six months (not shown, since this is not part of the Web form processing, but a later step using a separate Perl script).

Here is the annotated HTML Web form used to submit job information. Read it carefully.

```
<HTML>
<HEAD>
http://www.sdsc.edu/Xtal/ACA/Jobs/adv.html
<TITLE>Post a Position Available</TITLE>
</HEAD>

<BODY>
<P ALIGN=center>
<!-- Opening images with specific sizes and positions -->
 <IMG ALT="[SDSC Logo]" SRC="http://www.sdsc.edu/images/sdsc_logo.gif"
    WIDTH=112 HEIGHT=56 HSPACE=5 ALIGN=MIDDLE>
 <IMG SRC="http://www.sdsc.edu/Xtal/images/aca_logo.gif"
    ALT="American Crystallographic Association" ALIGN=MIDDLE
<P ALIGN=center>

<I>Supported jointly by the American Crystallography Association and
   the San Diego Supercomputer Center</I>

<!-- Begin form -->
    <FORM METHOD="POST"
    ACTION="http://www.sdsc.edu/CGI/Xtal/ACA/Jobs/postjob.cgi">

<HR>
<H2>Complete This Form To Post A Position</H2>
<STRONG>
 Caution - please carefully check over the information you have
 provided before submitting the form, as all job submissions will be
 automatically posted to the job lists.
</STRONG>
<HR>

<!-- Pop-up lists for type of position and location in US -->
Type of Position
    <SELECT NAME="type">
        <OPTION> Post Doc.
        <OPTION> Faculty
        <OPTION> Industrial
        <OPTION> Other
    </SELECT>

    <SELECT NAME="area">
        <OPTION> Eastern U.S.
        <OPTION> Central U.S.
```

```
            <OPTION> Western U.S.
            <OPTION> International
     </SELECT>

Geographical Area
<P>

<!-- Series of text boxes of set size -->
     <INPUT SIZE=50 NAME="title" > Title of Position <p>
     <INPUT SIZE=50 NAME="institution"> Institution <p>
     <INPUT SIZE=50 NAME="location"> Institutional Location <p>
     <INPUT SIZE=50 NAME="dept"> Institutional Dept. <p>
     <INPUT SIZE=50 NAME="site"> URL to which a candidate may refer
        (if known)
<P>
    <INPUT SIZE=20 NAME="start"> Start date <p>
    <INPUT SIZE=20 NAME="end"> Duration (if applicable) <p>

Job Description
<P>
<!-- Text area of specific size to contain job description -->
    <TEXTAREA NAME = "details" ROWS=10 COLS=60>
    </TEXTAREA>

<P>
 <INPUT SIZE=50 NAME="contact_name"> Person to Contact <p>
 <INPUT SIZE=50 NAME="contact_address"> Contact's Surface Mail
  Address<P>
 <INPUT SIZE=50 NAME="contact_email"> Contact's Email Address<P>
 <INPUT SIZE=50 NAME="contact_phone"> Contact's Phone Number<P>
 <INPUT SIZE=50 NAME="contact_fax"> Contact's Fax Number<P>
 <INPUT SIZE=50 NAME="requirements"> What is to be submitted
    (CV, 3 references, etc.) <P>

Any other details (affirmative action, etc.) <P>
 <TEXTAREA NAME = "other_details" ROWS=5 COLS=40>
 </TEXTAREA>

<P>
<!-- Submit and clear buttons -->
<INPUT TYPE="submit" VALUE="Submit Position">
<INPUT TYPE="reset" VALUE="Reset Form">
<HR>

If you submit a position and later wish to change it or have it disap-
pear from the list please contact the
```

```
  <A HREF = "MAILTO:toscano@sdsc.edu">Job List Editor</a>.
<HR>
</BODY>
```

The top half of the Web form is shown in Figure 10–4.

Here is the annotated version of the Perl script used to process the input to the Web form.

```
#!/usr/local/bin/perl
# Adapted from code written by Rich Toscano.
# Define the specific directory and URL
$directory = "/var/spool/gn/CompSci/Xtal/ACA/Jobs";
$url = "http://www.sdsc.edu/CompSci/Xtal/ACA/Jobs";
```

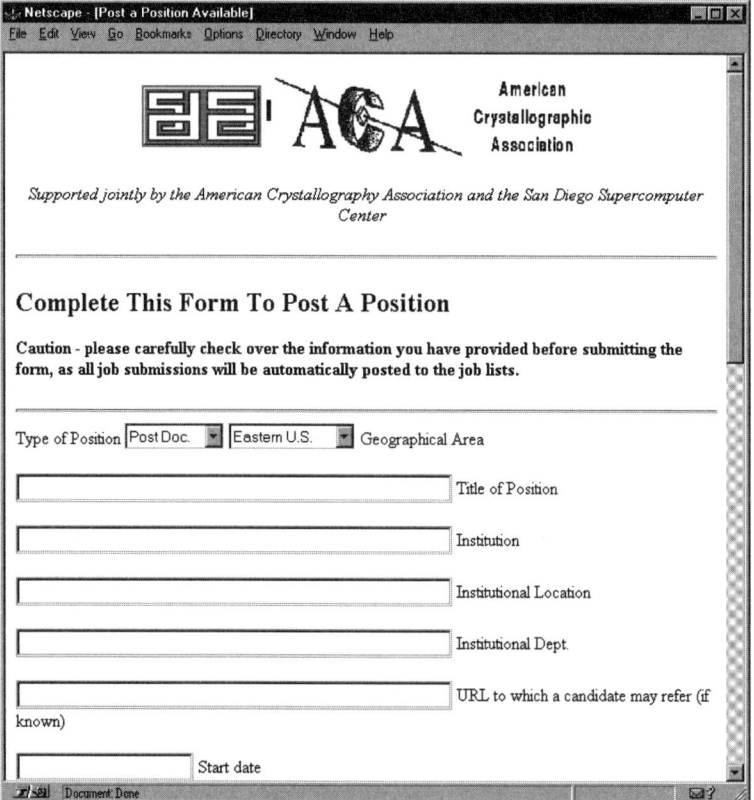

Fig. 10–4 Another Web Form—The Self-sustaining Archive

```
# Parse input - uses different parsing code than the previous example
# and is specific to the POST method.
# Read "CONTENT_LENGTH" bytes into a variable called buffer
read (STDIN, $buffer, $ENV{'CONTENT_LENGTH'});
# Define an array pairs of name=value pairs split on the & boundary
@pairs = split (/&/, $buffer);
# Define an associative array VALUE containing each value with an
# index of name.
foreach $pair (@pairs) {
        ($name, $value) = split (/=/, $pair);
        $value =~ tr/+/ /;
        $value =~ s/%([a-fA-F0-9][a-fA-F0-9])/pack("C", hex($1))/eg;
        $VALUE{$name} = $value;
}

# Modifies the appropriate job category file based on job type.
# Allowable job types are Post Doc, Faculty, Industrial, and Other.
# Begin by defining the appropriate file to modify by equating it with
# "oldfilename"
if ($VALUE{type} =~ /Post Doc\./) {
        $oldfilename = "pd.html";
}
elsif ($VALUE{type} =~ /Faculty/) {
        $oldfilename = "faculty.html";
}
elsif ($VALUE{type} =~ /Industrial/) {
        $oldfilename = "industry.html";
}
elsif ($VALUE{type} =~ /Other/) {
        $oldfilename = "other.html";
}
else {
        die;
}
# Define a new file - this way if there is a screw up we can recover
# the previously intact file!
$newfilename = "$oldfilename.tmp";
# Get the date and time in an appropriate format.
$date = `/bin/date +%D`;
chop $date;
$anchor = time;
# Open the existing and new file.
open (OLDFILE, "$directory/$oldfilename") || die "Can't open job file
$directory/$oldfilename: $!\n";
```

```
open (NEWFILE, ">$directory/$newfilename") || die "Can't open job file
$directory/$newfilename: $!\n";

while ($line=<OLDFILE>)
{
# If the "<!start shortlist>" string is found make a new entry
# immediately following it in the new file. Thus, this is a flag
# indicating where in the file to place the update. We retain inverse
# chronological order, i.e., the user sees the newest entries first
# when scrolling through the file.

        if ($line =~ /^<!start shortlist>/) {
                    print NEWFILE $line;
                    print NEWFILE "<LI><A HREF =
\"\#$anchor\">\n$VALUE{'title'},
$VALUE{'institution'}, $VALUE{'location'} [$date]</A>\n";
                    next
            }
# If the "<!end listings>" string is found write summary information.
# Thus, this is a flag after which summary information is written.
        if ($line =~ /^<!end listings>/) {
                    print NEWFILE $line;
                    print NEWFILE "<p><HR><I>Last posting: $date</I><P>";
                    print NEWFILE "Problems? Send mail to <A
HREF=\"mailto:toscano\@sdsc.edu\">toscano\@sdsc.edu</A>.\n";
                last;
            }
# If the "<!start listings>" string is found enter the full job
# description,formatting it based on the variables collected from the
# Web form.

        elsif ($line =~ /^<!start listings>/) {
                    print NEWFILE $line;
                    print NEWFILE "<HR><H3><A NAME=\"$anchor\">\n";
                    print NEWFILE "$VALUE{'title'}</H3>\n";

                    print NEWFILE "<H3>$VALUE{'institution'}</H3>\n";
                    if ($VALUE{'dept'} ne '') {
                    print NEWFILE "<B>Department:</B>
                    $VALUE{'dept'}<br>\n";}

                    if ($VALUE{'location'} ne ''){
                    print NEWFILE "<B>Location:</B>
                    $VALUE{'location'}<br>\n";      }
                    if ($VALUE{'site'} ne ''){
                    print NEWFILE "<B>URL:</B> <A
HREF=\"$VALUE{'site'}\">$VALUE{'site'}</A><br>\n";  }
```

```
                      if ($VALUE{'start'} ne ''){
                      print NEWFILE "<B>Start Date:</B>
                      $VALUE{'start'}<br>\n"; }
                      if ($VALUE{'end'} ne ''){
                      print NEWFILE "<B>Duration:</B>
                      $VALUE{'end'}<br>\n";   }
                      if ($VALUE{'details'} ne ''){
                      print NEWFILE "<B>Description:</B>
                      $VALUE{'details'}<br>\n";        }
          }

                      if ($VALUE{'other_details'} ne ''){
                      print NEWFILE "<B>Other details:</B>
                            $VALUE{'other_details'}<br>\n";      }
                      if ($VALUE{'requirements'} ne ''){
                      print NEWFILE "<B>Please submit:</B>
                            $VALUE{'requirements'}<br>\n";        }
                      if ($VALUE{'contact_name'} ne ''){
                      print NEWFILE "<B>Person to contact:</B>
                      $VALUE{'contact_name'}<br>\n"; }
                      if ($VALUE{'contact_address'} ne ''){
                      print NEWFILE "<B>Surface mail address:</B>
                            $VALUE{'contact_address'}<br>\n";    }
                      if ($VALUE{'contact_email'} ne ''){
                      print NEWFILE "<B>Email address:</B>
                            $VALUE{'contact_email'}<br>\n";       }
                      if ($VALUE{'contact_phone'} ne ''){
                      print NEWFILE "<B>Phone number:</B>
                            $VALUE{'contact_phone'}<br>\n";       }
                      if ($VALUE{'contact_fax'} ne ''){
                      print NEWFILE "<B>Fax number:</B>
                            $VALUE{'contact_fax'}<br>\n"; }
                      print NEWFILE "<B>Job Posted:</B> $date<br>\n";
                      print NEWFILE "<B>Job ID Number:</B>
                      $anchor<br>\n";
                      next;
          }
# Finally if nothing else write an existing line from OLDFILE to
NEWFILE.
          else {
                  print NEWFILE $line;
          }


}

close OLDFILE;
close NEWFILE;
```

```
open (OLDFILE, ">$directory/$oldfilename") || die "Can't open job file
$directory/$oldfilename: $!\n";
open (NEWFILE, "$directory/$newfilename") || die "Can't open job file
$directory/$newfilename: $!\n";

# Now that NEWFILE has been updated copy it back to the original file.
while (<NEWFILE>) {
        print OLDFILE;
}

close OLDFILE;
close NEWFILE;

# This section makes a pointer to the job listing in the appropriate
# location file which is accessed via the clickable map.
# Define the appropriate file to update.
if ($VALUE{area} =~ /Eastern U\.S\./) {
      $oldlfilename = "east.html";
}
elsif ($VALUE{area} =~ /Central U\.S\./) {
      $oldlfilename = "central.html";
}
elsif ($VALUE{area} =~ /Western U\.S\./) {
      $oldlfilename = "pacific.html";
}
else {
      $oldlfilename = "international.html";
}

$newlfilename = "$oldlfilename.tmp";

# Open the original file and a new file.
open (OLDFILE, "$directory/$oldlfilename") || die "Can't open job file
$directory/$oldlfilename: $!\n";
open (NEWFILE, ">$directory/$newlfilename") || die "Can't open job file
$directory/$newlfilename: $!\n";

# Append an entry with the appropriate URL to the listing when the
# flag "<!end> is found.
while ($line=<OLDFILE>)
{
        if ($line =~ /^<!end $VALUE{type}>/) {
                print NEWFILE "<LI><A
HREF=\"$url/$oldfilename\#$anchor\">$VALUE{location}</A>\n";
        print NEWFILE $line;
        next
```

```
 }
# Reestablish the flag after the last member of the list.
        elsif ($line =~ /^<!end list>/) {
                    print NEWFILE $line;
                    last;
        }
# Otherwise just copy the line to the newfile.
        else {
            print NEWFILE $line;
        }
}
# Include some ending information
print NEWFILE "<p><I>Last modified: $date</I><P>";
print NEWFILE "Problems? Send mail to <A
HREF=\"mailto:toscano\@sdsc.edu\">toscano\@sdsc.edu</A>.\n";

close OLDFILE;
close NEWFILE;

open (OLDFILE, ">$directory/$oldlfilename") || die "Can't open job file
$directory/$oldlfilename: $!\n";
open (NEWFILE, "$directory/$newlfilename") || die "Can't open job file
$directory/$newlfilename: $!\n";
# Now this has been done successfully copy the new file to the origi-
nal file.
while (<NEWFILE>) {
      print OLDFILE;
}

# Print out a message which is sent back to the employee.

print "Content-type: text/html\n\n";
print "<TITLE>Job Posting Results</TITLE>\n";
print "<H1>Job Posting Results</H1>\n";
print "<HR><P>Your job was successfully posted to our <A
HREF=\"http://www.sdsc.edu/CompSci/Xtal/ACA/Jobs/$oldfilename\">$VALUE{
type} job list</A>. For further assistance, send mail to the <A
HREF=\"mailto:toscano\@sdsc.edu\">Job List Editor</A>. If you would
like a job removed from the listings, please make sure to include the
\"Job ID Number.\"\n";
```

Figure 10–5 illustrates the result of posting an industrial type position.

A brief summary for each available job appears at the top of the Web page which includes position title, location of position, and date posted. The summary is a link to a name anchor in the same file. Thus, it is easy to find details of a specific posting in a large list of available positions.

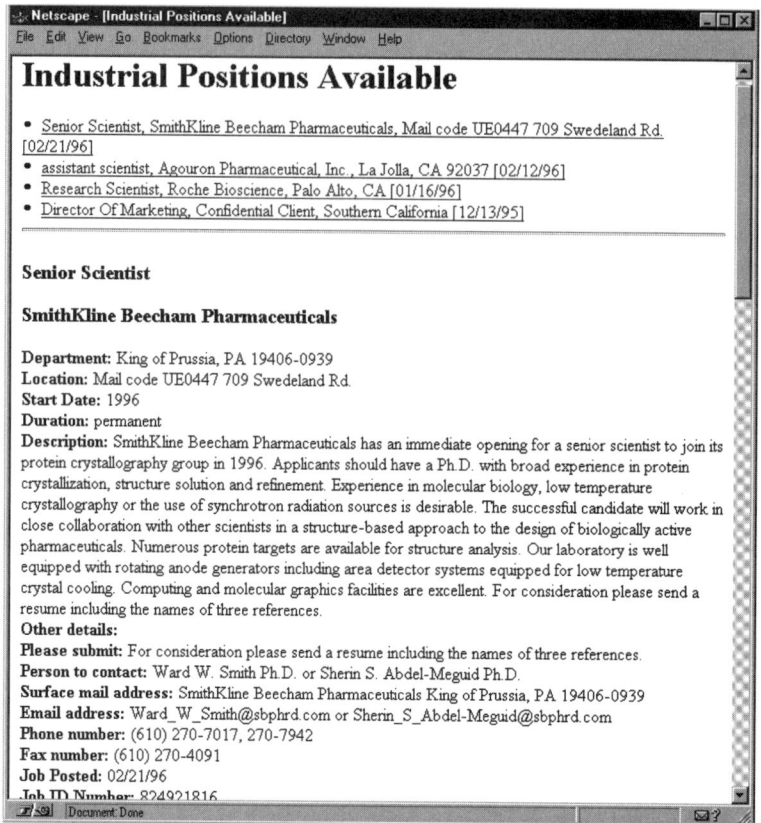

Fig. 10–5   A Web Page from the Self-sustaining Archive

10.4.4 Overcoming The Stateless Interaction

Overcoming the stateless interaction of the Web server using the idea of a client identifier (as introduced in Section 10.1) is only one way of imposing state, and therefore an ongoing dialog between client and server. Java (Chapter Eleven) makes it straightforward to open a socket (a direct line of communication) between client and server.

A good example of using a client identifier (Table 10–5) has been developed by Rob Hooft and Michael Scharf from the European Molecular Biology Laboratory (EMBL).

They developed this application because the program run on the server requires too much time to compute to be executed interactively through a Web browser. The basic idea is that you upload your data to the server, have computations performed on that data, and view the results at a later time. An alternative, not implemented, would be to have the server e-mail you the results, Here are the basic steps, from the user's perspective, which you can adopt in developing similar applications.

TABLE 10–5 An Example of Overcoming the Stateless Web Interaction

Location	Description
http://biotech.embl-heidelberg.de:8400/	Original site.
http://biotech.pdb.bnl.gov:8400/	U.S. mirror.

1. Download the designated Perl script from the server using the "Save As…" feature of your client browser.

2. Execute the script on your client, providing the name of a file containing the data that will be uploaded to the server for processing. *This represents a security risk and you should carefully examine this script before executing it on your client.*

3. Processing begins on the server and the Perl script creates a local HTML file. This file contains an identifier (which happens to be derived from the server's process id that created the file) and which is the key to accessing your results on the server.

4. Later, by accessing the local HTML file with your Web browser, you can follow a link to your output on the server, review the material and, optionally, download the results. The output remains on the server for a designated period of time.

Beyond the client side security risk mentioned in Step 2, there are server side security issues associated with this application. Precautions are taken to allow access to the original input data and the output generated by that input by only the user who submitted it. That is, the person accessing the data must know the identifier and be from the same Internet subdomain. However, the process is not fool-proof. *Sensitive data should not be uploaded to a server in this way.*

A less elegant version of the above procedure would be to upload a file to an ftp location on the server, either via ftp, or using a capability supported by some Web browsers. Then, from a Web form downloaded from the server, indicate to a CGI script the name of the file you uploaded. The script would provide you with a reference number that you could later use to locate your output on the Web server.

None of these approaches are as secure as using a socket, and we shall see the beginnings of how to do that in the next chapter.

These four examples can serve as templates for developing your own Web forms interface. You should now be able to create your own Web form, and, if you are already familiar with Perl, have input to that form processed by a CGI script you have written. If you are not already familiar with Perl you should at least be able to process Web forms data using the modifications to the templates I have given. The templates are available from the book's Web site.

11

The Global Computer

Ingredients:

- *Javascript*
- *Java*

For some dinners no meal is complete without a good cup of coffee. Coffee can be instant or ground and percolated slowly. The more effort that goes into the making, the better the taste.

11.1 COMPUTING VIA THE INTERNET

What we have learned to do so far is to serve information in the form of text, graphics, and, to a lesser extent, sound and video, and to accept and process information submitted via Web forms from client users. The information is processed by a CGI script or program on the server and a response is sent to the client Web browser as new Web pages.

We now move on to the next logical step in the development of your information server. This step could be described as permitting users to compute via the Internet. The basic idea is that your client user downloads a piece of code from your server and runs it locally on the client, or invokes it on the server from the client, or both, as part of an ongoing dialog between server and client. There are many possible applications of this technology. For some of the latest examples of what can be done refer to

http://www.gamelan.com/pages/Cool.html

What these examples show you, the information provider, is a wealth of new capabilities to enhance the information you deliver. Here are some examples of these capabilities.

- Inline sounds that play in real-time whenever a user loads a page. That is, the sound does not have to be invoked separately. An example is music that plays in the background on a page as it is being read.

- Cartoon style animation, once downloaded, is displayed in real-time, since it does not depend on continuous downloading from the server to view each consecutive frame.
- Objects rendered (moved in real-time) on a Web page, for example, the mouse can be used to direct the rotation of an object.
- Web pages made more interactive. In other words, an ongoing dialog maintained between the user of a client Web browser and the server, bypassing the stateless nature of a Web interaction. An example would be an iterative database query— the output from one query is used as input to the next.

While these capabilities are impressive, they are just the beginning. Future developments will only be limited by our imaginations, programming skills, and network bandwidth. Network computing, as I have called it, has the potential to completely change the way we compute. In this book there are many examples of downloading applications, configuring them, and executing them. In the future, when you choose to run an application, it will be fetched from an Internet server, configured without your even knowing it, and run. This will happen *each time you invoke the application*. In this way you will always be running the latest and greatest version of software, since the software is maintained at a remote site. The remote site has the expertise and resources to develop and maintain that application.

The current tools that make this new type of computing feasible are the Java programming language from Sun Microsystems Inc., and JavaScript from Netscape Communications. It is beyond the scope of this book to teach you how to program in Java and JavaScript. There are many books on this subject already (see Table 11–1 for a pointer). It is within the scope, however, to provide you with an overview of the capabilities of Java and JavaScript, give you very simple examples of how to use these tools, and point you at additional information. After reading this chapter you should be able to state one of the following.

- Yes, I will develop applications in Java or JavaScript.
- No, my server does not need to provide Java or JavaScript capability.
- I do not need Java or JavaScript today, but will revisit using these tools at a later date.

11.2 JAVA ☞

Java is a programming language akin to C, C++, FORTRAN, Basic, Pascal, Perl, Tcl, and so on. In many ways Java combines the best features of all of these languages while remaining lightweight, that is, not overburdened with esoteric syntax. A powerful feature is the ability to invoke Java programs from a Web page, as we shall see subsequently.

Make no mistake, Java is a programming language and requires programming skills to use it effectively. It is much more complex than using HTML, and about as complex as C++. Moreover, like C++, Java is an object-oriented and not a structured language like C or FORTRAN. If you are not familiar with the techniques of object-oriented programming using languages like C++, Smalltalk, and Objective C, there will be an additional learning curve. Do not be deterred, however. First, if you are not familiar with object-oriented programming, Java is a good language in which to get your feet wet, particularly since there is a flood of free Internet-accessible documentation, tutorials, and general help. Second, JavaScript is an intermediate approach between HTML and Java, so you can begin with JavaScript and make the further transition to Java as your needs become more complex.

It is beyond the scope of this book to teach you the principles of object-oriented programming. However, to understand what Java has to offer I will touch on some of the basic principles. Additional sources of information on the capabilities and shortcomings of Java can be found in Table 11–1.

TABLE 11–1   Sources of Additional Information on Java

Location	Description
http://java.sun.com/doc/-language_environment/	A white paper written by the Java developers summarizing the features and motivation behind the Java language.
http://www.arlut.utexas.edu/-~rfmpwww/wag/slides/javabl/-presentation/index.html	A set of slides summarizing features of Java and the HotJava browser.
http://www.connect.hawaii.com/hc/-webmasters/books/index.java.html	Reviews of recent books on Java.
http://java.sun.com/doc/-tutorial.html	Java tutorial from Sun Microsystems Inc.
http://sunsite.unc.edu/javafaq/-javatutorial.html	Another very good tutorial, but still under development at the time of writing.
http://www.yahoo.com/-Computers_and_Internet/-Programming_Languages/Java/-Guides__Tutorials_-and_Documentation/	Entry point to Java from Yahoo.
http://java.sun.com/doc/-general.html	Entry point to a wide variety of Java information.
http://www.well.com/user/yimmit/-hworld.html	Examples of Java applets.

11.2.1 Overview

To develop applications in Java you need the Java Developer's Kit (JDK) which is free and can be found at

http://java.sun.com/products/JDK/CurrentRelease/

At the time of writing this is available for only one UNIX platform, Sun's Solaris operating system, as well as Windows NT, Windows95 and MacOS. For UNIX users this means if you do not have access to a Solaris system, you cannot write Java applications, but you can use existing applications. The reason for the difference between the compile and run-time environments will become apparent as you read further. This is restrictive and current details of ports of JDK to other platforms can be found at

http://java.sun.com/Mail/external_lists.html

The JDK consists of the following components:

- class libraries—libraries needed by the Java compiler
- source code of the compiler and libraries
- a Java compiler
- a Java interpreter
- a Java debugger
- a Java applet viewer

With the exception of the Java applet viewer, these are standard components for use with any programming language. The need for an applet viewer is explained with the help of Figure 11–1.

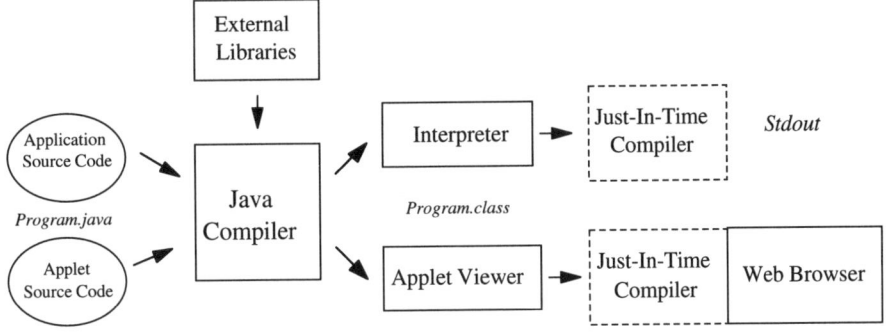

Fig. 11–1   Java Components

Moving from left to right, the first thing to understand is that there are two types of Java source code, one written to be run as an application and one written to run as an *applet*. We have met the term applet at other points in this book. Recall that an applet is Java code that is to be run from a a Web browser. An application will be run from the UNIX command line. The main difference, as we shall see in Section 11.4.2, between an applet and an application is the libraries you use as part of your code. Either way the source code, which I assume is in a file *program.java* (*java* is the standard file extension for Java code) is compiled using the Java compiler and produces a file, *program.class*. The file *program.class* is in *byte code* and will run on any computer for which a Java interpreter is available. In other words, the interpreter interprets the byte code, which can be thought of as machine independent code. Java interpreters are available for many UNIX platforms. If your source code produces an applet then, as we shall see in Section 11.4.2, that applet can be wrapped in HTML and passed to a Web browser. Thus, Web browsers that can make sense of Java code (most of them) have their own built-in Java interpreters.

The applet viewer (Figure 11–1) lets you test your applets locally before making them part of a Web page.

Byte code is a major feature of Java, since it is hardware independent. The price you pay for this independence is performance. That is, the code is not optimized to take advantage of the specific hardware architecture. This may or may not be a problem, it depends on the application. It will be a problem for a CPU-intensive application, but less of a problem for a simple display program. Enter the *just-in-time compilers* (Figure 11–1). Just-in-time compilers take the Java byte code and convert it to more efficient machine-specific code that takes advantage of the specific hardware features of the UNIX platform. This happens just prior to running the application, hence the name. At the time of writing, just-in-time compilers are just starting to appear in Web browsers. The impact of just-in-time compilers is considered in Section 11.5, which summarizes my colleagues' and my experiences with Java to date.

You should now have some sense of the various Java components and be ready to consider some of the major features of Java. We will then move on to a couple of simple examples of writing, compiling, and using Java, both from an application and an applet standpoint.

11.2.2 Major Features

The major features of Java are introduced here. These features should indicate why there is considerable excitement about Java. Other languages have some of these features, but only Java has them *all*.

11.2.2.1 Network Ready

Java was designed with the network in mind. Self-contained blocks of code are easily transferred from server to client using the http protocol, and subsequently executed by including references to them in your Web pages. As we saw in the previous section, these blocks of code are called applets and can only be executed by Java-ready browsers like HotJava (itself written in Java) and Netscape version 2.0 and above.

You can write standalone applications using Java which are interpreted by a separate Java interpreter (Figure 11–1).

Assuming a Web browser is Java-ready, that is, can interpret an applet, how it handles the applet is browser and configuration dependent. Most browsers will not permit the applet, when read as part of a remote URL, to read or write to the local client disk, since this poses a security risk. Browsers that access the applet as part of a Web page that is a local file often behave differently.

11.2.2.2 Hardware Neutral

As indicated in the previous section, this is a great feature of Java. When you compile a piece of Java code you are not compiling it into machine-specific code, but rather into byte code. This is possible because Java is statically typed. Which is a fancy way of saying that you declare all objects (numbers, variables, arrays, etc.) in Java to have an explicit data type (e.g., char, int) and that char and int (and other simple types) are defined explicitly by the language to have a specific storage requirement, for example, an integer is 32 bits and a long 64 bits. It is this explicit typing that helps give Java byte code its portability across multiple hardware types. It is the byte code that is passed from the server to the client. Thus, the client must be running a Java interpreter to use the Java code.

As indicated above, the Java interpreter is built-in to some Web browsers, but, for security reasons, may be available in a restricted form relative to a native interpreter. Whether there is a native interpreter available for your UNIX platform needs to be determined. Take a look at *http://java.sun.com/faq2.html#A* for the latest release information.

11.2.2.3 GUI Neutral

Only a single graphical user interface need be developed—a major accomplishment. That interface can be displayed and used on all UNIX platforms, PCs and Macintosh computers, since all these platforms support Java-ready browsers. This is a major accomplishment since up to 90 percent of the coding effort can be expended on interface development, particularly when using X/Motif. In the future, more computing is likely to be done through a Java-ready browser.

11.2.2.4 Extensive Class Library, Language Support, and Documentation ☞

Java is enabling the use of the Internet, and, conversely, the Internet is enabling the use of Java. This is possible because Java is evolving with the Internet, rather than predating it. For example, there are extensive Java-shared class libraries (see Section 11.2.2.7 for a definition) and applet libraries are being developed and shared. The documentation covering

TABLE 11–2   Java Libraries

Location	Description
http://java.sun.com/products/JDK/	The Java Developer's Kit (JDK) from Sun Microsystems Inc.
http://www.jars.com/	Starting point for locating useful applets.
http://the-inter.net/www/-future21/java/applets.html	Applets that can be simply used to enhance the appearance and usability of Web pages.

these developments is available worldwide, since it is written in HTML and available on the Web. Table 11–2 indicates where to find useful Java libraries.

11.2.2.5 Standard Compliant

The architecture-neutral and portable language platform of Java is known as the Java Virtual Machine. The Java Virtual Machine is based primarily on the POSIX interface specification, an industry-standard definition of a portable system interface.

11.2.2.6 Support for Threads

For the purposes of this discussion, threads can be thought of as lightweight processes. That is, when you start an application in UNIX this constitutes a process which may itself fork further processes. A process is the element to which the UNIX kernel allocates resources (e.g., CPU time and memory). A process has a certain overhead that must be incurred when it is started. In this era of multiprocessor computers a process can be broken down into threads of execution that are executed simultaneously and, therefore, in less wall clock time than on a single processor. The overhead in starting a thread is less than that of starting a process, hence the term "lightweight." Java supports threads and the results can be seen in applications like the HotJava browser that can simultaneously download multiple animation sequences while scrolling and displaying graphics.

Java supports multithreading at the language level with the addition of sophisticated synchronization primitives to manage concurrent and dependent threads of execution. The language library provides the *Thread* class, and the run-time system provides monitor and condition lock primitives, again necessary to synchronize multiple dependent threads of execution. At the library level, Java system libraries have been written to be thread safe. That is, the functionality provided by the libraries is available without conflict to multiple concurrent threads of execution.

11.2.2.7 Object-Oriented and Other Language Features

Classes and Inheritance are of proven value in shortening the software development cycle, since, if done properly, these object-oriented features facilitate code reuse. The downside is that you need to put more thought into the initial design, so you have bits of code that you can reuse. Those "bits" come in the form of *classes*. Classes have *attributes*, that is, variables with static or dynamic values, and *methods*, code that performs some function. Classes, with their associated attributes and methods are inherited, modified, and reused for a variety of purposes. An object is an *instance* of a class.

Encapsulation hides complex programming in objects that have a simple calling interface and, hence, can be used in a straightforward manner.

Polymorphism implies that the same message is sent to different objects. This results in behavior that is dependent on the nature of the object receiving the message.

Strong Typing helps make Java portable. Other than the primitive data types, everything in Java is an object. Even the primitive data types can be encapsulated inside library-supplied objects, if required. There are only three groups of primitive data types, namely, numeric types, Boolean types, and arrays.

11.2.2.8 Security

The following features help define the security features of Java.

- Memory layout is determined at run-time and is not defined by the code itself. Without a knowledge of how the application maps to memory, interfering with the application is made more difficult.
- The notion of pointers to other memory locations does not exist in Java and, hence, interfering with memory mapping is difficult.
- The byte code verifier and vetter analyze byte code coming across the network. Further networked byte code is treated differently to local byte code by memory partitioning.
- There is user level control over what byte code is run and from what machines.

These features, taken together, indicate that Java is an evolutionary step in programming. Java retains the best features of previous languages, while discarding those features affecting portability, security and ease of programming. Moveover, it is designed specifically for use via the Internet.

11.3 JAVASCRIPT ☞

JavaScript is to Java what C shell scripts are to the C language. That is, JavaScript is simpler, less functional, yet easier to program than Java. Further, it is an interpreted and not a compiled language. JavaScript code is embedded in your HTML documents and is interpreted by your Web browser, hence the Web browser is the JavaScript interpreter. JavaScript was developed by Netscape Communications Inc., in collaboration with Sun Microsystems Inc., and at the time of writing only functions with the Netscape client

TABLE 11–3   Comparison of Java and JavaScript

Java	JavaScript
Compiled on server.	Interpreted on client.
Complex but powerful.	Simple but limited.
Run-time support by several Web browsers.	Run-time support limited.
Full-blown object-oriented language.	Uses built-in extensible objects, but no classes or hierarchies.
Strong typing.	Weak typing.

TABLE 11–4   Sources of Additional Information on JavaScript

Location	Description
http://www.yahoo.com/- Computers_and_Internet/- Programming_Languages/JavaScript/	The Yahoo starting point for more information on JavaScript.
http://intergalactinet.com/javascript/	Excellent staring point for FAQs, tutorials, example scripts, and books.
http://home.netscape.com/eng/- mozilla/Gold/handbook/javascript/- index.html	Netscape's introduction to JavaScript basics.

browser, version 2.0 or later. Table 11–3 summarizes the similarities and differences between Java and JavaScript.

Table 11–4 contains pointers to additional information on JavaScript. The following section makes the capabilities of Java and JavaScript clearer by way of several annotated examples.

11.4 SIMPLE EXAMPLES

Since JavaScript is simpler than Java we begin with it.

11.4.1 JavaScript

Our first example is about as simple as it gets with JavaScript.

```
<HTML>
<HEAD>
<SCRIPT LANGUAGE="JavaScript">
<!-- For non-JavaScript supporting browsers
document.write("Hello World.")
```

```
// -->
</SCRIPT>
</HEAD>
<BODY>
That's all, folks.
</BODY>
</HTML>
```

What the user sees in their Web browser is the following:

Hello World. That's all, folks.

Note the following

- The <SCRIPT> … </SCRIPT> HTML tags delimit JavaScript code within an HTML document.
- The LANGUAGE attribute to the <SCRIPT> tag defines the language to be used to interpret the embedded code—a promise of more languages in the future.
- The <!-- … --> (comment delimiter) prevents Web browsers unable to recognize JavaScript from displaying the code in the browser window.
- The statement

```
document.write("Hello World.")
```

declares the document object with the write method and assumes to write to an HTML document defined within <BODY> … </BODY> tags. There are assumed attributes of the document object that can be explicitly overwritten. The use of objects and methods is made clearer in the discussion of Java in the next section.
- The HTML code wraps around the JavaScript.

In our simple introduction this covers the basics of how HTML and JavaScript work together. Let us now look at a couple of examples that introduce features of the JavaScript language. First, the concept of declaring a function and then using that function.

```
<HTML>
<HEAD>
<SCRIPT LANGUAGE="JavaScript">
<!-- for non-supporting browsers
   function square(i) {
```

```
         document.write("The call passed ", i ," to the
             function.","&lt;BR&gt;")
         return i * i
     }
     document.write("The function returned",
             square(2),".")
// end hiding contents from old browsers ->
</SCRIPT>
</HEAD>
<BODY>
<BR>
All done.
</BODY>
</HTML>
```

The result seen in the Web browser is

We passed 2 to the function.
The function returned 4.
All done.

Note the following new feature of this script

- A function, square(i), has been declared, which is subsequently called with a specific value of i (2 in this example).

Now let us look at an example that works with features of the browser itself by popping up a separate alert window.

```
<HTML>
<HEAD>
<SCRIPT LANGUAGE="JavaScript">
<!-- for non-supporting browsers
  function helloworld() {
          alert("Hello World!")
                            }
// end hiding contents from old browsers -->
</SCRIPT>
</HEAD>
<BODY>
<FORM>
<INPUT TYPE="BUTTON" VALUE="Press Me"
ONLICK="helloworld()">
```

```
</FORM>
</BODY>
</HTML>
```

Note the following new features

- Again we defined a function—helloworld(), but this time that function calls another built-in function (i.e., available as part of the JavaScript libraries) called alert(), which takes a single text string argument and pops-up an alert window with that text string returned along with a dismiss button.
- The ONCLICK attribute of the <INPUT> tag defines what happens when a button (specified with the TYPE attribute) is pressed. In this case it invokes the helloworld() function.

These examples gives you a feel for what you might do with JavaScript. Table 11–4 will take you to the next step with a variety of useful pointers to learning JavaScript.

11.4.2 Java

Let us look at our simple "Hello World" example in Java.

```
/*
 * File: HelloWorld.java
 */
public class HelloWorld {
      public static void main(String args[])   {
             System.out.println("Hello World!");
                                              }
                        }
```

If you are a C++ programmer, or to a lesser extent, a C programmer, the features of this example will be apparent, if you are not, note the following

- Comments are contained within /* ... */.
- The first thing we have done is to declare a class called "HelloWorld" which is public. By being public it is accessible to other classes, but has the requirement that only one public class is available per file and that the file be called, in this example, *HelloWorld.java.*
- Next, we have declared a method main. Since it is public it is available to other methods. Since it is static it is shared by all instances of this class and (in principle) could be invoked as HelloWorld.main.

- System.out.println() is a method that takes as an argument a single string that is output to UNIX standard out (stdout), usually the display screen.

Our simple program is compiled with the command

% **javac HelloWorld.java**

This produces a file of byte code *HelloWorld.class*

    This file can be executed on any computer that supports a Java interpreter—the code is machine independent. The command to run it is:

% **java HelloWorld**

You should see "Hello World!" appear on your display screen.

    This is an example of a Java application; a Java applet has a slightly different structure. Here is the same application, coded as an applet.

```
import java.awt.Graphics;

public class HelloWorldApplet extends
   java.applet.Applet {

 public.void.paint(Graphics g) {
        g.drawstring("Hello World!", 5, 25) ;
                                         }
                      }
```

You should see similarities and differences between the applet and the application.

- The import statement was not found in the Java application and is used to gain access to classes from the JDK to handle the applet itself and to draw to the screen.
- We have declared a public class, as was true of the application. Here, however, we extend a basic applet class java.applet.Applet, which implies that the HelloWorldApplet takes on the basic characteristics of the basic applet supplied with the JDK.
- The paint() method is used to display the text string "Hello World!" to the screen, The paint() method replaces main() in our Java application example. More specifically:
- The paint() method takes an instance of the Graphics class as its single argument. We then used the drawstring() method from the Graphics class to display

the string. The string is displayed on the screen starting at 5 pixels across and 25 pixels down. As we shall see in the subsequent example, there are other methods of the Graphics class that we could have used to control font size, color, etc.

Just as with the Java application, the applet must be compiled as follows

% **javac HelloWorldApplet.java**

This produces a file of byte code *HelloWorldApplet.class* which can be included in a Web page and executed by a Java ready browser when the Web page is loaded. To include the applet in an application you use the <APPLET> ... </APPLET> HTML tags.

```
<HTML>
<HEAD>
<TITLE>A Simple Java Applet </TITLE>
<!-- File: HelloWorldApplet.html -->
</HEAD>
<BODY>
<P> Here is my Java Applet: <BR>
<APPLET CODE="HelloWorldApplet.class"
   WIDTH=125          HEIGHT=30> </APPLET>
</BODY>
</HTML>
```

Note the following:

- The CODE attribute of the <APPLET> tag defines the name of the applet file.
- The WIDTH and HEIGHT attributes of the <APPLET> tag define the space reserved on the Web page (in pixels) to display the applet.

Applets can also be viewed with the appletviewer that comes as part of the JDK. The command would be

% **appletviewer HelloWorldApplet.html**

Let us take this simple applet to the next level which, first, gives you more details on how to control the look of text produced by an applet, and second, shows you how to pass a parameter from HTML to an applet.

```
import java.awt.Graphics;
import java.awt.Font;
import java.awt.Color;
```

```
public class HelloNameApplet extends
    java.applet.Applet {

Font f = new Font("TimesRoman", Font.BOLD, 24) ;
String name;

public void init() {
  name = getParameter("name");
  if (name == null) name = "Phil" ;

  name = "Hello " + name + "!" ;
                      }
public void paint(Graphics g) {
  g.setFont(f);
  g.setColor(Color.red);
  g.drawString(name, 5, 30);
                                }
                      }
```

This applet code can then be used as follows:

```
<HTML>
<HEAD>
<TITLE>Another Simple Java Applet </TITLE>
<!-- File: HelloNameApplet.html -->
</HEAD>
<BODY>
<P> Here is my Java Applet: <BR>
<APPLET CODE="HelloNameApplet.class" WIDTH=125
  HEIGHT=30>
<PARAM NAME=name VALUE="Fred">
</APPLET>
</BODY>
</HTML>
```

Note the following:

- We have imported additional classes to handle fonts and color.
- We have created an individual font object (f) using the "new" constructor of the Font class. That font object has attributes that define it as a 24 point, bold, Times Roman font.
- The init() method will get the parameter "name" from the HTML file. If name is not defined, the string "Phil" will be used.

- The "name" variable will have a text string "Hello " prepended to it and the text string "!" appended to it.
- The complete text string will be displayed in red, starting 5 pixels to the right of the top left hand corner of the assigned applet space and 30 pixels down.
- The <PARAM> tag defines parameters to be passed to the applet for use. The attributes NAME and VALUE define the name-value pair to be used by the applet.
- If the <PARAM> tag had been missing, the Web page would contain "Hello Phil!"

Basic examples like these can be found in the introductory chapters of most books on Java or JavaScript or in the online information. They are not included here to attempt to teach you Java. Rather they are intended to provide the context for when and how to use Java to supplement the information you are providing through the Web.

11.5 THOUGHTS ON DEVELOPING WITH JAVA

For any software developer, on first glance, Java and JavaScript are compelling. Java, particularly, has all the features one would like to see in a programming language and, hence, has generated a great deal of excitement. This is evident when visiting the Internet section in any bookstore—there are many books on Java. A downside of this rise to fame is there has been little opportunity for the product to mature. Bugs and non-uniform behavior are common. Non-uniform behavior implies, for example, graphical user interfaces that appear different from one hardware type to another. Or even appear different from one release of the Web browser to another on the same hardware platform. I anticipate this situation will improve with each new release of the Java Developer's Kit (JDK).

Another issue to consider is performance. As an experiment we took a commonly-used scientific algorithm, which we had coded in C++ and converted it to Java (a trivial process). The Java code ran ten times slower that the C++ code using the same input data set and hardware. Using the just in time compiler made the Java code run approximately ten times faster, roughly equaling the performance of the C++ code. Thus, *the just-in-time compiler is important for CPU-intensive applications written in Java.*

At this point your server should be fully operational and you should be excited at the prospect of what you might do with Java and JavaScript. It is now time to consider the mundane, yet important task of server maintenance.

12

Server Maintenance

Ingredients:

- *Server log files and their formats*
- *Tools to manage log files*
- *Handling errors found in log files*

That terrible moment has arrived—washing-up time. An unfitting end to a wonderful meal. You can defer the chore, but sooner or later you have to deal with it. The longer you have waited, the more unpleasant it will be. You can wash-up by hand or use a dishwasher.

Each type of information server I have covered in this book—ftp servers, Listservers, and Web servers—requires ongoing maintenance. Each type of server produces log files that record access to the server and any warnings or errors relating to server operation. These log files are both your friend and your enemy. They are your friend since they enable you to analyze problems and monitor usage. The latter may be important for justifying the resources spent in developing the server and for planning how to expand the server. The log files are your enemy because you cannot ignore them. On heavily loaded servers these log files grow until they consume all available disk space. For example, a Web server receiving one million hits per month can produce approximately 300 MB worth of log files each month.

We begin with a discussion of which log files get created for each server and their format. We then look at tools available for analyzing these log files to summarize usage, and conclude with errors and warnings contained in these files and how you should respond to these messages.

12.1. LOG AND ERROR FILE FORMATS

As before, I introduce server types in order of increasing complexity—ftp server, Listserver, and, finally, Web server.

12.1.1 ftp

The location and format of the ftp log file is dependent on the versions of UNIX and *ftpd* running on your information server. The location may also be defined by the system administrator, either explicitly, or by having *syslog* handle ftp error logging. This is done when *ftpd* is started, usually at boot time. You can find the default location for ftp log files by reading the man page for either ftp, *syslogd*, or *ftpd*.

As an example of a specific location and format, consider *wu-ftpd* (Section 7.1.2) running on a SunOS system. The log file can be found at */usr/adm/xferlog*. The format of this particular version of the log file is described in the man page for *xferlog* distributed with the *wu-ftpd* software. I summarize this format using the following typical entry from the file.

> Mon Mar 18 01:38:00 1996 161 dido.scij.ulst.ac.uk 433861
> /pub/sdsc/biology/WPDB/wpdbbin.zip b _ o a b.mccullough@ulst.ac.uk ftp 0 *

This is a single record with fields delimited by white space, where:

- *Mon Mar 18 01:38:00 1996* is the date and time the transfer began
- *161* is the time it took to complete the transfer in seconds
- *dido.scij.ulst.ac.uk* is the remote client initiating the transfer
- *433861* is the size of the file transferred in bytes
- */pub/sdsc/biology/WPDB/wpdbbin.zip* is the file transferred
- *b_o* is the type of transfer (b = binary) and special action flag (o = none)
- *b.mccullough@ulst.ac.uk* is the user initiating the request.
- *ftp* is the transfer method
- *0* is the authentification level (0 = none)

12.1.2 Listserver

Again, as with ftp, the format of the log file is dependent on the Listserver you are using. Taking Majordomo (Section 7.2), the log file format is described at the URL

> *http://www.lanl.gov:8010/computerinformation/user/nmug/2dec93/more/email-lists/major-domo/majordomo.manual*

and not repeated here.

The location of the log file is defined by the *$log* variable in the *majordomo.cf* file.

12.1.3 Web Server

Like ftp servers and Listservers, not all Web servers use the same log file format. Fortunately, most popular Web servers (e.g., NCSA's httpd and Cern httpd) do use the same format, and a conversion utility has been written by John Franks (the author of wn) to convert the wn log file format into that produced by the NSCA and Cern Web servers. This format is widely referred to as *common log file format.* A record in this format appears as

hercules.sdsc.edu - - [12/Mar/1996:18:54:15 -0800] "GET /moose/moose.html HTTP/1.0" 200 2238

where

- *hercules.sdsc.edu* is the client requesting the page from the server
- *[12/Mar/1996:18:54:15 -0800]* is the date and time the request was made, noting that the time zone (U.S. Pacific Standard Time) is 8 hours behind GMT
- *"GET /moose/moose.html HTTP/1.0"* is the request made to get the file using version 1.0 of the HTTP protocol where the file is *DocumentRoot/moose/moose.html*
- *200* is the return status for the request (i.e., normal completion)
- *2238* is the number of bytes transferred

The log files for most Web servers are found in the directory *ServerRoot/logs*. For example, the NCSA httpd server has a file called *access_log* with this format in this directory. You will find additional files in this directory, namely:

- *agent_log* that contains the name and version of the client software making the request to the Web server. For example,

Mozilla/2.0 (X11; I; OSF1 V3.2 alpha)

where Mozilla is the name of the Netscape browser. The browser was version 2.0 and was running on a DEC Alpha client with v3.2 of the OSF1 (alias DEC UNIX) operating system.
- *error_log* that contains any errors or warnings. For example,

[Tue Mar 12 19:15:37 1996] HTTPd: caught SIGTERM, shutting down

The time the server was shutdown.
- *httpd.pid* that contains the process identifier for the process running the server.
- *referer_log* that contains the URLs that referenced your server's Web pages. For example,

http://xtal1.sdsc.edu/ -> /icons/menu.gif

An inline image (DocumentRoot/icons/*menu.gif*), was referenced from the URL *http://xtal1.sdsc.edu/*. The file *referer_log* is useful in tracing who is referencing your pages and where pointers to your pages exist on other Web sites.

12.2. MONITORING USAGE

Monitoring the usage of each type of information server requires running programs that read files containing the log formats defined above and providing appropriate summaries. You would first divide the log files up into manageable components based on a given time period. That is, typically, once per week or once per month, depending on amount of usage and, hence, log file size, the existing log files are renamed and a new file is created (if necessary) to contain new logging. I say "if necessary," since some servers will create the file automatically the first time they need to write something, if it does not already exist.

Updating log files requires write access to those files, and, depending on who configured the server (Chapter Seven), may require access to the UNIX root account. Updating log files is usually automated by placing appropriate commands in the system or user *crontab* file. If you are not familiar with *crontab*, refer to the UNIX man page. Here is a trivial annotated example of appropriately renaming the NCSA *access_log* file on a monthly basis.

```
#!/bin/sh
# File: new_http_log
# Move to the location of the log file
cd /usr/local/etc/httpd/logs
# Define the current month as variable MONTH
MONTH = `date | cut -c5-7`
# Rename access_log to, for example, access_log.mar
mv access_log access_log.$MONTH
# Create a new, empty log file
touch access_log

# crontab entry to run the above script at the beginning of the month
0 0 1 * * /usr/local/bin/new_http_log
```

With the log files in manageable components based on a specific time period, you are now ready to summarize the information using a program appropriate to the information type.

We consider FTPWebLog (Section 12.2.1) for summarizing either ftp or Web log files, *logsummary.pl* for use with Majordomo log files (Section 12.2.2) and various tools, notably WWWstat (Section 12.2.3) for analyzing Web log files.

TABLE 12–1   FTPWebLog Software Snapshot

Location	*http://www.netimages.com/*
	~snowhare/utilities/ftpweblog/
Source	Yes (Perl)
Bugs	*snowhare@netimages.com*

12.2.1 ftp with FTPWebLog ☞

Table 12–1 provides information on FTPWebLog.

FTPWebLog, written by Benjamin Franz, was inspired by *WWWstat*, which I shall discuss shortly. *FTPWebLog* will satisfy most information manager's needs for processing ftp log files (and possibly http log files). The output of *FTPWebLog* is an HTML file that can be subsequently graphed with an additional program, *graphftpweblog*, included with the distribution, but not discussed here.

Installation is straightforward and requires that you

1. Download the compressed tar file distribution.
2. Uncompress and untar the tar file.
3. Modify the variables in the *ftpweblog* Perl script to suit your needs. Some of these variables may be redefined at run time as command line arguments. This is fully described in the Web page that comes with the distribution. Here are some features that may be defined:
   - Whether you want to process an ftp log file or a Web common log format file.
   - Whether you want to include daily statistics.
   - Whether you want to include hourly statistics.
   - Whether you want to include domain information.
   - Whether you want to exclude entries in the log file based on Regex expressions.
   - Whether you want to summarize files based on the number of accesses and bytes downloaded.
4. Run the Perl script.
5. Look at the results with a Web browser.

Figure 12–1 is an example of a report generated with *FTPWebLog*.

The summary is self-explanatory. Note that the summary reports on which files are being accessed by which sites and the volume of information transferred. Additionally, when the server is being accessed is also available.

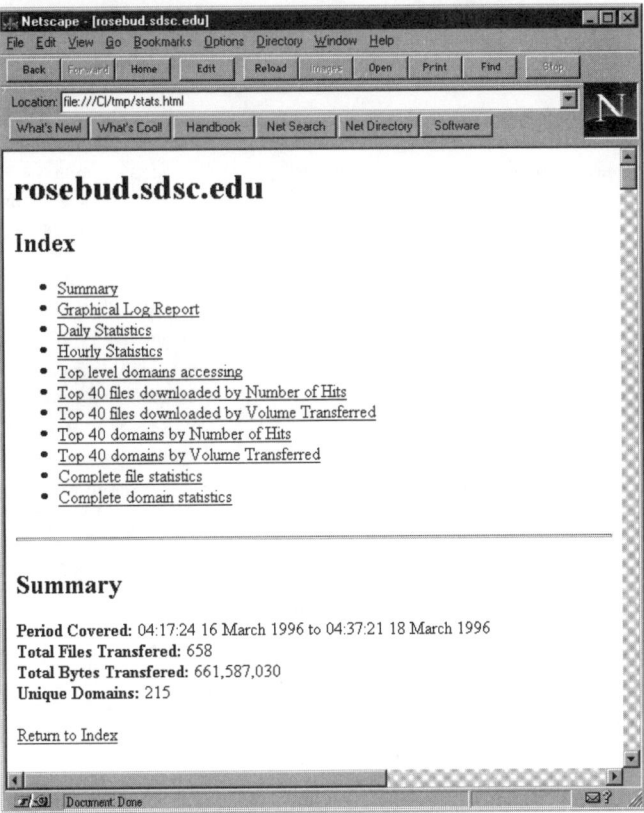

Fig. 12–1 A Report of ftp Access Statistics Generated with FTPWebLog

12.2.2 Majordomo with logsummary.pl

The *contrib* directory of the majordomo distribution (Section 7.2) contains a Perl script *logsummary.pl,* written by Paul Close, which summarizes the contents of the log file produced by Majordomo. The summary includes statistics on who subscribed, who unsubscribed, who requested an index, etc., for each list. I will not consider it further here.

12.2.3 WWW with Various Tools

Section 12.1.3 introduced the various log files produced by NCSA httpd and other Web servers. Here we look at the tools available to summarize each of those files and the results they produce.

TABLE 12–2   Programs for Summarizing Web Server Log Files

Location	Description
http://www.statslab.cam.ac.uk/-~sret1/analog/	Analog provides multiple report options.
http://www.eit.com/software/getstats/	Getstats compiles on many platforms supporting the *gcc* compiler. Also processes common log files produced by Plexus and gn.
http://dis.cs.umass.edu/stats/-gwstat.html	Gwstat processes HTML output from WWWstat producing graphical summaries as GIF files.
http://www.netgen.com/products/-net.Analysis/	net.Analysis from net.Genesis is an example of a commercial product.
http://www.boutell.com/wusage/	Wusage from Boutell.Com Inc. is available free and is widely used.
http://www.ics.uci.edu/WebSoft/-wwwstat/	WWWstat from the University of California, Irvine, produces HTML summaries and is widely used.

12.2.3.1 Common Log Format ☞

There are a number of options for processing and summarizing Web server logs written in common log format. Table 12–2 summarizes a few.

See

http://www.gsn.org/web/html/wwwfaq/stats.htm

for additional options. A commonly used log file summarizer for Web servers is the Perl script *WWWstat,* written by Roy Fielding of the University of California, Irvine. A discussion of this tool provides us with an overview of the capabilities of this class of *httpd* log file processing software.

12.2.3.1.1 WWWstat ☞   Table 12–3 provides the software snapshot for the WWWstat program.

TABLE 12–3   WWWstat Software Snapshot

Location	*http://www.ics.uci.edu/WebSoft/-wwwstat/*
	ftp://liege.ics.uci.edu/pub/arcadia/-wwwstat/
Source	Yes (Perl)
Documentation	*http://hpux.ee.ualberta.ca/man/-Networking/WWW/wwwstat-1.0/ wwwstat-1.0.README.html*
Bugs, Suggestions	*fielding@ics.uci.edu*

Since *FtpWebLog* (described above) was inspired by *WWWstat,* it is not surprising that the installation is similar. Installation requires that you

1. Download the compressed tar file.
2. Decompress and extract from the tar file.
3. Edit the *wwwstat* Perl script as needed. Some configurable items are
   - the title to appear on the report
   - the Web server's default home page
   - the location of the Web server's log file, (e.g., *ServerRoot/logs/access_log* for NCSA's httpd)
   - the location of the Web server's configuration file, (e.g., *ServerRoot/logs/conf/srm.conf* for NCSA's httpd)
   - if log files are compressed, the command to use to decompress them, and the file extensions that represent compressed files
   - the domain of your Web server, so this can be summarized separately in the output.
   - whether full IP addresses should be displayed
4. Execute the script with a command similar to

wwwstat > stats.html

Figure 12–2 illustrates the beginning of the file *stats.html* produced by the above command when viewed through a Web browser.

The following items are summarized by *WWWstat*

- total transmission statistics
- hourly transmission statistics
- daily transmission statistics
- transmissions by domain
- transmissions of each Web page

Transmission statistics include

- total number of requests
- total bytes sent
- percentage of the total requests for the time period
- percentage of total bytes for the time period

As for *FTPWebLog*, there is a graphical option, called *gwstat*, written by Qiegang Long, which takes the output of WWWstat and post-processes it, producing graphs that

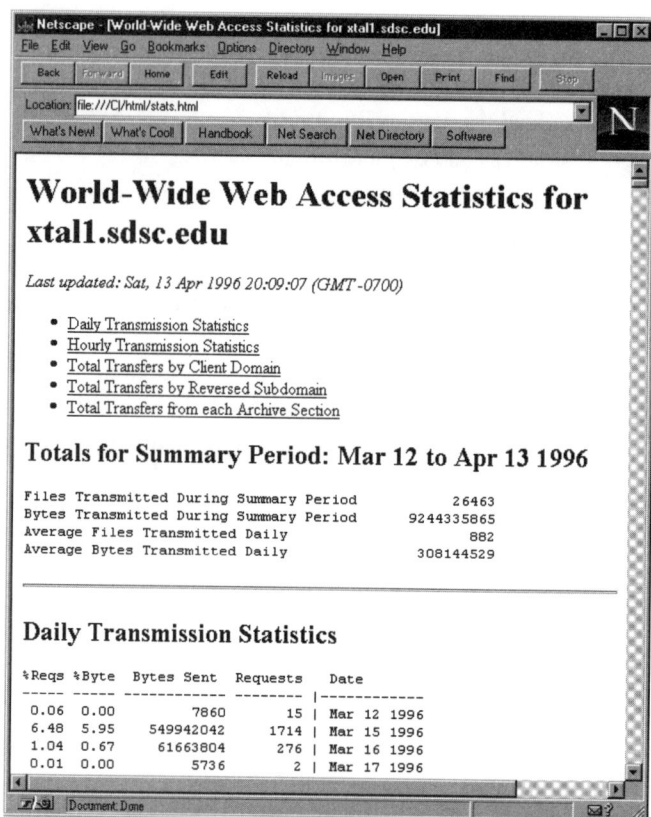

Fig. 12–2 Output from the *WWWstat* Program

can be viewed with an X/Motif XY plotting program called *xmgr*. The *xmgr* program may be obtained from Paul Turner at

http://www.teleport.com/~pturner/acegr/

Figure 12–3 shows sample output, produced by *gwstat* and displayed with *xmgr.* The output is taken from the Web page

http://dis.cs.umass.edu/stats/summary.html

12.2.3.2 Error Logs

As with other log files, the exact location and format of the error log files produced by a Web server depends on the specific Web server. For example, the NCSA httpd server will

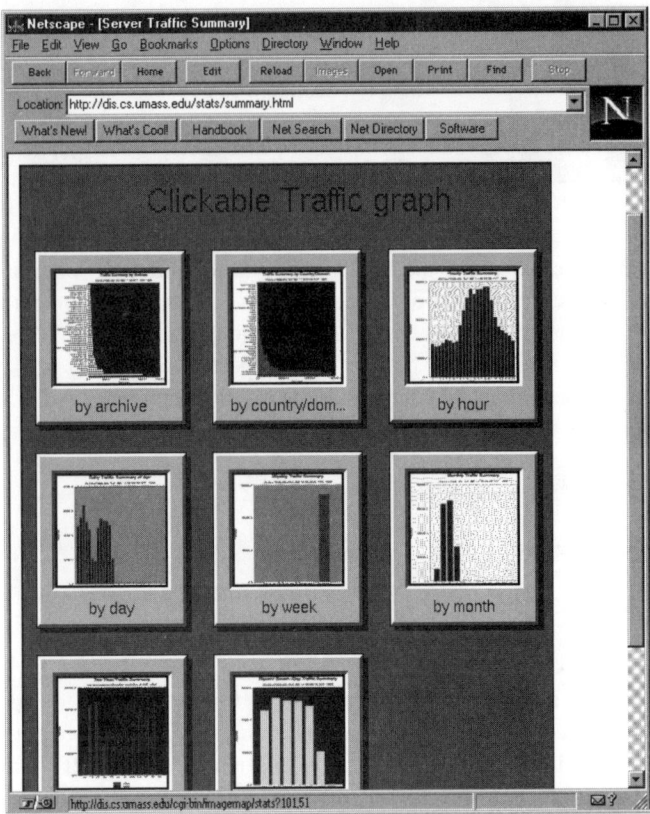

Fig. 12–3   Graphical Summary of a Web Common Log Format File

write, by default, to the file *ServerRoot/logs/error_log*. Details of what gets logged to that file can be found at

> *http://hoohoo.ncsa.uiuc.edu/docs-1.4/-*
> *setup/httpd/ErrorLog.html*

Here is an example.

```
❶[Tue Mar 12 19:17:03 1996] HTTPd: Starting as /usr/ncsa/httpd -d /usr/ncsa
❷[Tue Mar 12 19:19:58 1996] httpd: access to
/usr/htdocs/moose/images/moose.gif
       failed for hercules.sdsc.edu, reason: No file matching URL:
       /moose/images/moose.gif from http://xtal1.sdsc.edu/moose/moose.html
```

```
❸[Wed Mar 13 11:28:14 1996] HTTPd: caught SIGTERM, shutting down
❹[Fri Mar 15 07:57:04 1996] httpd: send aborted for 896ed78a.extern.ucsd.edu,
        URL: /Harvest/cgi-bin/HarvestGather.cgi
❺[Fri Mar 15 17:33:54 1996] httpd: access to /usr/htdocs/PDB/ failed for
        xtal1.sdsc.edu, reason: No file matching URL: /PDB/ from -
```

The records ❶ through ❺ cover the major features found in this error log file.

❶ indicates when the server was started and what command line options where used. In this case, the -d option indicates an alternative document root directory from the default was used. The server is usually started at boot time.

❷ is very useful for finding dead hypertext links, that is, those links for which the pointer still exists, but the page that the pointer references is no longer available. In this example this implies that a request from the host *hercules.sdsc.edu* failed. The Web page

   http://xtal1.sdsc.edu/moose/moose.html

references the file

   /usr/htdocs/moose/images/moose.gif

but that file is not available.

❸ indicates when the server was shutdown.

❹ indicates that a download from the server to the client was aborted. Whether the problem lies with the server or with client is unclear. It should be taken as a warning of a possible problem and monitoring for other such occurrences would be judicious.

❺ indicates that a client attempted to access *http://xtal1.sdsc.edu/PDB* and failed, since this URL did not exist. This could be a mistake by the client user mistyping a URL in the Web browser "Locator" text box. Alternatively, it could indicate you changed a real link at some point and a user is trying to access that obsolete link through a Web browser hot list entry that predates your change. Corrective action may be warranted, that is, you may wish to regenerate the obsolete page and navigate the user to the new page via the old page with a message similar to

   "This page has been moved. The new page is <A HREF = "*http://www.server.edu/-newpage.html*">*http://www.server.edu/newpage.html*</A>".

12.2.3.3 Agent Logs

Tools that summarize agent logs, that is, tools that summarize what client Web browsers have been used to access your Web server and with what frequency, need not be complicated. Here is a simple C shell script that provides summary information to satisfy most needs.

```
#!/bin/csh
echo "BROWSER STATISTICS FOR THE LAST 50,000 HITS ON \
XTAL1.SDSC.EDU" > browsers.txt
date >> browsers.txt

tail -50000 agent_log | sort | uniq -c | sort -nr >> browsers.txt
```

The results written to the file *browsers.txt* are

```
                BROWSER STATISTICS FOR THE LAST 50,000 HITS ON
                               XTAL1.SDSC.EDU
                        Sat Jun 29 08:37:57 PDT 1996
44612 Harvest/1.4.pl2
2068 Slurp/1.0 (http://www.inktomi.com/slurp.html)
 604 Mozilla/2.02 (X11; I; SunOS 4.1.4 sun4m)
 602 Mozilla/2.02 (X11; I; OSF1 V3.2 alpha)
 310 Mozilla/2.01Gold (Win95; I)
 201 Mozilla/2.0 (Macintosh; I; PPC)
 170 Mozilla/2.02 (X11; I; OSF1 V3.0 alpha)
 76 Mozilla/2.02 (X11; I; IRIX 5.3 IP22)
 75 Mozilla/1.1N (Windows; I; 16bit)
 74 Mozilla/2.0 (Macintosh; I; 68K)
 66 Mozilla/2.02 (X11; I; IRIX64 6.1 IP21)
 65 Mozilla/3.0b4 (Win95; I)
 62 Mozilla/2.02 (X11; I; SunOS 4.1.3_U1 sun4m)
 52 Mozilla/1.1N (Macintosh; I; PPC)
 51 Mozilla/2.01 (Macintosh; I; PPC)
 40 Mozilla/2.0 (X11; I; IRIX 5.3 IP22)
 40 Mozilla/2.0 (Win16; I)
 39 Mozilla/2.01 (Macintosh; I; 68K)
 34 Mozilla/2.02 (X11; I; IRIX 5.3 IP7)
 32 BackRub/0.5
 31 Mozilla/2.01 (X11; I; IRIX 5.3 IP22)
 30 ArchitextSpider
 28 Mozilla/2.0 (Win95; I)
 26 Mozilla/3.0b4Gold (Win95; I) via Squid Cache version 1.0.beta7
 24 Scooter/1.0 scooter@pa.dec.com
 23 Mozilla/2.02 (X11; I; IRIX64 6.0.1 IP26)
........
```

Excluding Harvest (Section 7.5), which is run each night and which accesses many of the server's pages, Slurp has the next highest access rate. Slurp is a *Web robot* that collects pages and builds a searchable index. There is no indication of who was using this robot to search the server's pages, although it is interesting to see how often robots are reaching your pages. If you think it is not often enough you should register your pages yourself (Section 8.4) The remaining entries are dominated by versions of Mozilla for different hardware platforms and operating system versions. Mozilla is the name given to the Netscape browser.

12.2.3.4 Referer Logs

Recall from Section 12.1.3 that the file *referer.log* indicates the hosts that have accessed the various URLs on your server. Using the frequencies with which specific hosts access your pages is useful for determining who has likely made links to your pages. Brian Exelbierd has written a nice Perl script for summarizing this information. It can be found at

http://www.catt.ncsu.edu/users/bex/www/scripts/ref.pl

It is reproduced here with Brian's kind permission.

```
#!/usr/local/bin/perl
# By Brian Exelbierd (bex@ncsu.edu)
# Copyright 1995 Brian Exelbierd
#    Except the match_any subroutine
#
# ref.pl
#
# Description:
#    uses the references log to create a hyperlist of what site
#    referenced which pages, how many times
#
# Version 1.2--Reversed the indexing, added better restrictions on counted
#        pages
#        Tuesday July 11, 1995
#
# Version 1.0--Initial Release
#        Sun May 14 05:06:50 EDT 1995
#
# Permission given for use per the GNU-Public License. Credit the script
# and its web page http://www.catt.ncsu.edu/users/bex/programs/ref.html
# and the author (Brian Exelbierd) and my web page
# http://www.catt.ncsu.edu/users/bex/www/index.html. Please also mail
```

```
# me, bex@ncsu.edu and let me know you are using it. Thanks.
#
# Expansions
#
# A jump list to the pages being referred to
# Verification of page existence

# specify a / escaped pattern for from host exclusions
@frompatterns = ('^www$', '^www\/$', 'catt.ncsu.edu', 'www.catt.ncsu',
     'www.catt', '^152.1.43');

# specify a / escaped pattern for referred to page exclusions
@topatterns = ('^\/cgi-bin', 'gif$', 'jpg$', 'xbm$');

$output = "test.html";
$referer_log = "/var/log/www/referer_log";
$header = "/p/www/scripts/ref_pre.html";
$footer = "/p/www/scripts/gen_footer.html";


#
# No changes needed below here
#

use POSIX;
$date = strftime( '%d %h %Y', localtime time );

$f = match_any(@frompatterns);
$t = match_any(@topatterns);

open(LOG,"<$referer_log");
open(OUT,">$output");

while (<LOG>) {
 ($from, $to) = split(" -> ",$_,2);
 ($trash, $sitestart) = split("://",$from,2);
 ($sitestart, $trash) = split("/",$sitestart,2);
 $_ = $sitestart;
 if (($from !~ /^file/) && ! &$f() && ($from ne "")) {
   if ($from =~ /\/$/) {
     chop($from);
     }
   chop($to);
   $_ = $to;
   if (!&$t()) {
     if (($to =~ /\/$/) && ($to ne "/")) {
```

```perl
            chop($to);
            }
        $refs{"$to -> $from"}++;
        }
    }
 }

open(FILE,"<$header");
while (<FILE>) {
 $_ =~ s/<!-DATE->/$date/g;
 print OUT $_;
 }
close(FILE);

print OUT "<UL>\n";
$last = "";
foreach $i (sort(keys(%refs))) {
 ($from, $to) = split(" -> ",$i,2);
if ($from ne $last) {
 print OUT " </UL>\n" unless ($last eq "");
 print OUT
     "<LI><a href=\"http://www.catt.ncsu.edu$from\">$from</a>\n <UL>\n";
 $last = $from;
 }
if ($refs{$i} > 5) {
   print OUT " <LI><STRONG>$refs{$i} - <a
href=\"$to\">$to</a></STRONG>\n";
   }
 else {
   print OUT " <LI>$refs{$i} - <a href=\"$to\">$to</a>\n";
   }
 }
print OUT " </UL>\n";
print OUT "</UL>\n";

open(FILE,"<$footer");
while (<FILE>) {
 chop;
 $_ =~ s/<!-DATE->/$date/g;
 print OUT $_;
 }
close(FILE);

close(OUT);
exit;
```

```
# From: Tom Christiansen <tchrist@mox.perl.com>

sub match_any {
  die "usage: match_any pats" unless @_;

  my $code = <<EOCODE;
sub {
EOCODE

 $code .= <<EOCODE if @_ > 5;
 study;
EOCODE

 for $pat (@_) {
    $code .= <<EOCODE;
 return 1 if /$pat/io;
EOCODE
 }

 $code .= "}\n";

#  print "CODE: $code\n";

 my $func = eval $code;
 die "bad pattern: $@" if $@;

 return $func;
}
```

Features of this script that may be modified are

- the output file name
- the location of *referer_log*
- text defining the header and footer
- specific pages to be excluded

The output from this script appears as an HTML document like that shown in Figure 12–4.

The bullets in Figure 12–4 highlight each Web server URL that has been accessed. The squares show the remote URL from which the access was made and the number of times that link was followed. A significant number of accesses from the same remote site are highlighted automatically. This number is set to five in the version of *ref.pl* shown

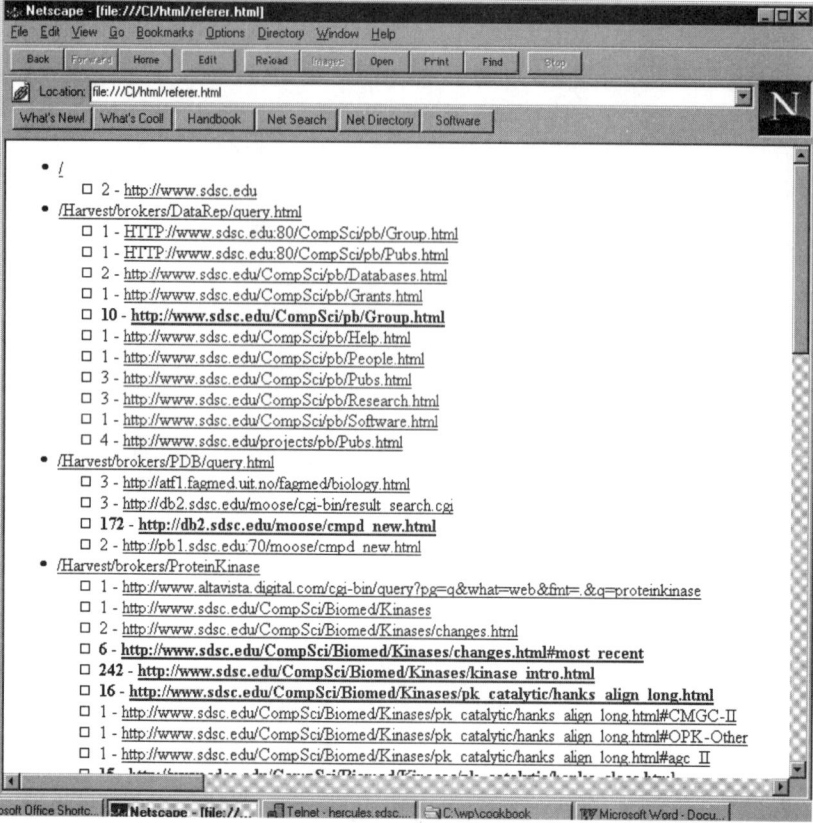

Fig. 12–4   Output from *ref.pl*

above. A large number may indicate that someone has included a link to one of your pages on their server. All URLs in the list can be immediately accessed from the Web browser, so you can check on the sites that are frequently linking to your server pages.

12.3. PREVENTIVE MAINTENANCE

Beyond the log files we have already encountered, analyzing problems on your information server (hopefully before they happen and not afterwards) takes you to the UNIX system log files. Much of the server software is configured to generate errors to be interpreted and logged by *syslogd*, the standard UNIX error log program. Accessing the logs produced by *syslogd* is UNIX operating system dependent and not discussed here. See the UNIX man pages for *syslogd* for further details.

That's it. These are the basics for building an Internet information server. If you have enjoyed the experience of putting the server together, fear not, the experience is not over. The technology is changing so fast that there will be lots of new and useful software to install in the future. You can go on implementing software as long as you like, thanks to a world of generous programmers. Check out this book's associated Web site for the latest.

Epilogue

The feast is over and you should be full. The nature of the human condition is such that tomorrow you will be back at the table wanting another helping. A good cookbook should still have something delicious to offer.

The large, yet select, group of URLs provided in this book resulted from an extended period of Internet surfing. This surfing has left me with two lingering feelings.

The first feeling is sheer awe at the ever-increasing amount of information that is available. The Internet has already become a great reference source for the average family. What is currently lacking is a fast, cheap, and convenient delivery mechanism akin to television. This will come through cable TV modems, blanket satellite coverage, frame relay, or by some other yet unimaginable medium. At that time we will see a quantum jump in usage, and correspondingly, a quantum jump in the amount of information available to the average family at home. Where the Internet differs from television is that anyone is able to broadcast. I can't wait to have such things as my son's little league game schedule and price comparisons from the local supermarkets at my fingertips.

The second feeling is that the Internet is becoming more commercial in orientation. Many more companies are advertising on the Internet and making product literature available. As long as this remains information on demand, I personally welcome these changes.

If these trends continue, it is not hard to image that future generations will have a large part of human collective knowledge at their fingertips.

It is my hope that, in a small way, this book and the associated Web site will help you become an information provider and continue to be a useful reference source for some time.

We have so much to offer each other, and with the Internet, there is less excuse than ever before for not giving of ourselves.

Appendix A

Internet-based Resources for Learning UNIX and UNIX Administration

The following are popular Internet-based sources for learning UNIX and UNIX administration. If your time is limited, start with the last item on this list.

- The UNIX Shell Commands Reference Card by Robert Evans at the University of Wales

  http://www.cm.cf.ac.uk/System/Intro.0994/2/2.html

  provides a good overview and is similar to an introductory UNIX text.

- The UNIX Help/Tutorial from the University of Cincinnati

  http://www.ece.uc.edu/unix-info.html

  is a good "get you started" guide. Many other sites reference this page, a testament to its quality and usefulness.

- A good set of online documentation, including material specific to Ultrix

  gopher://jake.esu.edu/11/Help/Tutorials

- A brief history of UNIX and the original philosophy behind it from Michigan State University

  http://wxweb.msu.edu:80/ucgdocuments/misc/unixtut.html

- Another good UNIX overview from the originators of the World Wide Web

  http://wsspinfo.cern.ch/file/doc/unixguide/unixguide.html

  A bibliography of UNIX books with 513 entries as of September 1996

  http://bavi.unice.fr/Biblio/Os/unix.2.html

- The UNIX index, a service of Proper Publishing Inc., provides a very comprehensive entry point to various aspects of UNIX, including answers to frequently asked questions on all aspects of UNIX

  http://proper.com:70/O/unix/welcome/welcome-unix

- The UNIX Reference Desk. Based on what I have discovered, the best entry point to the definitive guide on all aspects of UNIX. The reference desk is put together by Jennifer Meyers (believe it or not, she is a neuroscience major) at Northwestern University

  http://www.eecs.nwu.edu/unix.html

  This page has it all, here are a few highlights.
    - Documentation specific to different versions of UNIX
    - Keyword searching of help files
    - Acronym searching
    - Jargon searching
    - Online versions of many popular manuals
    - Sources of UNIX-based free software
    - UNIX for PCs
    - UNIX humor

While there is a wealth of information out there on learning or brushing up on UNIX and UNIX administration, the question to ask is whether this information is better than an introductory or more advanced UNIX text book. The short answer is yes and no. Yes, because there is a wealth of information, much more that can be contained in a single book. No, because this information may be repetitive and not exactly to the point (also true of some books, but not this one of course).

As far as UNIX is concerned, it would seem that at the time of writing we have yet to unleash the full power of the current interactive capability of the Web on learning and brushing up on UNIX. The current offerings, while very useful, are for the most part static. That is, browsing of text with the occasional ability to search for text strings. However, tools exist to make a UNIX course much more engaging for the student. This type of capability exists locally in products like the Silicon Graphics bookshelf, distributed as part of the Irix operating system. Using the Irix bookshelf, the user can read about a specific command or function, and then press a button to try it out as part of a captive process.

What we need are Web servers that support this type of interaction so that the student can learn by making mistakes. The simple-minded approach would be to have a list of options that simulate the most common mistakes that the student can make. An ambitious idea would be to have an intelligent interpreter that parses what the student has entered and makes a stab at determining what is wrong with it.

Keep your eye on the Web server associated with this book, because I'll bet some folks are working on just these approaches right now!

Appendix B

HTML Reference Guide

If you wish to be write HTML that conforms strictly to the standard for a particular version of HTML refer to

http://www.ozemail.com.au/~dkgsoft/html/index.html

Alternatively, if you do not care about the standard, it is suggested that before you invest heavily in the use of an HTML tag, you check its functionality, first with the Web browser(s) you use, and then with the Web browsers you anticipate being used to access your information server.

This is not a summary of all the features of HTML, Chapter Eight covers where to go for that information. Rather, it is intended as a quick reference to the *major* features of HTML. If you need more details in a hurry refer to the Yahoo page on HTML

*http://www.yahoo.com/Computers_and_Internet/Software/-
Data_Formats/HTML/Guides_and_Tutorials/*

The nomenclature used in this Appendix, which extends the conventions used throughout this book, is as follows:

<IMG ALIGN={TOP/MIDDLE/BOTTOM/LEFT/RIGHT} SRC="filename">

Curly braces {} indicate one of a number of options is permissible—in this case delimited by slashes (/). Common attributes to each tag are provided. HTML tags and their attributes are in uppercase, variables are in lowercase. Where necessary, variables are surrounded by double quotes (" ").

Page Layout

\<BANNER\> ... \</BANNER\>	Region of text that does not scroll (browser dependent).
\<BODY\> ... \</BODY\>	Main body of the document.
\<DIV\> ... \</DIV\>	Standard sections of a document.
\<HEAD\> ... \</HEAD\>	Document header information.
\<Hn\> ... \</Hn\>	Header level where n=1-6.
\<HTML\> ... \</HTML\>	Entire HTML document.
\<RANGE {attributes}\>	Define a section of content for use by a STYLE.
\<STYLE {attributes}\> ... \</STYLE\>	Impose a style.
\<TITLE\> ... \</TITLE\>	Appears in the Web browser's title field.

Paragraph Layout

\<BR\>	Line break, i.e., begin a new line.
\<P\>	Paragraph break, as \<BR\> but leave a blank line.

Text Layout

\<ABBREV\> ... \</ABBREV\>	An abbreviation.
\<ACRONYM\> ... \</ACRONYM\>	An acronym.
\<AU\> ... \</AU\>	Name of an author.
\<BLOCKQUOTE\> ... \</BLOCKQUOTE\>	Text quoted from some other source; left and right margins are indented.
\<B\> ... \</B\>	Bold.
\<BIG\> ... \</BIG\>	Big print.
\<CITE\> ... \</CITE\>	A citation.
\<CODE\> ... \</CODE\>	An HTML directive.
\<DEL\> ... \</DEL\>	Text deleted since a previous version of the document.
\<DFN\> ... \</DFN\>	A definition.
\<DIR\> ... \<LI\> ... \</DIR\>	Directory list of items.
\<DL\> ... \<DT\> ... \<DD\> ... \</DL\>	Definition list, where \<DT\> is the term and \<DD\> the definition.
\<EM\> ... \</EM\>	Emphasize text.
\<FN\> ... \</FN\>	A footnote.
\<I\> ... \</I\>	Italics.
\<INS\> ... \</INS\>	Text inserted since a previous version.
\<KBD\> ... \</KBD\>	A keyboard key.
\<LANG\> ... \</LANG\>	Language.
\<LH\> ... \</LH\>	The header for a list of elements.

continued

Text Layout *(continued)*

<LISTING> ... </LISTING>	Computer listing.
<MENU> ... <LI> ... </MENU>	Menu of items.
<NOTE> ... </NOTE>	Admonishment—a note or warning.
<OL> ... <LI> ... </OL>	Ordered (numbered) lists.
<PERSON> ... </PERSON>	Name of a person.
<PRE> ... </PRE>	Preformatted text, i.e., text is presented literally, except hyperlinks are interpreted.
<Q> ... </Q>	Quotation.
<STRIKE> ... </STRIKE>	Strikethrough text.
<SAMP> ... </SAMP>	Include sample output.
<SMALL> ... </SMALL>	Small print.
<STRONG> ... </STRONG>	Place strong emphasis.
_{...}	Subscript.
^{...}	Superscript.
<TAB>	Force a tab.
<TT> ... </TT>	Typewriter font.
<U> ... </U>	Underline.
<UL> ... <LI> ... </UL>	Unordered (bulleted) list.
<VAR> ... </VAR>	Define a variable.
<XMP> ... </XMP>	As <PRE>, but hyperlinks are ignored.

Links

<A HREF="URL">anchor_text </A>	A link via anchor_text to another HTML document designated by URL.
<A NAME="anchor_name">- anchor _text </A>	A named point in an HTML document to which other links point.
<A HREF="URL#anchor_name"> anchor_text </A>	A link via anchor_text to a point #anchor_name in URL.

Images and Figures

<CAPTION> ... </CAPTION>	Descriptive label for a table or figure.
<CREDIT> ... </CREDIT>	Credit a figure.
<IMG HEIGHT=n WIDTH=m ALIGN={TOP/MIDDLE/BOTTOM/LEFT/ RIGHT} ALT = "image_description" SRC="URL">	Inlined image defined by URL, either a GIF or XBM, ALIGNed with respect to text, and ALT displayed in text-only browsers.
<OVERLAY>	Superimpose an image on a figure.

Miscellaneous

<!-- comment_string -->	Comment completely ignored by browsers, regardless of content.
<!--#command VAR="variable"-->	Execute command with the associated VAR (server dependent).
<!--#INCLUDE FILE="filename"-->	Include the contents of FILE (server dependent).
&ascii_equivilent;	Use a character literally, e.g., < for less than (<).
<ADDRESS> ... </ADDRESS>	A closing address on a Web page. Has nothing to do with postal addresses.
<BASE HREF="URL">	Base part of a URL prepended to all relative URLs in the document.
<HR SIZE=n WIDTH="m%">	Insert a horizontal rule of optional thickness SIZE and covering WIDTH percent of the browser window.
<ISINDEX>	Describes a database or searchable index.
<LINK REV="RELATIONSHIP" REL="RELATIONSHIP" HREF="URL">	Identifies the e-mail address of the document owner; it is not displayed in the browser.
<META attribute_value>	Meta information provided between <HEAD> ... </HEAD> tags, e.g., to define the expiration date of a page.

Table Layout

<TABLE BORDER= n ALIGN={LEFT/RIGHT/CENTER/JUSTIFY /CHAR} CELLSPACING= n CELLPADDING= m BGCOLOR= #bbffee> ... </TABLE>	Define a table with optional BORDER of thickness n. ALIGN contents in cells, leaving CELLSPACING between CELLS and CELL PADDING between text and cell edge. Optionally set the background color of the table with BGCOLOR.
<CAPTION ALIGN = {TOP/BOTTOM}> ... </CAPTION>	Define a centered, optionally ALIGNed caption.
<TR ALIGN={LEFT/RIGHT/CENTER/JUSTIFY /CHAR} VALIGN = {TOP/MIDDLE/BOTTOM/BASELINE} BGCOLOR = #bbffee> ... </TR>	Define a table row, vertically aligning contents (VALIGN).
<TD COLSPAN=n ROWSPAN=m ALIGN={LEFT/RIGHT/CENTER/JUSTIFY/ CHAR} VALIGN = {TOP/MIDDLE/BOTTOM/BASELINE} BGCOLOR = #bbffee NOWRAP> ... </TD>	Define a data cell that optionally spans n columns (COLSPAN) and m rows (ROWSPAN).Optionally prevent contents from wrapping (NOWRAP).

continued

Table Layout *(continued)*

<TH>COLSPAN=n ROWSPAN=m ALIGN={LEFT/RIGHT/CENTER/JUSTIFY/ CHAR} VALIGN = {TOP/MIDDLE/BOTTOM/BASELINE} BGCOLOR = #bbffee NOWRAP> ... </TH>	As <TD> but for column headers only.

Forms Layout

<FORM METHOD={GET/POST} ACTION="URL"> ... </FORM>	Define a form for processing by URL using METHOD.
<INPUT TYPE=TEXT NAME="name" SIZE=n>	A text entry box of n characters with the text associated with the variable NAME.
<INPUT TYPE=PASSWORD NAME ="name" SIZE=n>	As TYPE=TEXT, but with the text not echoed for security reasons.
<INPUT TYPE=CHECKBOX NAME="name" VALUE={CHECKED/ NONCHECKED}>	A checked (VALUE=CHECKED) or non-checked (VALUE=NONCHECKED) checkbox.
<INPUT TYPE=RADIO NAME="name" VALUE={CHECKED/ NONCHECKED}>	A radio button (on if VALUE=CHECKED). Radio buttons with the same NAME are grouped.
<INPUT TYPE=SUBMIT VALUE="button_text">	Send form contents to the Web server. VALUE is the text within the button.
<INPUT TYPE=RESET VALUE="button_text">	Clear a form of all information and reset radio buttons, checkboxes, etc. VALUE is the text within the button.
<INPUT TYPE=HIDDEN NAME="text" VALUE="text">	Submit a hidden (i.e., not seen on the form) NAME to the server with VALUE.
<SELECT NAME="name"> <OPTION> "option_text" <OPTION SELECTED>"option_text" ... </SELECT>	Pop-up menu with multiple <OPTION> tags. SELECTED defines the default <OPTION>. If SELECTED is not specified, the first <OPTION> is the default.
<SELECT NAME="name" MULTIPLE SIZE=n> <OPTION> "option_text" <OPTION SELECTED>"option_text" ... </SELECT>	Scrollable list of OPTIONs with SIZE rows displayed. MULTIPLE indicates multiple options may be selected. SELECTED defines the default selection, which may be more than one row if MULTIPLE is specified.

continued

Forms Layout *(continued)*

<TEXTAREA NAME="name" ROWS=n COLS=m> "optional_text" ... </TEXTAREA>	Scrollable text area of n ROWS and m COLS (columns), optionally containing "optional_text".

Frames Layout

<FRAMESET COLS="n,m" ROWS ="n,m"> ... </FRAMESET>	Defines a set of frames, within which each individual frame is defined with the <FRAME> tag. The dimensions of the area containing frames, ROWS and COLUMNS can be optionally specified.
<FRAME SRC="URL" NAME="name" MARGINHEIGHT=n MARGINWIDTH=m SCROLLING={YES/NO} NORESIZE>	Display the URL in a frame of specified MARGINHEIGHT and MARGINWIDTH, with or without SCROLLING. The frame will resize to remain proportional to the overall window size unless NORESIZE is specified.
<NOFRAME> ... </NOFRAME>	Defines behavior in cases when the Web client recognizes the <NOFRAME> tag, but not the <FRAME> tag.
<A HREF="URL" TARGET="name">	Update the target FRAME with URL.

JavaScript

<SCRIPT LANGUAGE="JavaScript" SRC="JavaScriptCode.js"> ... </SCRIPT>	Block of JavaScript code. Use either the LANGUAGE or SRC attributes. LANGUAGE if the code is embedded; SRC if it is in a separate file with the extension *.js*.
<INPUT TYPE={BUTTON/CHECKBOX} NAME="name" ONCLICK="JavaScript function">	As the regular <INPUT> tag but with the ONCLICK attribute to define the JavaScript function to be executed.

Java

<APPLET CODE="code.class" WIDTH=n HEIGHT=m ALIGN={TEXTTOP/TOP/ ABSMIDDLE/MIDDLE/BASELINE/ ABSBOTTOM} HSPACE=n VSPACE=m CODEBASE="directory"> ... </APPLET>	Include an applet called *code.class*, optionally from the directory CODEBASE. Reserve a WIDTH on n pixels and a HEIGHT of m pixels for the applet on the Web page. ALIGN the applet with respect to the text on the Web page. Leave HSPACE (horizontal space) and VSPACE (vertical space) between the applet and the Web page contents.
<PARAM NAME="name" VALUE="value">	Pass the VALUE associated with NAME to an applet. The <PARAM...> tag lies between <APPLET> ... </APPLET> tags.

Glossary

A general and more extensive list of terms is available from

- Free Online Dictionary of Computing
  http://wfn-shop.Princeton.EDU/foldoc/ (US)
  http://wombat.doc.ic.ac.uk/ (Europe)
- Dictionary of Dictionaries
  http://www.refdesk.com/facts.html#dict
- The Cook Report—An Internet Monthly
  http://pobox.com/cook/glossary.html

Note: The definitions here relate to how the terms are used in this book and may differ slightly from the definitions used by others.

101 A basic introduction to a topic.

Anonymous ftp A mechanism to get files from, or put files to, a remote computer, when you do not have an account on that remote computer.

Applet Code written in the Java language that is downloaded to the client via a *Web browser* and executed. Frequently used to support animation and continuous client server interaction.

ASCII American Standard Code for Information Interchange. A set of 8-bit binary numbers representing the alphabet, punctuation, numerals, and other characters used in text representation.

Bit-mapped Display A display that supports addressing of pixels (points on the screen) rather than specific characters on a line of length 80 or 132 characters.

Byte Code Machine independent code generated by the Java compiler.

CERT Computer Emergency Response Team. A government funded group which, among other things, produces bulletins of known security problems on the more popular operating systems and issues patches (fixes) from the vendors and others. See *ftp://info.cert.org/pub/* for further details.

CGI Common Gateway Interface. A means of passing information from a Web client browser to a CGI-compliant script resident on a Web server. The CGI script will invoke some action, like the generation of HTML pages, that are sent back to the client browser.

CGI program Used interchangeably with *CGI Script*. Strictly speaking, a CGI script uses an interpretive language and a CGI program uses a compiled program.

CGI Script A file containing an executable program, code interpreted by an interpretable language, (e.g., Tcl, Perl) or code interpreted by the UNIX shell, which is invoked by the Web client and executed on the Web server.

Clickable Map An image that has a series of URLs mapped to different regions of the drawing, thereby providing visual navigation.

Common Gateway Interface See *CGI*.

Common Log File Format The *de facto* log file format produced by popular Web servers when logging access to the server.

Daemon A program important to the functioning of a UNIX system. Rather than being part of the kernel, daemons run as standalone programs, usually started at boot time. Daemon, not to be confused with demon, is taken from the Greek meaning something, neither good nor evil, that helps define personality and character, that is, spirit.

Document Root Directory The top level directory recognized by the Web server that contains documents to be served. All documents served are found in this directory or below it in the directory tree. Symbolic links to files being served outside of this tree may be allowed. Support for symbolic links is Web server dependent.

FAQ Frequently Asked Questions. A useful means of quickly asking the most obvious questions on a particular subject by way of a Listserver.

File Extension Any characters following (and including) the last period in a UNIX file name.

Filter Software that converts information in one format to the same information in another format.

Ftp File transfer protocol. Part of the TCP/IP stack of protocols controlling file transfer between two computers.

Ftp Archive Files accessible by *anonymous ftp,* hopefully organized in a way to make it easy for the user to find the information she needs.

GIF   Graphics Interchange Format, developed by CompuServe. A popular and free graphics format supported by Internet information servers.

Gopher   Text-based predecessor to the Web. Used a different protocol to http, but supported the idea of hyperlinks.

GUI   A Graphical User Interface (GUI) is the hardware and software needed to address (by way of a mouse or some other pointing device) an individual point on the display device and solicit a particular response.

Helper Applications   Applications configured and subsequently invoked from a Web browser to process a MIME type not recognized by the browser itself.

Hit   A single access to an information server. For example: the downloading of a single *Web page* or graphic image from a Web server; a single mail message sent to a Listserver; a single file transfer using *ftp*. The number of hits is an approximate measure of the amount of activity on a server.

Home Page   A particular Web page. A point in the World Wide Web that represents the starting point for viewing a specific body of information.

HotJava   A *Web browser* written in the *Java* programming Language, developed by Sun Microsystems Inc.

Hot List   A list of *URLs* to which the user refers frequently and which are maintained by the client *Web browser.*

http   HyperText Transfer Protocol, the protocol used by the World Wide Web.

Hyperlink (or Hypertext Link)   A virtual connection between two pieces of information accessible via the Internet.

HyperText Markup Language (HTML)   "The language of the Web" used to define Web pages.

IP Address   A number and associated name by which Internet hosts are recognized.

Internet   Conglomeration of interconnected computer networks all using the *TCP/IP* protocol.

Intranet   Conglomeration of interconnected computer networks within a specific organization.

ISDN   Integrated Services Digital Network, a fast network connection available through many telecommunications companies.

Internet Service Provider (ISP)   A commercial organization that provides Internet access to commercial and private users.

Java   *Object-oriented programming language* designed by Sun Microsystems Inc., with network access and portability in mind.

JavaScript   Simplified version of Java designed by Netscape Communications Inc., for use with Netscape Web browsers and Web servers.

Just-in-Time Compiler   A compiler that takes *Java byte code* and converts it to more efficient machine-specific code. This is done at run-time.

LaTeX   Word processing system derived from TeX.

Line Interface   An interaction with the computer on a line-by-line basis. You enter a text string followed by <enter>. The <enter> signifies that the computer should process the line(s) and produce a response. Contrast this to a *GUI*. All display devices support a line interface.

Link   See *hyperlink*.

Listserver   Software that serves lists of users. A user subscribes to the list and thereafter any e-mail postings sent to the list are forwarded to the user. This continues until the user unsubscribes from the list.

Markup   The act of adding information to a document to control how it will be formatted for a printer or display device.

Methods   Also called *procedures*. A term loosely taken from *object-oriented programming* and meant to imply a piece of reusable code for performing a specific task.

MIME Type   Multipurpose Internet Mail Extension is a standardized method of assigning types to documents. It was originally developed for use with mail messages. That is, mailers could recognize specific types of documents embedded in mail messages by their MIME types. This same mechanism has now been adopted as the mechanism for assigning and detecting the formats of Internet documents.

Mirror Site   An information server that keeps a current copy of all or part of the information found on another information server. The prime purpose of a mirror site is to make the same information easily accessible from different global locations, thereby avoiding slow Internet connections.

Moderated List   A list available on a Listserver, where each incoming message to that list is examined by the person referred to as the List Moderator, before being optionally broadcast to all subscribers to that list after possible modification.

Netiquette   Undefined rules for how to behave when accessing the Internet. Common sense on the Internet.

NNTP   Network News Transport Protocol, the protocol used to access Usenet newsgroups and associated articles.

PC   Personal Computer. Any computer using the Intel 386, 486, Pentium, or other Intel chip.

Plug-in   A Netscape term for an application that "plugs-in" to the Netscape browser and extends the capabilities of the browser. Refer to *http://home.netscape.com/eng/mozilla/2.0/-handbook/docs/appans.html#C13* for details.

PPP   Point to Point Protocol, another protocol with similar functionality to *SLIP*.

Procedures   See *Methods*.

README   The name of a file commonly found in *ftp archives* and software distributions. Usually contains information important to the installation or information that was written too late to be placed in the formal documentation.

Rich Text Format (RTF)   ASCII-based text interchange format developed by Microsoft Inc. Works well for exchanging text between word processing systems that read and write RTF, but is not so good for exchanging graphics and mathematical equations.

Robot   See *Web Robot*.

SLIP   Simple Line Interface Protocol, a protocol used to support asynchronous connections to the Internet, typically over telephone lines.

SHTP   Secure Hypertext Transport Protocol, extension to e-mail that provides privacy and authentication over the World Wide Web.

SGML   Standard Generalized Markup Language, used by the publishing industry to describe the final appearance of a document. *HTML* is a subset of SGML.

SMTP   Simple Mail Transport Protocol, the e-mail protocol used on the Internet.

Style Guide   A reference document and possibly software templates that define common characteristics to be used in developing Web pages.

Swapping   The moving of pages (i.e., 512 byte chunks of information) between physical memory and disk.

TCP/IP   Transmission Control Protocol/Internet Protocol. The protocol suite that allows communication on the Internet. That is, all computers connected to the Internet support this protocol.

TCP/IP Protocol Stack   The specific protocols included in TCP/IP.

URL   Uniform Resource Locator. A global reference point to a piece of information. That information can exist in a variety of formats. All Web browsers recognize and display the contents of URLs.

Usenet Newsgroups   Discussion groups on the Internet, each centered around a specific topic. There are currently about 15,000 Usenet newsgroups. Users post messages by e-mail to newsgroups and review newsgroups either via e-mail or special newsreader software.

Virtual Reality Modeling Language (VRML)   Can be thought of as a 3-D version of *HTML*. VRML defines behaviors through which the user navigates using a VRML browser.

Web   See *World Wide Web*.

Web Browser   Client software capable of reading, interpreting, and displaying information in HyperText Markup Language (*HTML*).

Web Client   Software resident on client hardware for interpreting *Web pages* downloaded from a *Web server*.

Web Form   A particular type of *Web page* for sending information to the Web server for processing.

Webmaster   The generic name given to the person responsible for maintaining *Web pages* on a *Web server*.

Web Page   A discrete piece of information read by a *Web browser*. That information resides between <HTML> and </HTML> tags and is usually contained in a single file.

Web Robot   Software that moves around the Internet gathering and indexing *Web pages*. Most commonly used to support Internet search services like Yahoo, Alta Vista, and Magellan.

Web Server   Computer running software (or the software itself) capable of serving requests from Web clients for documents in HTML format.

Web Site   Computer maintaining a set of Web pages with a related theme.

WYSIWYG   What-You-See-Is-What-You-Get. Usually refers to an editor that allows you to work with the document in the form in which it will appear on the printed page.

World Wide Web   Computers attached to the *Internet* that support the *http protocol* used in global information exchange.

WWW   An acronym for *World Wide Web*.

Index

A

Access
  internet, 55–64. *See also* Internet access
  server, 11–14
Account security
  prerequisite infrastructure and, 69
Addresses
  basics of, 9–11
  domain name services, 10
  types of, 11
Administrative interface
  Harvest and, 147. *See also* Harvest server
Advanced web documents, 185–209
  clickable maps, 203–209. *See also* Clickable maps
  frames, 189–197, 284
  server side includes, 197–203. *See also* Server
    side includes
  tables, 186–189. *See also* Tables
Agents
  mail user, 16
Agents logs, 268–270
Aliases
  mail, 66
Anchors
  HTML, 157–159
  modified, 167
Anonymous ftp
  basic server configuration, 117–119. *See also*
    Basic server configuration
  enhanced ftp, 119
  file permissions for, 118
  ftp archive registration with archie, 119
  installation notes, 120–123
  security, 119
  server installation and, 116–123
  wu-ftpd, 119
  wu-ftpd software snapshot, 119

Archie
  ftp archive registration with, 119
  ftp archive search using, 18–19
  installing, 86–87
  software snapshot, 87
  use of, 87–88
Archive
  archie and, 18–19
  automated, 231–240
  self-sustaining, 234, 240
Audio players, 23
Authoring tools, 24
Automated archive
  web forms and, 231–240

B

Background
  control of, 176–177
  image sources, 177
Basic server configuration
  anonymous ftp and, 117–119
  file permissions for anonymous ftp, 118
  ftp archive registration with archie, 119
  security, 119
Basics
  client server, 15–17
  internet, 8–15
  internet information related tools, 17–24
Binary files, 35, 39
BODY tag
  text-based attributes of, 178
Browsers, 42–44. *See also* Web browsers
  compute capable, 22–23
  popular, 44
  3-D, 44
  2-D, 43–44